Jules Stewart is an historian and author. His books include *On Afghanistan's Plains: The Story of Britain's Afghan Wars* (I.B.Tauris, 2011), *Crimson Snow: Britain's First Disaster in Afghanistan* (2008); *The Savage Border: The Story of the North-West Frontier* (2007); *Spying for the Raj: The Pundits and the Mapping of the Himalaya* (2006) and *The Khyber Rifles: From the British Raj to Al Qaeda* (2005).

To Helen

ALBERT
A LIFE

Jules Stewart

I.B. TAURIS
LONDON · NEW YORK

Published in 2012 by I.B.Tauris & Co. Ltd
6 Salem Road, London W2 4BU
175 Fifth Avenue, New York NY 10010
www.ibtauris.com

Distributed in the United States and Canada Exclusively by Palgrave Macmillan,
175 Fifth Avenue, New York NY 10010

ISBN 978 1 84885 977 7

A full CIP record for this book is available from the British Library
A full CIP record for this book is available from the Library of Congress
Library of Congress catalog card: available

Typeset in Caslon by Dexter Haven Associates Ltd, London
Printed and bound in Sweden by ScandBook AB

'Princes have only to behave with common decency and prudence, and they are sure to be popular, for there is a great and general disposition to pay court to them.'

Charles Greville, *The Greville Memoirs*, vol. I, p. 159

Contents

House of Saxe-Coburg Saalfeld and Saxe-Coburg Gotha

House of Hanover

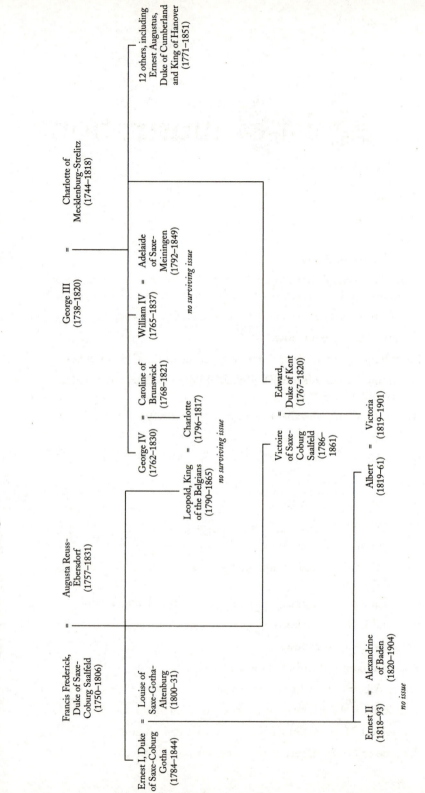

List of illustrations

cknowledgements

I am deeply indebted to Helen Crisp for taking the time to read through my manuscript and offer her insightful appraisal and suggestions. Hearty thanks are also due to my agent, Duncan McAra, for having enabled, several books ago, my seamless transition from journalism to authorship. Joanna Godfrey at I.B.Tauris has once again provided her superb editing skills. Several people opened doors to me, in this country and in Germany. I would particularly like to thank Michael Hunter at Osborne House, Malcolm Hay at the Palace of Westminster, Nigel Williams at the Royal Commission for the Exhibition of 1851, Michael Eckstein at the Prince Albert Society, Jutta Stumm at Rosenau Castle, Horst Gehringer at Staatsarchiv Coburg and Gerhard Hartan at Tourismus Coburg.

Introduction

In 1848, angry mobs took to the streets of Paris, Berlin, Prague, Budapest and Vienna, in a widespread uprising that became known as Europe's Year of Revolution. Many thousands were killed in the clashes, and many more suffered torture in police dungeons. In May of that year, Prince Albert wrote from the serenity of London's Buckingham Palace to his mentor in Germany, Christian Friedrich Stockmar, 'All is well with us, and the throne has never stood higher in England than at this moment.'[1]

Queen Victoria's young German husband, who was three months short of his thirtieth birthday, was too modest a man to take credit for having restored the British monarchy's esteem after decades of discreditable Hanoverian rule. By then the Prince had already assumed the role of monarch without a crown. The burden he was obliged to shoulder as intermediary between the Government and the Crown pushed him to the brink of exhaustion: fully 28,000 dispatches concerning the uprisings were sent out or received at the Foreign Office in that year, and as the Prime Minister, Lord John Russell stated in a letter to Albert, 'These dispatches ... Lord Palmerston must recollect, come to you and the Queen, as well as to himself.'[2] Had Albert not appeared on the scene when he did, it is more than likely that the Crown would have found itself besieged by the same crowds that had ousted the Orleans monarchy across the Channel.

It is said that behind every great man there stands a woman: in the case of Albert and Victoria, the roles were reversed. True enough, had the Queen of England not been there to provide the symbol of greatness, Albert's genius would surely have withered into obscurity, living out his days as a collector of fine art and accomplished organist in his native Coburg, whose dukedom by right of primogeniture went to his elder brother Ernest. But Albert's uncle, King Leopold I of the Belgians, working in league with the astute Baron Stockmar, had in 1840 successfully engineered the marriage of their protégé to his first cousin, Victoria.

It was by no means a case of greatness comfortably falling into the lap of a little-known German prince from a minor ducal seat of the German Confederation. Albert fought an uphill battle every step of the way to make himself acceptable to a mistrustful, xenophobic British establishment and, more importantly, to the British people.

Albert fell in love with Britain, its constitution, to which he devoted months of diligent study, the wild Scottish Highlands, where he stalked stag and revelled in the invigorating mountain air, the grandeur of an empire which at its height held sway over a quarter of the world's landmass and ruled more than 450 million people, and of course his family, which grew to number nine children by the time of the Prince's death.

Albert was awed by the magnificence of imperial Britain, and he was equally appalled by the squalid horrors of its factories, the destitution of workers who slaved in those 'dark satanic mills', the fetid slums of the mining towns and industrial cities. Never had he come across such deprivation in the pastoral Coburg of his boyhood, and he could scarcely have imagined its existence in the world's most powerful and scientifically advanced country. Albert the devout Christian and humanist realised early on that he could not stand idly by, luxuriating in courtly splendour, while only a few minutes' ride from Buckingham Palace people were forced to live out an existence of terrible penury.

In the 21 years he spent in Britain before his death at only 43 years of age, there was hardly a corner of British society that remained untouched by Albert's enlightened hand. Look about you on a stroll through London: the vast South Kensington museums complex, the lions at the base of Nelson's Column, Cleopatra's Needle on the Embankment, the giant frescoes that decorate the Houses of Parliament – these are a very few examples of the Prince's tangible labours. In the arts, Albert was definitely the intellectual, as opposed to Victoria the sensualist. But it was through the Prince's work to bring art to the general public and his efforts to add a new dynamic to traditional university disciplines that the study of art history has gained a large academic following. Albert the Teuton was rather more prudish than Victoria in his tastes. The Prince thought the great mural of sea nymphs above the grand staircase at Osborne House a trifle too nude, but Victoria waxed enthusiastic over the work. Albert considered the kilt too short on a Highlander statue that stands on the landing, but here again Victoria thought it beautiful. Despite these discrepancies, their tastes in art complemented one another's. Albert was a romantic, and together they read the novels of Sir Walter Scott. They both loved the rich, voluptuous court portraiture of the Prince's countryman, Franz Xaver

Winterhalter, who executed some of the most sensuous paintings of the royal couple held in the Royal Collection. Albert's world was one of Schubert and Byron, his wife's that of Gilbert and Sullivan. His was the face of a cultured, enlightened monarchy, something almost revolutionary in Hanoverian times.

Then there are Albert's less visible bequests, and to him we owe the army's present-day regimental system, Cambridge University's modern curriculum, his leadership in building decent, affordable working-class housing, improved farming techniques and the fight for humane factory conditions – again, to name but a handful of initiatives.

The work he left behind and his modernising accomplishments serve to underpin Albert's greatest gift to the nation. This was the advent of a new concept of royalty, with unprecedented close ties to the common people, with a determination to raise the standards of education, the public awareness of science and the arts, a compassion for the poorest, in a way that no monarch in the past had ever imagined should be part of the sovereign's role.

It was a life that inspired many biographers to sing the praises of this extraordinary man. Theodore Martin laboured for years to produce the five-volume 'official' history that had been commissioned by Victoria. Anyone who has since endeavoured to chronicle the life of Albert owes a major debt of gratitude to Martin's colossal undertaking. Hermione Hobhouse, Robert Rhodes James, Daphne Bennett, Hector Bolitho and Stanley Weintraub have all made significant contributions, based extensively on Martin's *magnum opus*, to our knowledge of the Prince's life, and all have treated Albert with the highest admiration. The objective of the present work, which comes to light in the hundred-and-fiftieth anniversary year of Albert's death, is to relate the life and works of a man about whom too little is known and appreciated by the present generation.

In carrying out his task, the Prince secured for Victoria a revitalised monarchy that during the four decades she had left to reign in her widowhood, enjoyed an unprecedented popularity and respect. It has come to be known as the 'Victorian age'. Considering the legacy that has come down to us from the Prince's endeavours, 'Albertine' would seem a more appropriate title. However, there is no need to quibble over historical labels: the Prince's prominence in nineteenth-century British, and indeed European, history remains secure. Let it be said, then, that Albert was the greatest of the Victorians.

1

The Suitor from Saxony

The two young brothers were tucked up in bed with whooping cough at the Rosenau, their father's stately summer home four miles from the medieval town of Coburg, the family ducal seat. The boys, Albert and Ernest, were happiest at this fifteenth-century Gothic-revival castle, where they could give free rein to their fantasies of playing at knights in armour, acting out heroic jousts in the romantic English landscaped park that surrounds the house, or on rainy days under the vaulted ceiling of the colonnaded great marble hall, its walls suitably decorated with Saxon coats of arms. Albert, the younger brother by a year, in particular dreaded the end-of-summer return to Coburg and life at the vast, inhibiting Ehrenburg Palace that dominates the town square.

It was just as well that the boys were ill that late September day in 1824, for had they been on their feet they would have witnessed the most traumatic sight of their lives. On that chill autumn morning, a carriage slowly passed through the tall iron gates and across the frost-covered, gravelled palace courtyard, disappearing into the rolling, wooded countryside of northern Bavaria. In the coach sat a young, strikingly beautiful and desperately unhappy German noblewoman. This was the boys' mother, Princess Louise of Saxe-Coburg-Altenburg. Months after abandoning the family home, Louise wrote in despair of her ordeal: 'Leaving my children was the most painful thing of all…they had whooping cough and said, "Mamma cries because she has got to go, now, when we are ill."'[1] Never again were they to see her, for Louise's infidelities had been unmasked and she had been sent away by her enraged husband who, after divorcing his wife, in December 1832 married his niece and Albert's cousin, the Duchess Marie of Württemberg. The Duke's rage, one might add, needed to be taken with a substantial pinch of hypocrisy, for Ernest of Saxe-Coburg-Saalfeld was himself an inveterate womaniser who never let pass an opportunity to flit like a butterfly from one mistress to another, a character flaw that was passed on to his son Ernest. The Duke's lecherous activities began almost immediately after his marriage. His sons knew nothing of their father's escapades at the time, but the loss of their mother came as a terrible blow, for the two boys were only four and five years of age when she left home.

Princess Louise had been Ernest's 16-year-old bride. She was less than half his age, and a lonelier and more miserable existence for a young bride could not have been imagined. Not only did her husband ignore as well as betray her, she was aware that he also coveted the Duchy of Gotha which she had brought to the marriage. Three years after being forced to abandon her home and children, Louise found herself a 27-year-old divorcee living in St Wendel in the Lichtenberg jurisdiction of Germany with her lover, now husband, the dashing Lieutenant

Count Alexander von Hanstein. Some time the following year she began to suffer from severe stomach pains and bleeding. The couple travelled to Paris to consult an eminent gynaecologist, but one August evening on their return to St Wendel, she collapsed and died in her bedroom. There is a story told by the German philologist Max Müller that after her banishment Louise caught a glimpse of her sons only once, when disguised as a peasant woman she slipped into a crowd at a harvest festival they were attending.[2] But it is more than likely that neither Albert nor his brother Ernest ever laid eyes on their mother from the day she was driven out of the family home.

The elder of Duke Ernest's children was given the name Ernest and his younger brother Albert, following the tradition of the sons of Frederick III the Wise, Elector of Saxony, who bestowed these names on the two branches of the dynasty into which the ancient Saxon family was thenceforward divided. Albert was described by his mother as 'superb, an extraordinary beauty, with large blue eyes…and always jolly'. Princess Louise's portrayal of Albert's elder brother was of a less fulsome nature. 'Ernest is quite large for his age, lively and intelligent,' was all she had to say.[3] At that wretched moment in Albert's life, scarcely could anyone imagine that this tearful, trembling little boy, imagining himself forsaken by his mother, was destined to marry his first cousin and become the power behind the throne of England.

*　　　　*　　　　*

Franz Albrecht August Karl Emanuel was born on 26 August 1819 at the Rosenau. Three months previously the Duchess of Kent, Duke Ernest's sister, had given birth to a girl in London's

Kensington Palace. She was christened Victoria, and was to become the Queen of Great Britain and Empress of India. By a remarkable coincidence, Albert and Victoria were brought into the world by the same midwife, Frau Charlotte Siebold. This distinguished midwife accompanied the Duke of Kent and his pregnant wife, along with several coachloads of servants and assorted pets, on the rough journey back from Germany to London, where Victoria was born on 24 May 1819. A few weeks later, Frau Siebold journeyed back to Germany to bring Victoria's future husband, Albert, into the world.

Before he divorced Louise, Ernest had become the reigning Duke of Saxe-Coburg and Gotha in a reshuffle of the Saxon duchies following the death of Albert's great-uncle, the Duke of Saxe-Coburg-Altenburg. From then onwards, and later when Ernest's younger son's name was Anglicised, he became known as Prince Albert of Saxe-Coburg and Gotha. The preacher officiating at Albert's christening at the Rosenau in September 1820 undoubtedly believed he was uttering a standard deference intended to please the Duke when he spoke of the will of God calling the infant Prince to fulfil a high position in life. Never in his wildest dreams could the good, simple Superintendent Genzler have imagined how high the child he had just baptised into the Lutheran Evangelical Church was one day destined to rise.

Albert's inherent goodness and intelligence were recognised at a very early age by his uncle, Duke Ernest's brother Prince Leopold, who in 1831 was chosen to be the first King of the Belgians. Leopold left England for Germany in 1820 after the coronation of George IV. This was his first trip abroad since the death three years previously of his wife Princess Charlotte, who had been heiress presumptive to the throne of England. Leopold had spent but a day with Albert when he pronounced him a person of a humane and benevolent character, much like that of Leopold's own mother, the Dowager Duchess Augusta of Reuss-Ebersdorf. 'No one else in the family possesses them (these qualities) to the same degree,' Leopold wrote after his visit to Coburg.[4] Albert was only a one-year-old infant at the time, yet less than a year later his grandmother the Duchess mentioned, as if in some dark prophesy, that while Ernest struck her as a vigorous lad who easily got over the normal run of child illnesses, Albert was not. 'Albert is teething like his little cousin (Victoria) but he is feverish with it and not at all well. He is not a strong child.'[5]

Albert's rather delicate constitution, which in no way impeded his boyish enthusiasm for athletic activities like gymnastics and hunting forest animals, was manifested in 'a slow and somewhat feeble pulse, low blood pressure…even as a child he fatigued easily'.[6] Even at the age of four, he insisted on being carried up and down stairs. He found it a torture to have to stay up late, doing lessons or greeting his father's guests. 'If prevented from going to bed, he would suddenly disappear and was generally found sleeping quietly in the recess of the window – for repose of some kind, though but for a quarter of an hour, was then indispensable.'[7] This abhorrence of nightly activities was something that stuck with him throughout life. His inability to last out a formal ball on his feet was noted with amusement by Queen Victoria in the early days of their relationship. He was often overcome by sudden exhaustion – it was not unusual for him to fall asleep and slip from his chair. Yet in spite of being less robust than his brother and most of his friends, he displayed an extraordinary intellectual energy. He spent many hours adding to the specimens of his 'science collection', consisting mostly of rocks, plants and garden creatures. These he gathered on long rambles with his brother through the woodlands around the Rosenau, when he was at his happiest.

Albert never got over the loss of his mother, who bequeathed to her younger son a personality full of cleverness and talent, as well as a striking physical resemblance, in his early youth, of sparkling blue eyes and a fair complexion. She also passed on a love of classical music, a pastime of little interest to his father, but which Albert cultivated with a passion and made an intrinsic part of his life. Albert missed Louise deeply, and for a long time the young Prince could not bear the sight of strangers in the house. His young mind had no inkling of the reason behind his mother's sudden disappearance, but at the approach of visitors outside his immediate family he would dash into a corner of the room and cover his face with his hands, refusing to look up or utter a word. When his father tried to force him to respond with courtesy, Albert would break into violent fits of screaming. He recoiled when confronted with the unknown, such as an unfamiliar face, which would have conjured up the memory of this upheaval in his life.

There was little time for reminiscing, for now it was time for him and his brother to begin their formal education. It was imperative to have the boys prepared for a life of responsibility, in particular Ernest, who would one day inherit the title of Duke of Saxe-Coburg and Gotha, a relatively insignificant duchy of the German Confederation, but one which boasted dynastic links through marriage to the royal families of Portugal, Belgium, Bulgaria and, in due course, Great Britain. As for Albert, his early intellectual aptitudes and natural refinement spoke of princely years ahead devoted perhaps to music, following his mother's talents, or the arts, philosophy – who could say? The boys were adored by their grandmothers, Caroline of Saxe-Coburg-Altenburg and the Duchess Augusta. In the absence of a mother, these aristocratic matrons spared no effort to see to the children's well-being. But more than the smothering affection of two elderly women, what Albert and Ernest were missing was a father figure. Albert in particular had a strong dislike of being under the wing of overbearing women.

Most people can point to friends or relations in their childhood who had a lasting influence on their lives. For Albert, the first but by no means the greatest of his early mentors outside the immediate family was his tutor Johan Christoph Florschütz. Prince (later King) Leopold knew his brother Ernest only too well. He was under no illusions about the Duke's suitability to bring up two small boys. Duke Ernest and his brother had been on hunting trips together, including one almost immediately after Louise's departure. The time spent with Ernest in those trying days before the marriage break-up had given Leopold ample opportunity to take stock of the situation at Coburg and decide what should be done. There was a family friend, the commanding figure of Leopold's physician and adviser Baron Christian Friedrich Stockmar, who later played an active role in the negotiations to place Leopold on the throne of Belgium. Leopold trusted Stockmar more than any other of his collaborators, and he therefore dispatched the doctor to the Rosenau to find out what could be done to ensure the boys' welfare. Stockmar took one look at their precarious situation and made his recommendation: Florschütz was required on the scene, the sooner the better.

In 1823, the 25-year-old philosophy and theology graduate of Jena, whose celebrated sixteenth-century university was founded in the spirit of the Protestant Reformation that arrived in the city at roughly the same time, was appointed tutor to Albert and Ernest. As well as imparting the gifts of the Enlightenment to his charges, Florschütz came to fill an emotional gap in Albert's craving for parental love. The Duke was not a cruel or heartless father: he desired, in classic bourgeois fashion, the 'very best' for his children. Sadly this did not involve giving very much of himself, rather what he could extract from his none-too-deep pockets. He could happily enjoy the boys' company, over breakfast, at story-telling time, or for that matter on a shooting trip. But his chief ambition was to see them impeccably tutored, groomed and worthy of a jaunt to the fashionable capitals of Europe to be paraded before eligible young women of high birth, and preferably of affluent parentage. Duke Ernest was nevertheless a cold and aloof man, and while Ernest could tough it out as a motherless child under the shadow of such a father, life in a broken home turned Albert into a melancholy, more sensitive youth than his brother, and one who at times expressed a morbid fascination with death.

Outwardly, however, Albert's early childhood was a joyful time of life, with few signs of the anguish he must have felt at the lack of a mother's presence. With his intellectual capacity and passion for order in all things, he looked forward to his daily lessons, eagerly absorbing every bit of knowledge that Florschütz had to impart to his pupil. 'To do something was with him a necessity,' Florschütz noted.[8]

Albert was not yet five when he began to keep a journal, a practice he regrettably gave up at an early age. Most of the entries are mundane commonplaces of a young boy's daily routine – we learn that on a certain day Albert got up, washed himself, was dressed and was happy. Other times he speaks affectionately of 'dear Papa', for, though largely unrequited, the Prince never abandoned his love and respect for his father, with whom he maintained an affectionate correspondence until Ernest's death in 1844 at the age of 60. The young boy's susceptibility to illness sent him into attacks of anxiety. 'When I awoke this morning I was ill. My cough was worse. I was so frightened that I cried.'[9] Florschütz was alert to the younger brother's predisposition to come down with all sorts of ailments as a matter of course: 'He was rather delicate than robust,' he noted. Yet the tutor was impressed by Albert's 'powers of perseverance and endurance'.[10]

That something strange was taking place under Albert's normally cheerful exterior was evident, and it was manifested in these sudden outbursts over trifles. The tears flowed over regrets at having left his books scattered about the room. He wept during a lesson because he could not find a verb that he was expected to know. The spelling mistakes he discovered in a letter he had written to his father brought on another gush of tears. Leaving aside the weeping sessions brought on by illness, there is a common thread running through each and every one of these breakdowns. Even at the age of five, Albert was developing an acute sense of duty. The young Prince cried when he failed to perform according to expectations: he was untidy, he could not recite his lessons – he even flew into a rage when his friends proposed sneaking up on a play castle from the rear instead of launching a chivalrous frontal attack. In adolescence Albert began to display an extraordinarily rigorous, self-imposed standard of high moral behaviour, the character trait that was to guide him throughout life. Albert's contemporary friend Count Arthur von

Mensdorff described his boyhood companion as 'a child of mild, benevolent disposition. It was only what he thought unjust or dishonest that could make him angry.'[11]

The Prince's journal is strongly indicative of a singular trait, not commonly found in children born to high rank, which was his awareness of the well-being of others. When a downpour of rain put a stop to a village festival, the nine-year-old Prince wrote of his disappointment that other less fortunate children were to be deprived of having fun that day. Albert's temperament always showed this fervent concern for those of whose existence most of his playmates would scarcely be aware. At around the same age, the Prince was so shocked to watch a peasant's cottage burn to the ground near the Rosenau that he took up a collection to have the house rebuilt. This act was a forerunner of the many charitable works that Albert, as the future Prince Consort, was to endow and the benevolent societies founded in his name.

Albert followed a strict daily routine all through the years of his adolescence. In summer, he rose between six and seven, an hour later in winter. He and Ernest breakfasted with their father and stepmother, then it was time to meet Florschütz to begin the daily lessons. The brothers took lunch alone with their tutor at one o'clock, and this was followed by more lessons, supper at seven and, for Albert at least, bed as soon after as possible. 'An irresistible feeling of sleepiness would come over him [Albert] in the evening, which he found it difficult to resist even in later life.'[12] The Prince was burning off intellectual as well as physical energy faster than it could be replenished without the benefit of a sound night's sleep. This was a teacher's delight for Florschütz, whose capable hand brought to the surface Albert's vast range of scholarly interests. The tutor struggled to keep up with his pupil's voracious appetite for learning. His classes took in Latin, modern languages, mathematics, philosophy and religion, all of which Albert systematised in a daily routine of his own design. The regime started in the early hours of the morning with French, history, Latin, English and mathematics. An afternoon break, spent playing outdoors or revising, led into an evening of more French language practice, finishing off at seven or eight o'clock with another round of Latin. These academic disciplines were relieved by lighter moments of music and drawing, two pursuits in which he excelled and would later share with Victoria, with equal passion. Music seemed to take Albert into a dream world, and it was one of the greatest comforts of his life. He became an accomplished organist and composer, and his *Chorale*, now known as *Gotha in A*, was played at his funeral as the coffin was lowered into the vault.

Albert and his brother embarked on their first trip abroad in the summer of 1832, when they paid a brief visit to their uncle Leopold in Brussels. This took place eight months after the death of their grandmother, the Dowager Duchess, who had been one of the most ardent supporters of a marriage between Albert and Princess Victoria, whom she always referred to affectionately as 'little Mayflower'. Three years later, the two brothers' had their confirmation at Coburg on Palm Sunday, 1835, Albert having now turned 16, his brother being a year older. The time had now come for them to broaden their education and social contacts by embarking on the classic nineteenth-century European Grand Tour.

The first stage of the journey took them to Berlin to join their father, who had his sons paraded before all the right people at Court. From there the brothers carried on to Dresden, Prague,

Vienna and Budapest, much to the alarm of their grandmother the Duchess of Gotha, who wrote to the Duke entreating him to be gentle with the boys and not oblige them to put up with rough coach journeys by night. But exhaust themselves they did, and far more than his sturdy brother, Albert was suffering the effects of travel-weariness. 'It requires a giant's strength to bear all the fatigue we have had to undergo,' he wrote to his stepmother, the Duchess Marie, on his return to Berlin. 'Visits, parades, déjeuners, dinners, suppers, balls and concerts follow each other in rapid succession, and we have not been allowed to miss any of the festivities.'[13] One senses that the term 'festivities' may have been expressed somewhat tongue-in-cheek, for Albert at that time and in future would sooner have shut himself up with a book, or simply sat and contemplated a tree, than be drawn into sumptuous banquets and courtly merrymaking.

The young Prince found himself in far more congenial surroundings on his return to Gotha, where he launched back into his studies with relish. Here, in February 1836, Albert wrote a most astonishing letter to Dr Seebode, Director of the Coburg High School. In spite of all the distractions, the social visits he was obliged to attend, even as he put it 'the howling of the wind and the winter storms', Albert had 'at length completed the framework of my Essay on the Mode of Thought of the Germans',[14] a document that traces the historical progress of German civilisation – no insignificant feat for a 16-year-old. This gives us a glimpse into one of the greatest ambitions Albert cherished, but never lived to see fulfilled, the creation of a united German state.

The year 1836 marked a turning point in Albert's life. It was by that time a foregone conclusion that Victoria would inherit the throne of Great Britain. In 1818, her father, the Duke of Kent, fourth son of George III, had married Duke Ernest's youngest and widowed sister, Victoire Maria Louise, Princess Leiningen. The year after their marriage, the Duchess of Kent gave birth to a daughter. From the first days of Princess Victoria's infancy, the Duke was in the habit of boasting to visitors at Kensington Palace, 'Look at her well, for she will be Queen of England.'[15] Victoria's father met an untimely death two years later at the age of 53, passing away the same year as his own father King George III. By an uncanny twist of fate, the Duke's three elder brothers died without surviving legitimate issue. It was left to Leopold to look after his twice-widowed sister and, most crucially, his infant niece, the future Queen Victoria. Leopold's mother, the Dowager Duchess of Coburg, died in 1831, leaving her son with the lingering memory of her hope that the young Albert, always so dear to her heart, might one day be chosen to forge a union between the House of Saxe-Coburg and the throne of England. Albert recalled in later life that even as a child of three his nurse had always told him 'that he should marry the Queen [Victoria] and that when he first thought of marrying at all, he always thought of her'.[16]

Certainly there were historical precedents for such a bond through matrimony. Leopold's marriage in 1816 to Princess Charlotte, and that of Victoria's father to Duke Ernest's sister Victoire stand as examples. Leopold was from the outset eager to bring about a formal link between the Saxe-Coburg family and the British royal family. What a splendid stratagem to ensure that the family seat achieved prominence in the future merger of the fragmented ducal states into a strong German Confederation. The obvious candidates to mould this alliance, to his mind, were Albert and Victoria, the first cousins who were only three months apart in age. The only potential fly in the ointment was the list of keen-as-mustard suitors for Victoria's hand that was growing apace across the courts of Europe, and even Albert's father believed that his elder son, Ernest, might make a more suitable candidate.

At this point, Leopold turned for advice to his friend and adviser, the canny Stockmar, a man who was to wield a decisive influence in most facets of Albert's life. Stockmar was a native of Coburg, 32 years Albert's senior, who had entered Leopold's service as family physician at the time of his marriage to Princess Charlotte in 1819. This stern yet kindly individual rose from being the bookish son of a well-to-do but otherwise unremarkable family of merchants and lawyers to become the confessor, intimate friend and mentor of persons in high political positions in several European capitals. 'It was a clever stroke to have originally studied medicine,' Stockmar reflected in later life. 'Without the knowledge thus acquired, without the psychological and physiological experiences which I thus obtained, my *savoir faire* would often have gone a begging.'[17]

Stockmar inspired trust and confidence in all who came into close contact with him.[18] He excelled as a negotiator at the very highest levels. As the person who had held Charlotte's hand until the last moment, and subsequently had to break the news of her death to Leopold, Stockmar was welcomed into the household as private secretary, spending most of his time in England. Always to be found by Leopold's side, the Coburg doctor occupied a key position in the complex diplomatic negotiations between the great European powers that eventually resulted in the independence of Belgium, with Leopold I as the new country's sovereign. In England, 'he acquired a thorough knowledge of the country, its people and Constitution'.[19] His views, which carried an enormous weight in London as well as Coburg, were therefore eagerly sought regarding the question of a match between Albert and Victoria.

Leopold would as a matter of course have been expected to call upon Stockmar for advice regarding his plan to promote Albert's marital candidacy at Kensington Palace. Stockmar had formed a favourable impression of the lad from their meetings at Coburg. The Baron's letters to Leopold provide a unique and intimate glimpse into Albert's character. In Stockmar's assessment, Albert in many respects took after his mother, displaying 'the same intellectual quickness and adroitness, the same cleverness, the same desire to appear good natured and amiable to others'.[20] Albert and Stockmar developed a friendship that was to last more than twenty-five years, and grow into a relationship of deep mutual admiration. 'The society of a man so highly distinguished as Baron Stockmar,' wrote Albert in 1839, 'was most precious and valuable to me. Above all, that complete harmony which is so necessary for any enjoyment of life always existed amongst us.'[21] In the same year he confided to his brother Ernest that what he owed to Stockmar was the teaching of 'several big principles of life, which brought me to a state of clarity and the awareness that if they are absorbed, these principles act as a support for one's character and behaviour'.[22]

The great moment arrived in April of 1836, when Duke Ernest received a letter from his sister the Duchess of Kent. He summoned Albert and Ernest to the richly appointed drawing-room in the Rosenau to inform them that father and sons were to embark on a journey to England, a country that Albert held in the highest esteem as 'the mightiest land of Europe', in whose hands 'lies the happiness of millions'.[23] They were to travel to Kensington Palace, where the boys, now young men, would be guests at their cousin Victoria's seventeenth birthday party. This was ostensibly nothing more than a courtesy call, a long-overdue gathering of the Saxe-Coburg clan, which also had the aim of giving the two brothers first-hand exposure to the world's most powerful empire. Not surprisingly, the wily Stockmar was pulling the strings, and with a camouflaged agenda in mind. The Duchess's letter had in fact been written at the good doctor's instigation. But, he insisted, 'it must be a *condition sine qua non* that the real intention of the visit should be kept secret from the Princess as well as the Prince [Albert], that they may be perfectly at ease with each other.'[24]

It mattered little that young Ernest was to make his life at Coburg, for despite the rustic existence awaiting him in this parochial backwater, he was to inherit the title to a dukedom that would assure him a station in society. Albert was a different matter: it was necessary to extract the younger and exceedingly gifted brother from the confinement of a petty German principality a tenth the size of Wales, to place him in a position that would enable him to make his mark on the world. In a word, he had to be married to the Queen of England. In contemplating Albert's maiden voyage to London, Stockmar calculated that 'If the first favourable impression is now made, the foundation stone is laid for the future edifice.'[25]

It soon came to light that Albert was not the only eligible bachelor being put forward as a suitor for the 16-year-old Princess. Britain's last Hanoverian monarch, the dissolute William IV, held the Coburg clan in utmost contempt, and he spared no effort to throw a spanner in the Leopold–Stockmar works. Albert's candidacy must be nipped in the bud, and to this end the ailing King drew up a shortlist of several rival pretenders. These were the two sons of Leopold's sworn enemy the Prince of Orange[26] and the Prussian Duke William of Brunswick, to all of whom he threw open the doors of St James's Palace for a sojourn in the capital. King William harboured a particular hatred of Victoria's mother, his sister-in-law the Duchess of Kent, who in his opinion was an unworthy and presumptuous seeker after royal privilege.[27] The fatally ill monarch's objective was to cling to life until Victoria reached her majority, which fell on 24 May 1837, in order to prevent her mother from stepping in as regent. It was rumoured that Victoria's mother was in league with Sir John Conroy, who had been the chief attendant of the late Duke of Kent, and later comptroller of the Duchess's household. Together they designed a system of rules intended to render Victoria weak and dependent upon them, in the hopes of allowing the pair to wield power through her.[28] This plan of course hinged on the King dying before Victoria reached her majority. William had no surviving heirs − not counting the eight illegitimate children he fathered from a premarital twenty-year cohabitation with the actress Dorothea Jordan − since his two legitimate daughters had both died in infancy.

One of the more picturesque bidders for Victoria's hand, if we choose to accept American newspaper gossip of the day, was the US President Martin Van Buren, who at 54 was rumoured to have thrown his hat into the ring.[29] If Van Buren had ever seriously contemplated marrying the Queen of England, his attention was soon diverted to other more pressing matters, such as the threatened collapse of the country's banking system and the onset of one of the worst economic depressions in its young history.

William's efforts to scupper the arrival of the Saxe-Coburg contingent reached near hysterical proportions. So determined was the King to stop his sister-in-law receiving her relatives in London that he summoned Lord Palmerston, the Foreign Secretary, to demand that he prohibit Ernest and his sons from setting foot on British soil. 'They must not be allowed to land,' he thundered, 'and must go back whence they came.'[30] Palmerston's entreaties to Leopold to postpone the trip fell on deaf ears. Albert and his brother Ernest, with the Prince's black greyhound Eos in tow,[31] boarded a steamboat that took them swiftly down the Rhine to Rotterdam, aiming to make the Channel crossing in mid-May for a four-week stay with their aunt the Duchess of Kent. Albert recounted how he and his brother walked about incognito on a stopover in the Hague, which worked successfully until 'the chamberlain of the Princess of Orange, saluting us with a malicious smile, unmasked us'.[32] When not suffering from bouts of severe seasickness, Albert spent his time on board trying to practise his English by engaging some British passengers in conversation.

While the steamer bearing the Coburg party plied the choppy Channel seas on its way to England, the King was rolling out the red carpet for William and Alexander of Orange, with an eye in particular on the younger Alexander, the monarch's favoured candidate. Albert and Ernest, accompanied by their father, docked in London on 18 May, to learn that five days prior to their arrival the King had thrown a gala ball for the Orange brothers at St James's Palace. William needn't have taken the trouble to parade the Dutch princes before his niece: Victoria was singularly unimpressed by the brothers, whom she dismissed in a letter to Leopold as 'very plain … heavy, dull and frightened and not at all prepossessing. So much for the Oranges, dear Uncle.'[33]

Victoria's Coburg cousins, on the other hand, struck her as 'most delightful young people … very amiable, very kind and good, and extremely merry, just as young people should be'.[34] Her appraisal of her German brethren rings with childish frivolity, a teenager confiding to her journal the sort of giggly remarks someone of less exalted status would have shared with a close friend. Ernest had dark hair and fine eyes, but she was rather disappointed with his nose and mouth. Nevertheless, his face was quite kind and intelligent. Of the two Coburg brothers presented to Victoria, one immediately took the Princess's breath away, and that was Albert. They met at Victoria's gala birthday ball at Kensington Palace, at which Albert rubbed shoulders with the luckless Orange brothers and the equally rejected Duke of Brunswick. Victoria received Albert a moment after acknowledging with a nod Ernest's departing bow. The Princess lifted her eyes to find before her a young man who, she describes with breathless impetuosity, 'possesses every quality that could be desired to render me perfectly happy'.[35] She described him as extremely handsome, 'with large blue eyes, a very sweet mouth and fine teeth, but the charm of his countenance is his expression, which is most delightful'.[36]

Victoria was completely smitten by the striking young Prince, so much so, in fact, that no sooner had he quitted London than she dashed off a letter to her Uncle Leopold, confessing that on Albert's departure she had 'cried bitterly, very bitterly'. Precipitating events somewhat, the Princess took this encounter to be the promise of 'great happiness … in the person of dear

Albert'. She begged Leopold to look after the health of one 'now *so dear* to me, and to take him under *your special* protection [Victoria's emphasis]'.[37]

There is little mention of how Albert took to his excitable cousin, apart from a letter to Florschütz written during his London visit. The Princess would have been dismayed to learn that it was nothing like love at first sight on Albert's part. 'Cousin Victoria is always friendly towards us,' the Prince writes with a seeming lack of enthusiasm. 'She is not beautiful by any means, though extremely kind and bright.'[38] But there is evidence to suggest that his health did indeed require looking after. On 1 June, while still in London, he replied to a letter from his stepmother in Coburg: 'I would have answered you sooner if I had not been suffering for some days from a bilious fever. The climate of this country, the different way of living, and the late hours, do not agree with me.'[39] The culprit was not so much the English weather as the late hours and courtly merriment to which Victoria was so utterly given. In the same letter, Albert relates his tribulations at a levee, followed by a concert he was obliged to sit through until two in the morning. The next day found Albert at a reception for the King, standing in a receiving line with nearly four thousand guests, contemplating with a feeling of misery a great supper ahead, and another concert that was to last until one o'clock. 'You can well imagine that I had many hard battles to fight against sleepiness during these late entertainments.'[40] Then came the Duchess of Kent's ball, which had Albert on his feet until four in the morning, at which point he discreetly slipped out of the ballroom and dragged himself upstairs to bed.

It was a gruelling routine for Albert, and this gave Victoria some cause for alarm. After her birthday party, Albert spent a day in his room at Kensington Palace recovering his strength, and when at last he emerged into the light of day, Victoria was startled by his pale and delicate appearance. But in the days before his departure, the couple planted the seeds of what was to blossom into an intimate friendship first, and eventually a lasting love affair afterwards, playing piano duets and discussing together the next stage of Albert's progress, which would take him on a course of study in Brussels and then on to university at Bonn.

Albert and Ernest left London to spend the next ten months in Belgium, taking in Paris on the way. In Brussels they were placed under the care of Baron Wiechmann, a retired officer of the King's German Legion.[41] During this sojourn in Uncle Leopold's newly created kingdom, the boys occupied their time exploring further into the subjects of history and modern languages, though this alone did not suffice to quench Albert's thirst for knowledge. The eminent Belgian mathematician and astronomer Adolphe Quetelet was called in to broaden Albert's skills in higher mathematics. The 17-year-old Prince astonished his teacher by asking him for tutorials in highly advanced areas, such as the application of the law of probabilities to social and natural phenomena. Albert and Quetelet formed a friendship that was to last nearly a quarter of a century, until the Prince's death. Albert paid tribute to his maths tutor in his last public speech, in July 1860, an address to the opening of the International Statistical Congress. The knowledge the Prince had acquired in Brussels in his youth was transposed almost 15 years later to the Great Hall of the 1851 International Exhibition, where 'statistical science was earliest developed'.[42]

In April 1837, the brothers travelled to Bonn, where they were to embark on their university studies. Their living quarters were in a small detached cottage near the cathedral, which they shared in the amiable company of Florschütz. Bonn was a town steeped in history and learning, thus very much to Albert's liking: a place of Roman origin, picturesquely set on the Rhine, the birthplace of Beethoven, the seat of a renowned university founded in 1784 − it was everything a young seeker of knowledge could desire. In this idyllic setting Albert would throw himself into his favourite studies of natural sciences, philosophy and music. He took up the model life of the Student Prince, even carrying off first prize at a university fencing match. Here, too, Albert formed a number of lifelong friendships with fellow German patricians, most notably Prince William of Löwenstein-Wertheim. William, the future Duke of Mecklenburg-Strelitz, in later days praised Albert's intellectual gifts, prominent among which was his ability as a composer, 'a master of the art'. There were barely enough hours in the day for Albert to fill with his pursuit of knowledge and his love of art. On excursions to nearby Cologne, the Prince spent many happy and profitable hours scouring the galleries for artistic treasures, some of which he acquired for his personal collection, including drawings by van Dyck and Dürer. He threw himself with the greatest eagerness into every facet of his studies, whether in science or the arts. 'He spared no exertion either of mind or body,' said Prince William. 'On the contrary, he rather sought difficulties in order to overcome them.'[43]

Albert's time at Court in London was fading into a distant memory, but the image of his beguiling cousin Victoria never drifted far from his thoughts. What was to become of this encounter? The Princess was not, in Albert's view, a raging beauty − but there was chemistry between them, that much was certain. But his days were now fully occupied with the pleasures and excitement of university life. Apart from his scholarly and sporting talents, fellow students remembered the Prince's fondness for mimicry, at which he showed a great ability in later life as well. The university provided ample inspiration for caricature, and Albert was celebrated for impressing his friends with a recitation of whole passages from lectures, in the same pompous style as his professors.

In early summer of 1837, however, Albert could no longer remain indifferent to what was happening in England. By late May it was evident that King William was gravely ill and that the end was but a matter of weeks away. His devoted wife, Queen Adelaide, remained at his bedside for ten days. But with great obstinacy, the King achieved his final wish by clinging to life until Victoria's coming of age. William suffered an asthma attack that suffocated him, and he died of heart failure at a quarter past two on the morning of 20 June. The historic moment in Victoria's life came four hours later. The Princess was woken at six o'clock by her mother, who told her the Archbishop of Canterbury and Francis Conyngham, the Lord Chamberlain, were at Kensington Palace and wished to see her immediately. Victoria got out of bed and went to her sitting-room, alone, her hair loose and in her dressing gown, to find the two dignitaries bowed before her. Lord Conyngham then informed the startled 18-year-old that her uncle the King was no more, and that consequently she was now Queen of England. Drafts of the official documents prepared on the first day of her reign described her as Queen Alexandrina Victoria, as she had been christened, but the first name was withdrawn at her own wish and not used again.

When Albert learnt of the dramatic change that had taken place in his cousin's life, he wrote to the young Queen, his first letter in English, to offer his 'sincerest felicitations'. Her reign, he hoped, would be 'long, happy and glorious'. Keeping his iron in the fire, he then added, 'May I pray you think likewise sometimes of your cousins in Bonn, and to continue to them that kindness you favoured them with till now.'[44]

The Queen was crowned on 28 June 1838 in Westminster Abbey, wearing the Parliament Robes of crimson velvet, trimmed with ermine and gold lace and fastened with a golden cord. The five-hour ceremony was a great ordeal and not without hitches. The aged Archbishop of Canterbury forced the coronation ring on to her fourth finger, not noticing it had been made for her fifth. 'That evening, she only managed to remove the ring after bathing her finger in iced water.'[45] Victoria's accession raised the logical question of marriage and heirs to the throne. It was no secret in Court circles that she had been left completely cold by the hopefuls paraded before her at the time of her seventeenth birthday – with the outstanding exception of the Duke of Saxe-Coburg's younger son. Albert thus became, in the eyes of the gossip set and the press, the leading candidate to partner her in a royal marriage.

During the tense days of King William's final illness, Baron Stockmar, at Leopold's behest, had stood by the Princess as her confidential adviser. Victoria never suspected at the time that the kindly doctor was hatching a plan, for years the wish of the Coburg family, to secure the marriage of the Queen of England with Prince Albert. Stockmar was obliged to tread with extreme delicacy in the execution of this scheme – though barely five feet tall and slightly built, Victoria was a fiery-tempered woman with a will of her own, not one to be bullied into an arranged marriage. It was nevertheless a blessing for Victoria to be able to count on Stockmar's reassuring presence, for she came to the throne at a time of major political turbulence and feuding. Leopold kept Albert apprised of the acrimonious struggle for power between Lord Melbourne's Whigs and the Tories led by Sir Robert Peel. Melbourne's ministry had been saved from shipwreck only by the demise of the King and the accession of Victoria, who brought new enthusiasm for the monarchy. Leopold reasoned it was good for the Prince to be acquainted with the affairs of state and the party leaders of the country because he would, if all went according to plan, one day rule alongside Victoria. Albert had a strong dislike of politics, and he considered the machinations and personal clashes that made up the daily bread of Westminster as unseemly behaviour for the people's elected representatives. 'On every side there is nothing but a network of cabals and intrigues, and parties are arranged against each other in the most inexplicable manner,' he wrote to his father.[46]

Leopold could see from Stockmar's reports that this was not an opportune moment to send Albert off to England. For now, Victoria's determination to be her own woman precluded any clumsy attempts at matchmaking. On the morning of her accession, she had breakfast with Stockmar, alone. Later that day, Victoria also insisted on receiving her Prime Minister, Lord Melbourne, in private, without the presence of advisers. The same held true for her first Council and meetings with her Ministers of State. Her mother the Duchess of Kent was still living in Kensington Palace, but Victoria sat alone at the dinner table and, for the first time in her life, that night she slept in her own bedroom.

Leopold wisely decided to remove Albert from the limelight by sending his nephews off on a holiday jaunt through Switzerland

and northern Italy. Reports had been circulating even before Albert arrived in Bonn of a marriage contemplated between the Prince and Victoria. On 28 August, Albert and Ernest, under the watchful eye of Florschütz, set off through several German towns, battling a driving rain all the way, eventually making the border crossing into Switzerland a week later, at Basel. The tour of Switzerland took them to the top of the Rigi, overlooking the Zugersee and William Tell's village of Altdorf. The three travellers then tramped across high mountain passes and through deep snowdrifts, sleeping in hostels, completing their Swiss journey on 26 September in the sumptuous surroundings and comfort of Geneva. Then on they went, Albert drinking in with wild enthusiasm the spectacular mountain scenery of Chamonix and the towering peak of Mont Blanc, afterwards crossing into Italy for a short stopover at Milan and Venice.

Victoria, who had by now moved into Buckingham Palace, was delighted with the gifts Albert sent from his trip: an album of views of the most spectacular places he visited, a dried rose plucked at the summit of the Rigi, and a scrap of Voltaire's handwriting he had picked up at the writer's house in Ferney. Albert was back in Bonn by the first week in November, eager to resume his studies of Roman law, history and languages. 'This winter will be one of very hard work,' the Prince wrote to his father, 'for we are overwhelmed with lectures, papers and exercises.'[47]

The end of the two brothers' university days together also brought an inevitable parting of the ways. Albert and Ernest were of markedly different character, yet they had remained inseparable companions throughout their adolescence and early manhood. Now Ernest was to earn the military rank befitting the heir to a German ducal state by serving with the army in

Dresden, or 'to sacrifice himself to Mars', as Albert put it in a letter to his student friend Prince William of Löwenstein. Losing Ernest's companionship was a wrenching experience that Albert expressed to William in his youthful propensity to over-dramatise: 'The separation will be frightfully painful to us,' he says in the same letter. 'Up to this moment we have never… been a single day away from each other! I cannot bear to think of that moment!'[48]

There were other plans in the making for Albert. Leopold had discussed with his niece Victoria the idea of a marriage. The Queen demurred: she was too young, as was Albert, it was all too premature − he had not as yet even mastered the English language. Albert was very dear to her, very dear indeed, as she often confided to her diary, but in her opinion the Prince required more experience, polish, self-reliance. Then too, the young sovereign had already made it clear she was having no part of an arranged marriage. In spite of her strong feelings for Albert, it was no longer enough that her family wished them to marry.

Leopold had discussed the matter at length with Albert, and after his talk with Victoria he put the Prince in the picture. Albert was ready to marry his cousin, but equally he was prepared to accept a delay. His chief concern was the risk of the Queen's sentiments turning cool after a lengthy postponement. 'If after waiting, perhaps for three years, I should find that the Queen no longer desired the marriage, it would place me in a ridiculous position, and would to a certain extent ruin all my prospects for the future.'[49]

Victoria had not by any means given up on the prospect of a marriage with Albert. The astute young monarch decided that the way to gain time to think over her future, and also to round off Albert's cultural development, would be to have him packed off on another trip abroad. In the summer of 1838, Victoria charged Stockmar with accompanying Albert on a journey. The objective, apart from the educational advantages, would be to prepare the Prince under Stockmar's tutelage for his future duties. Albert and Stockmar had until that time maintained only a casual acquaintance, but by the time of their return from an extended tour of Italy, the friendship had been sealed for life.

Together, the Prince and his mentor visited Florence, where Albert gave free rein to his passion for music. He rose at six every morning and practised on the organ with such skill that the monks of the Church of the Badia Fiorentina were heard to remark that he played as well as their own organist. Albert played the piano as well, exhausting himself all day with difficult pieces, so that by nine in the evening he was ready to drop into bed. 'Oh! Florence, where I have been for two months,' he wrote to his friend Löwenstein, 'has gathered to herself noble treasures of art. I am often quite intoxicated with delight when I come out of one of the galleries.'[50]

Leopold sent a young British army junior officer (later Colonel), Francis Seymour, to Florence to keep the Prince company and to acquaint him with the type of people he was likely to come into contact with on visits to England. 'He [Seymour] is an ordinary and easygoing English infantry officer,' Albert wrote to his brother. 'Although he is twenty-five years old, he looks seventeen and I find him quite engaging.'[51] The match was a success, and Seymour remained Albert's close friend until the Prince's death, when Seymour placed his military accoutrements on the coffin.

In March 1839 Albert and Stockmar carried on from Florence to Rome, where the Prince was granted an audience with

Pope Gregory XVI. 'We conversed in Italian on the influence
the Egyptians had had on Greek art, and then again on Roman
art,' Albert wrote. 'The Pope asserted that the Greeks had taken
their models from the Etruscans. In spite of his infallibility I
ventured to assert that they had derived their lessons in art from
the Egyptians.'[52] Naples was next on the itinerary, then Tivoli,
Siena, Lucca and Genoa, and in each city they took in the glories
of the Renaissance, all of which left Albert agape with wonder.
The trip ended at Milan, where Stockmar left the Prince in the
hands of Duke Ernest, and father and son returned to Coburg.
In his home town Albert came across many familiar faces of
his childhood, among them Florschütz, now married. Albert
resumed his studies, paying particular attention to improving his
English. His zeal for music had been so fired by his tour of Italy
that in Gotha he formed a choral society, to which he himself
lent his solo bass voice, performing works by Beethoven and
Handel. But the Prince's idyll at the Rosenau was shortlived, for
in early October 1839 he was to leave home again, this time to
embark on an eventful visit to England.

*　　　　*　　　　*

Albert's arrival at Windsor Castle on 10 October 1839 coincided
with one of the most testing, indeed one might say *explosive*,
moments in Victoria's young reign. The start of their journey
was not an auspicious one. The two brothers landed deathly ill
from seasickness after a rough overnight sailing from Antwerp.
They were too out-of-sorts during the carriage ride to the rolling
Berkshire countryside to notice that their luggage had been left
behind at the Tower of London dock.

Victoria was miffed by her cousins' delayed departure from Coburg. She had invited them to be in London on 28 September, and family relations aside this was to be taken as a royal command. Albert had just turned 20, and his birthday had not been a particularly joyous occasion for him. His father had insisted he spend the day at Gotha, contrary to the Prince's wish to celebrate his birthday in more cheerful surroundings at the Rosenau. Victoria's imperious letter cast him deeper into a sulk, for it didn't require reading between the lines to realise that his cousin was not 'a defenceless girl in need of protection [and] he could be equally strong-willed. "Let her wait," he told Ernest, a trip to London could not be arranged overnight.'[53] The postponement of her cousins' trip was hardly likely to salve the ego of a young Queen bent on asserting her will, who had several months previously managed to get herself into a difficult spot in the notorious Lady Hastings affair. Flora Hastings was a 32-year-old lady-in-waiting to Victoria's mother, the Duchess of Kent. Victoria detested Hastings, who as far as the Queen was concerned belonged to the Kent–Conroy faction of plotters. Some weeks after Hastings' return from a trip to Scotland in the company of Conroy, a married man, her expanded girth began to raise eyebrows at Court. Speculation spread like wildfire that she was carrying Conroy's child, a hypothesis shared by Victoria. Hastings refused to submit to a medical examination, but when she bowed to pressure to do so, it revealed that her swollen midriff was more likely the result of the fatal illness she had contracted, and had nothing to do with any misdeeds of Conroy's. But the damage had been done: the Kensington Palace coterie, and most dangerously the power-seeking Tories, ganged up on Victoria. Things looked bleak for the Queen when on 7

July 1839 Flora Hastings died of liver cancer. The Queen was jeered at in the streets, and her close relationship with her Prime Minister, Lord Melbourne, aroused a good deal of indecorous public comment. The outcry by the press and opposition politicians eventually abated and the problem righted itself two years later, when Peel swept the general election and the machinery was set in motion that would eventually change the royal household completely.

No sooner had the Lady Hastings affair settled to a relative calm than the political tinderbox ignited anew. The young Queen was suddenly confronted with the first major challenge to her authority, known as the 'bedchamber crisis' of May 1839. Most of the ladies of Victoria's royal household were Melbourne appointees, with close links to the families of Whig grandees. When the Tories were poised to replace Melbourne, and Peel had been summoned to the Palace, he insisted that Victoria get rid of these Whig acolytes. Peel clearly foresaw the makings of an abrasive relationship with Victoria if she were allowed to remain under the influence of her bedchamber ladies, with their strong anti-Tory bias. Victoria so detested the Tories that her refusal to dismiss the women came as no surprise to anyone close to the affair − but her obstinacy backfired, and in later years she humbly admitted her error of judgement. Peel was having nothing to do with the ministry under these terms, thus leaving Melbourne to carry on in office for another two years. It was not a particularly happy period for the Whig leader, for he knew that this marked the finale of a distinguished public life. Sadder yet, Melbourne was to lose the Queen's ear, which had always been so attentive to his counsel. Victoria and her admired Whig friend continued to correspond, but this stopped soon enough, for it was considered inappropriate for them to carry on a close relationship.

Once the news of the bedchamber crisis hit Fleet Street, the Tory press lost no time in tearing into Melbourne and, by implication, the Queen.

> Lord Melbourne is quite grave in the announcement of his [namely *Victoria's*] objection to a removal of ladies about Her Majesty…Why did not Lord Melbourne, who had in his power the sole arrangement of the young Queen's household, form it of such persons as would be equally unconnected with his own Administration?[54]

What Victoria did not know was that in the latter stages of the crisis, with the approach of the Peel ministry, Albert − by then her husband − had been manoeuvring stealthily in a series of secret interviews with Peel that brought about a complete understanding on this difficult and complex question. The fledgling statesman from Coburg and the veteran Lancastrian politician agreed that the constitutional point should not be raised, but that on the formation of the Tory Government, which came about in February 1841, at least the principal Whig ladies should be dismissed and their places filled by others, who would be appointed by Peel. The pact brought Albert into close contact with the Prime Minister, and the two men formed a bond of friendship that was to remain steadfast until Peel's accidental death at the height of his political career. This also marked an important step forward in the Prince's future political career, and showed his great skill and tact in conducting talks at the highest level.

On the day that Albert and Ernest's carriage pulled into the courtyard of Windsor Castle, the earlier stages of the crisis were subsiding into a bad memory. Victoria's self-confidence had been shaken by the Hastings affair and the bedchamber crisis, coming as they did in quick succession. But she had been successful in retaining Melbourne, whom she treasured as her confidant and mentor and, one might add, the father she never knew. Six months before Albert's second visit to England, Victoria had revealed to Melbourne her feelings about a marriage. She thought it was not for her, in spite of constant prodding from Leopold, her other great male influence, to take Albert into her life. Having rid herself of her mother's unwelcome presence, Victoria was for now intent on remaining an independent woman. She would not entertain such a prospect for at least another two or three years, and she made her opinion known to Leopold three months before Albert's visit. The Queen was certain there existed no public pressure for her to wed, and that to do so precipitously might produce discontent.

> Though all the reports of Albert are most favourable … still one can never answer beforehand for *feelings*, and I may not have the *feeling* for him which is requisite to ensure happiness [Victoria's emphasis]. As it is, I am rather nervous about the visit, for the subject I allude to is not an agreeable one to me.[55]

That was what Victoria wrote to her uncle in Brussels in April 1839. On the evening of 10 October her first cousin, the wobbly and ashen Prince of Saxe-Coburg and Gotha, minus his formal attire, which sat in a trunk on the London dock, alighted from his carriage and was escorted to the foot of the high stone staircase, atop which stood Victoria, in speechless ecstasy. That night the Queen wrote in her diary, 'It was with some emotion that I beheld Albert – who is beautiful.'[56]

Three years had passed since Albert and Victoria had met. They spent the following four days together, albeit in the company of the Duchess of Kent, Melbourne and the usual courtiers, in what for Albert amounted to an exhausting round of riding, dinner parties and dancing, but most importantly in rekindling the flame that had been ignited when they first met on the occasion of Victoria's seventeenth birthday.

On 14 October, Victoria summoned Lord Melbourne to inform him that there had been a change of plan: she had made up her mind to marry Albert. 'I think it will be very well received,' was the startled Prime Minister's reply. He then remarked paternalistically, and to Victoria's chagrin, 'You will be much more comfortable, for a woman cannot stand alone, in whatever position she may be.'[57]

Albert returned to Windsor Castle from a hunting expedition at noon the next day, to find a summons from the Queen lying on his dressing table. Half an hour later, he stood before Victoria, who received him alone in her room. As sovereign, protocol made it imperative for the Queen to seek her husband's hand in marriage, so bidding Albert to sit by her side, this is what Victoria proceeded to do. The Prince accepted without hesitation, the couple embraced, and rushed to their respective writing desks to fire off a torrent of letters announcing the royal engagement.

Leopold's heart leapt for joy when he read the letter from his niece: 'My mind is quite made up – and I told Albert this morning of it. He seems *perfection* [Victoria's emphasis], and I think that I have the prospect of very great happiness before me. I love him more than I can say.'[58] Similar expressions of happiness were sent to Stockmar, her uncle the Duke of Sussex, William IV's widow Queen Adelaide and other relations, in each case begging them not to mention it outside the immediate family before the official declaration. The day before that event was to take place, Victoria met the Duchess of Gloucester, who asked if it was not a nervous thing to do. 'Yes, but I did a much more nervous thing a little while ago,' Victoria replied. 'I proposed to Prince Albert.'[59]

Albert's delight was equally unrestrained: 'I write to you on one of the happiest days of my life, to give you the most welcome news possible,' he told Stockmar, who hardly needed to be put in the picture. 'Victoria is so good and kind to me that I am often at a loss to believe that such affection should be shown to me.'[60] To the Duchess Caroline, Albert writes with some melancholy of having to take leave of his home and his grandmother. A letter to his stepmother is similarly tinged with Germanic angst. The Prince speaks of his future position having its 'dark sides'. Still, it is a great task that lies before him, 'decisive for the welfare of so many'.[61] There is no trace of reticence in his love letters to his fiancée, whom he addresses as 'Dearest, deeply loved Victoria' or 'Dear, beloved Victoria' in letters sent from Calais and Brussels, on his way to Coburg for a short visit.[62]

Testing days were in store for Albert as well as Victoria, who on 23 November had to confront the 80 stern members of the Privy Council to read out the formal declaration of her betrothal. Victoria received them in the bow room on the ground floor of Buckingham Palace, wearing a bracelet with Albert's portrait to give her courage. The Queen confessed afterwards that she hardly recognised a face in the room, except for that of Lord Melbourne, who had tears in his eyes. Victoria's hands trembled as she read the brief formal declaration, stating her intention to ally herself in marriage with Prince Albert of Saxe-Coburg and Gotha, and she assured those in the room that she had not come to this decision without mature consideration. Victoria was overcome with relief at the end of the ordeal, which had lasted all of three minutes, retiring to a small library to compose herself before the journey back to Windsor. But there was a hitch in the proceedings: Melbourne and the Cabinet had advised Victoria to omit the words 'a Protestant Prince' from the declaration. This was a mistake, for it would have silenced those who cast doubt on his faith. The Duke of Wellington stepped in to put things to rights, by successfully putting a motion to both Houses to have the word 'Protestant' inserted in the Queen's congratulatory address.

Albert was about to get a taste of the mixed reception awaiting him as the Queen's future Prince Consort. His first disappointment was to learn that Melbourne had decided the Prince should take over his own private secretary, George Anson, a staunch Whig. Albert had acquired sufficient knowledge of British politics to realise that this appointment would put him in bad odour with the opposition Tories, who would one day certainly become the governing party. The Prince complained to Victoria in a letter from Coburg that he knew nothing of Anson, apart from having seen him dance a quadrille. 'I give you to consider, dearest love, if my taking the secretary of the Prime Minister would not from the beginning make me a partisan in the eyes of many.'[63] Albert had no choice but to accept, at least in this instance, that the Queen's prerogative ranks above that of a Prince. Victoria wished her future consort to accept Melbourne's appointment, and so it came to pass. In time, Albert not only came to accept and confide in his Secretary, but there developed between the two men a deep, trusting alliance that was only cut short by Anson's untimely death, an event that prompted the Prince to lament, 'He was my only intimate friend. He was almost like a brother to me.'[64]

A more disheartening episode was the spate of rumours to the effect that Albert was a Roman Catholic, a radical, an infidel and a host of other accusations, notwithstanding the fact that his Saxon family had been an antagonist of Rome since the days of the Reformation. Stockmar and Leopold were so anxious to dispel the malicious gossip concerning the Prince's origins that the English journalist and editor Frederick Schoberl was commissioned to produce a book, in effect a 250-page genealogical treatise, affirming the unblemished Lutheran roots of the Saxe-Coburg dynasty.

Later came the debate in Parliament over the Prince's annuity, which in the cases of the wives of George II, George III and William IV had been set at £50,000. Albert, whose only source of personal income was a share in his mother's estate, which yielded around £2400 a year, had to face the humiliation of seeing his stipend voted down to £30,000 after a highly acrimonious debate in the House.

The Prince had been forewarned by Victoria, Stockmar and others that a German in Buckingham Palace would not be a welcome sight to England's many xenophobic politicians and the landed aristocracy. This only served to stiffen his resolve to prove himself the Queen's loyal subject, moreover one who would devote his entire life to improving living standards and cultural levels at home, while raising Britain's stature in the world.

On 16 January 1840, Victoria opened Parliament amid great expectation of the formal announcement of her marriage. Thousands lined the streets around Westminster, and not a seat in the House remained vacant, as the Queen implored in a clear voice the approval of Parliament to her proposed union. The fact of the Prince's Protestant faith was recorded in the address, giving satisfaction to the sceptics and some irritation to the Government's Irish supporters, and the declaration was accepted without dissention. The marriage ceremony was set for 10 February 1840, in the Chapel Royal of St James's Palace.

2

A blessing to Queen and Country

he morning of 10 February 1840 dawned over London with torrents of rain and violent gusts of wind as Albert entered his carriage for the short drive to St James's Palace amid the sound of trumpets and the presenting of arms. He was dressed in a scarlet and white British army Field Marshal's uniform, with the Collar of the Garter surmounted by two white roses hung over his shoulder. The Prince was escorted by a squadron of Life Guards. The press that day described his looks as 'attractive' and 'pensive', and his spirits were undoubtedly bolstered by the cheers drawn from the thousands of onlookers along the route from Buckingham Palace, who had ignored the foul weather to catch a glimpse of the event.

As Victoria emerged from Buckingham Palace at a quarter-past twelve to enter her carriage, the band struck up 'God Save the Queen'. She rode behind in the last of seven carriages, 'looking paler even than usual'.[1] The Queen was wedged into the carriage with her mother, the Mistress of the Robes and the Duchess of Sutherland, wearing a vast white satin dress trimmed with orange blossoms, wearing a wreath of the same design with a veil of lace on her head. Her 12 bridesmaids were attired exactly the same. Save for the Collar of the Garter, Victoria wore no others jewels, in keeping with her wish to shun royal ostentation.

Albert was ushered into the chapel, quite appropriately as later years were to prove, to the tune of Handel's *See, the Conquering Hero Comes*. Victoria walked in behind to great fanfare, on the arm of her uncle the Duke of Sussex, who was to give her away. As she entered, the trumpets ceased and the organ began to play. For a royal wedding, it was an imposing yet simple ceremony, 'gorgeous in the extreme, giving lustre and brilliancy to the whole'.[2] The wedding festivities were, however, overshadowed by political bickering, with the Tories calling for a celebration banquet for the royal couple, simply because the Whig ministry had voiced its opposition to having one. It was the sensible Duke of Wellington, as usual, who settled the matter, reminding both parties that a traditional banquet in the Palace of Westminster would not be feasible, simply because it had been gutted by fire in 1834. In the end, it was decided to follow up the service with a banquet at Buckingham Palace, where guests were treated to slices from a wedding cake weighing three hundred pounds. Once the festivities were over, the newlyweds drove to Windsor Castle, their old travelling coach slowed to a snail's pace by the great crowds that lined the road, so that they did not reach Windsor until eight o'clock. The honeymoon planned by Victoria was all too brief for Albert's taste – all of three days, and then back to work for the Queen, just as she had insisted in a letter to Albert before he arrived in England for the wedding. The Prince had nonchalantly ignored the petulant tone of his fiancée's letter reminding him of who was to assume the role of master, or in this case *mistress* of the household. 'You forget, my dearest love, that I am the Sovereign, and that business can stop and wait for nothing.'[3]

Albert did not respond – it was his way to keep a tight rein on his emotions, at least in the early days when he was finding his footing. Victoria was a good deal more excitable, and far less inhibited in most other respects. We do not know if Albert had acquired much sexual experience in the years prior to his marriage, but there is no reason to suspect that at Bonn he would have allowed his refined artistic temperament to stand in the way of an occasional caper in the company of his fellow students. Victoria's utterances after her bridal night speak of Albert as a man of 'excessive love and affection' who gave her 'feelings of heavenly love and happiness I could never have hoped to have felt before … His beauty, his sweetness and gentleness … to be called by names of tenderness, I have never yet heard used to me before was bliss beyond belief.'[4] Clearly the Prince was acquainted with the task before him.

If Albert can be accused of prudery in his public tastes, his intimate relationship with Victoria was of a far more passionate genre, and a stormier one as well, as he was soon to find out. Albert's overt stiffness and the Queen's fiery temperament were inevitably to clash at some point, but the Prince quickly learnt to master these squabbles, in most instances, with composure. After one of their arguments Albert locked himself in his room, ignoring Victoria's demand to be allowed to enter, in the name of the Queen of England. When after a few moments she calmed down and asked to be let in as his wife, the door opened immediately and marital bliss was restored to Buckingham Palace. Victoria almost always yielded to the Prince, in the confidence that his intellect and judgement were to be looked up to – quite literally, in fact. Albert was only five feet seven inches, yet he towered over the diminutive Queen, who stood barely five feet tall.

In the early months of Albert's new life in England, and indeed throughout his life, he never once showed any regrets at having taken the fateful step. 'I realise more and more each day that until one is married, one's mind is not settled, as a true and faithful match between two people gives life its right direction and balance,' he wrote to his brother.[5] Yet the Prince spent a good deal of time brooding over his lack of authority and the absence of a defined role as the Queen's Consort. 'In my home life I am very happy and contended,' he wrote to his university friend Prince William three months after the marriage. 'But the difficulty in filling my place with the proper dignity is that I am only the husband, and not the master in the house.'[6] Everything revolved around Victoria, who at this stage would not allow Albert to be present when she received her ministers. She did not let him see any official documents or discuss affairs of state with visiting politicians. To Albert's growing frustration, he rightly perceived the Queen to be firmly under the thumb of two individuals. Prime Minister Lord Melbourne dominated her political thinking, while the all-powerful Baroness Louise Lehzen, who had been Victoria's governess, held sway over the royal household and looked after the Queen's private correspondence and finances. Of the two, it was Albert's scheming countrywoman who caused him the greatest irritation.

Melbourne's influence, through ornate flattery and Victoria's adherence to him as a father figure, was in the end a self-righting problem: the Whigs' days as the country's ruling party were numbered. By August of the following year, Victoria's little-loved

Sir Robert Peel would be in power at the head of a Tory ministry. Lehzen was a more complex obstacle, but in good time the domineering Baroness would also be dealt with. For now, the Prince needed to find an outlet for his youthful energy and enquiring mind, both of which were shackled by a life of enforced and undesired leisure.

Albert had come to England at a time of national crisis on several fronts, events that stimulated his concern for public welfare and the downtrodden of society, as well as Britain's standing in Europe and throughout the Empire. The Prince took to riding through the streets for a daily 'airing', as the papers put it. His excursions took him to what where then comparatively distant corners of the city, from Regent's Park to Battersea and as far afield as Victoria Park. But he did not have to stray very far from the cloistered luxury of Buckingham Palace to be aware of misery and depravation on a scale he could not have imagined in his pastoral Coburg, or on his travels through the cultural havens of Italy or the sparkling valleys of Switzerland.

Soaring food prices following on from three years of poor harvests, and this, coupled with a manufacturing slump and plummeting trade, had brought the country's economy to its knees. The Government's budget had been in deficit since 1836, soaring to a record £1.5 million in 1840, with no improvement in sight. The Chartists had taken their campaign for political reform and working-class empowerment to the streets, bringing clashes so violent that even a battle-seasoned soldier like the Duke of Wellington was struck with horror by what he had witnessed in the riot-torn streets of Birmingham. Criminal gangs in Ireland were on the rampage, killing people by the hundreds, while the courts were capable of delivering only three convictions in one year. In Britain's overseas territories and beyond, the French colonists of Canada were in a state of revolt, the West Indies were seething with sedition, in Afghanistan Britain had plunged into a campaign that was to cost the army its worst ever military disaster, and a state of war existed with China.

Closer to home, Albert had an awareness, and often first-hand experience, of the destitution afflicting tens of thousands of London's poor. At that time upwards of twenty thousand prostitutes worked the streets, and some two thousand brothels were in operation, a state of licentiousness that leaves open to the imagination the extent of diseases like gonorrhoea and syphilis. Thousands barely survived in unbelievably squalid living conditions. In some neighbourhoods thirty people or more were crammed into a single room, and any respectable citizen straying into one of the city's gin-sodden slums stood a good chance of meeting a violent end. People with business in the East End would routinely don a metal spike-studded collar to avoid being garrotted or having their throats cut in an alley. As one contemporary observer put it, 'Pauperism prevailed throughout the kingdom to an extent hitherto unprecedented.'[7]

Albert looked about him, he listened to reports, and was deeply dismayed by what he saw and heard – this, after all, was the metropolis, the epicentre of the world's greatest empire. But he was equally pained by his own lack of an official position which would allow him to act in the name of the Crown, an institution, it must be said, that did not enjoy much public admiration. The identification of the monarchy with the government of the day had until then been more than a purely formal one. But now, 'There were ominous signs of a decline in the power of the Crown. It was no longer so easy...for the Crown to secure the return of its government at election time.'[8] The start of Victoria's reign did not bring an improvement in the Crown's standing. The Queen's unfortunate intervention in the Lady Hastings affair, Victoria's obstinacy in the bedchamber crisis, her close identification with the Whigs and in particular Lord Melbourne (there were occasions when she was heckled in public as 'Mrs Melbourne') cut deep into the resurgence of popularity that had heralded her accession to the throne. It would be Albert, and he alone, who in the next two decades would restore the monarchy's prestige by placing the Crown at the service of the people.

Duke Ernest and Albert's brother had been present at the wedding, staying on for three months as guests of the royal couple. They left for Gotha on 8 May, and their departure signalled the rupture of Albert's last tie with his native country. The Prince found himself, if not stateless, most definitely in want of official recognition of his status as the Queen's husband. There was no provision in the British constitution, which Albert took pains to study in depth in twice-weekly sessions,[9] for the title and precedence of the husband of a Queen Regnant, while the wife of a king enjoyed a high rank assigned by law. When this matter was brought before Parliament in January, a month before the wedding, it was decided that a simple Naturalisation Bill would suffice to confirm Albert's legal right of citizenship. A month later, Parliament took this a step further by conceding Albert 'place, pre-eminence and precedence next to Her Majesty'.[10] Queen Victoria at the time wanted the title of King Consort to be conferred upon her husband, but she was strongly urged by Stockmar, Lord Aberdeen and Peel to abandon the idea and so avoid a constitutional crisis. But it was not until 1857, four years before Albert's death, that the designation of Prince Consort was officially granted to him, though he had for many years everywhere been addressed by that title. In 1840 it was acknowledged in the Regency Bill that Albert was entitled to rule in the event of Victoria's death and her successor being under the age of 18. The controversial bill passed by Parliament in July of that year did not require a regency council to operate alongside the Prince, potentially giving him more power than earlier proposed regents.

Albert was overjoyed at this victory over those inside the Government, as well as many of the establishment grandees, who resented the intrusion of a foreigner in their country's public affairs. 'You will understand the significance of this matter and that it gives my position here in the country a fresh importance,' he wrote to his brother Ernest.[11] The bill had met with opposition even from Victoria's uncle the Duke of Sussex. However, thanks to Stockmar's persuasive arm-twisting and manoeuvring in the corridors of Westminster, its passage was secured without debate – and not a moment too soon, for at the end of March Victoria discovered that she was expecting her first child. This was the moment she had dreaded: finding herself pregnant so soon put her in a state of great anxiety. She was a young girl, a wife of less than two months who adored a life of dances, banquets and social gaiety until the early hours. That would soon be brought to a halt, and who knows what lay in store at the crucial moment? There was the awful memory of Uncle Leopold's wife Princess Charlotte of Wales, who had died giving birth to a stillborn son.

Albert was at a loss to comprehend his wife's tears, since coming as he did from a sturdy country background, childbirth was the most natural occurrence in a woman's life and nothing to be feared. Yet he was quick to rise to the occasion. 'Despite his youth and inexperience, he handled the situation with commonsense and kindness, singing and playing to her or reading aloud while she rested on her sofa.'[12]

As for Stockmar, it was mission accomplished, and now came the time for him to take his leave of England and return to the quiet life of Coburg. Stockmar had acted as a pivotal force in smoothing the way for Albert in three crucial stages of his life. He had brought Florschütz to the Rosenau to enlighten and educate the young Prince, he had promoted his marriage with Victoria, and finally he had secured for Albert the position in England for which his Uncle Leopold had once seemed destined. The old Baron had moreover instilled in Albert the conviction that his predestined task was to reunite the Crown with the nation, to ensure that the Palace set an example for the people, and that this labour required a strict adherence to principle and a separation of the Crown from party.

'This Act once passed,' Stockmar wrote in August 1840, 'my business here is at an end for the present, perhaps forever.'[13] His farewell message to Albert, on the eve of the Prince's twenty-first birthday, came with the sage counsel to 'Never lose self-possession or patience, but above all, at no time and in no way, fail in princely worth and nobleness. Continue, dear Prince, to insist upon honour, integrity and order in your household.'[14]

Albert's acceptance into the fabric of British society came early as far as his popularity with the public at large was concerned, but this had nothing to do with the conferral of titles. In fact, it was these very acts of official recognition that the upper classes found so irksome. Stiff resistance arose from the usual quarters – led by the Duke of Sussex – when the Queen asked for Albert's name to be included in the liturgy, which in due course it was, so that people would henceforth pray in church for himself, as well as for the Queen and her children. Victoria's uncle's hostility towards the Prince transcended significant issues like the Regency Bill, sticking on such petty matters as making room in St George's Chapel for Albert's banner. The landed aristocracy, a powerful force in nineteenth-century England, were mistrustful of this cerebral German. Yes, it had to be admitted, the Prince gave a good account of himself as a horseman, and there was no denying his ability as a marksman when out on a shoot, but he made himself thoroughly 'un-clubbable' by refusing to partake in their habits of swearing, wenching and drunkenness. Albert may have felt hurt at having been spurned by the patricians of British society, but to his credit he showed little interest in appeasing their xenophobic intolerance.

The Prince had now risen to a position which allowed him to occupy the seat next to the throne at functions presided over by the Queen, in spite of the customary grumbling by the Duke of Sussex and others. Speaking a few days after the prorogation of Parliament on 11 August, the Duke of Wellington, who never had much tolerance for Court etiquette when it conflicted with common sense, said it was quite appropriate for Albert to take his place alongside Victoria. 'Let the Queen put the Prince where she likes, and settle it herself – that is the best way.'[15] At this time, Albert had been appointed Colonel Commandant of the 11th Hussars; likewise he was made a member of the Privy Council, and had also been taken into Victoria's confidence by being granted access to all her foreign dispatches. This was done on Lord Melbourne's advice, a mark of growing appreciation by the political classes of Albert's importance and abilities.

The Prince enjoyed a status that encouraged him to strike out on his own. Being held up as the object of scorn by the nobility mattered little to him − indeed, in his view this segment of British society was part of the problem. Albert had his sights set on nobler endeavours. The baptism by fire came in June 1840, in the guise of an invitation to deliver his first public address, to the Society for the Abolition of the Slave Trade.[16] This was a golden opportunity for Albert to demonstrate that he shared the public interest in the great questions of the day, so on 1 June he presided at a meeting calling for the definitive abolition of this abominable practice. On the morning he was to deliver his speech, which in fact amounted only to a few brief introductory remarks, Albert came to the breakfast table overcome with nervousness. He had committed his comments to memory, and repeated them to Victoria. This was not only his maiden public speech, but the first he was to give in English. At the meeting hall, the Prince spoke passionately to a crowd of more than five thousand abolitionists, expressing his conviction that slavery was 'a stain upon civilised Europe' as well as 'a state of things repugnant to the state of Christianity'.[17] When he was finished, the audience rewarded him with a fervent ovation.

Albert abandoned the hall in triumph, conveying his exhilaration in a letter to his father in Coburg, with the boyish enthusiasm of a student who has just received an exam pass.

> My speech was received with great applause, and seems to have produced a good effect in the country. This rewards me sufficiently for the fear and nervousness I had to conquer before I began my speech. I composed it myself, and then learnt it by heart, for it is always difficult to have to speak in a foreign language before five or six thousand eager listeners.[18]

Albert's first appearance as a public speaker came very close to being his last. A little over a week after delivering his speech,

Albert and Victoria were out for their customary early-evening ride in a small phaeton. They had hardly gone a hundred yards from Buckingham Palace when Albert noticed on the footpath 'a little mean-looking man holding something towards us,' as he later wrote to his grandmother.[19] Before the Prince had time to realise the object the man was holding was a pistol, a shot was fired at barely six paces. The four horses drawing the open carriage took fright, and Albert seized Victoria's hands, but she had not spotted the assailant and had no idea why her ears were ringing. The man drew his second pistol and fired, but the bullet also went wide of the mark. This time Albert pulled Victoria below the seat. He then ordered the postilion to carry on as normal, and the couple arrived on time for a visit to the Duchess of Kent. 'From thence we took a short drive through the Park, partly to give Victoria a little air, partly also to show the public that we had not...lost all confidence in them.'[20]

The would-be assassin, Edward Oxford, was captured by an enraged crowd which the police struggled to prevent turning into a lynch mob. Oxford never denied his guilt, and was tried for high treason, declared to be insane and committed to an asylum for life. Albert's display of bravery brought results: in the days following the attack, he and Victoria were received with ovations everywhere they went. The Queen noted in her diary that when they entered the opera a few days later, the whole house rose and cheered, waving hats and handkerchiefs.

This was but the first of seven attacks on Albert and Victoria over a period of forty years, almost always involving a mentally deranged individual acting from some obscure motivation. Two years after the Edward Oxford incident, the royal couple were the intended victims of a gunman named John Francis, who leapt out of the crowd and fired at the royal carriage near St James's Palace. Francis managed to escape his pursuers, so Albert and Victoria rode out again the following afternoon in a heroic attempt to flush out their assailant and catch him in the act. The plan worked: Francis fired another shot at the carriage, and this time he was arrested by a waiting constable. It was an incredible act of bravery on the part of the Prince and Queen, but all it brought in the end was a death sentence commuted to transportation for life. Albert believed the attempt had been encouraged by Edward Oxford's acquittal two years earlier, a justifiable opinion given that less than a week after the Francis incident another would-be assassin, John William Bean, took a shot at the royal carriage. His gun was found to be loaded with paper and tobacco, but nevertheless the crime was still punishable by death. Albert thought this too harsh a sentence for a person of unsound mind. He petitioned the Government to change the statute making any offence against the Sovereign, short of assassination, punishable by seven years' imprisonment and flogging. Bean, a half-witted hunchback, got eighteen months, but neither he nor any person who violated the act in the future was flogged. Not long after the birth of her son Arthur, in May 1850, Victoria was riding up Constitution Hill for the christening when an Irish drifter, William Hamilton, opened fire on her carriage. His gun was powder-filled, but he was nevertheless convicted and given the mandatory sentence of seven years' penal transportation.

The most serious incident came a week later, when a former army officer, Robert Pate, struck Victoria with his cane as she was returning from a visit to Cambridge House. It was only the Queen's sturdy bonnet that saved her from serious head injuries, though she did sustain bruises to her forehead. Pate was caught and given the same sentence as Hamilton. There were two further assassination attempts, both of which occurred after Albert's death, in 1872 and 1882. In her widowhood, Victoria seemed to have given up caring for her personal security. Several years after Albert's death, the Queen's Secretary Sir Charles Grey warned of a plot to kidnap her while she was at Osborne. Victoria replied that she had no intention of changing her travel plans and 'must ask not to have this mentioned again'.[21]

*   *   *

Albert was lacking in political experience, most certainly the sort of high skulduggery that was wielded with such proficiency by the likes of Palmerston, Gladstone and Disraeli. On the other hand, the Prince knew full well that in order to raise the prestige of the Crown, which the last two Hanoverian monarchs had driven into the doldrums, the sovereign must be kept at a distance from party politics in the public perception. Shortly after his marriage, at the age of only 21, Albert made it a point of principle to avoid any semblance of partisanship in his public remarks or his dealings with politicians. However, this did not preclude his assuming an active role as what would today be termed an 'honest broker'. Albert defined this neutral position in a memorandum written on 15 April: 'My endeavour will be to form my opinions quite apart from politics and party, and I believe such an attempt may succeed.'[22] Victoria gradually succumbed to her adored husband's strict impartiality, and even Melbourne impressed upon her, through Albert, the need for the Queen to give up her hostility towards the Tories, for it was a foregone conclusion that

Peel was soon to win the general election. The Prince knew it was very much in his interest to cultivate the Crown's rapprochement with the Tories: with Peel back in power and Melbourne dispatched to the opposition benches, Albert no longer had a rival for the position of most trusted and influential adviser to the Queen.

The Prince was beginning to live up to the acclaim heaped on him by Lady Augusta Stanley,[23] a lady-in-waiting to the Duchess of Kent, who talks of him being a, 'blessing to the Queen and country', and describes his attributes as 'his kindness, his well-conditioned mind and tastes, and his anxious desire to do what is right and encourage and develop in others all that is good.'[24]

The final months of 1840, leading up to the year of the general election, were for Albert a time of consolidation of his growing political power in the Palace. To many of those who came into contact with him, the Prince gave the impression of being something of a prude, an overly devout Lutheran who seemed to hold himself prouder of this designation than any of the titles or privileges he had been granted since his marriage. This was an unfair judgement. It must not be forgotten that Albert's apparent puritanism stemmed from a sense of the responsibility that had been thrust upon him as Prince Consort. He never lost sight of his self-imposed obligation to be of service to others through diligent labour and exemplary conduct. This moral philanthropy, one writer argues, 'was born of an awareness of the consequences of irresponsibility which he had witnessed in his own family'.[25] There may have lurked in Albert's psyche a desire to atone for his father's, and later his brother's, moral failings. But it would be wrong to dismiss out of hand the sincerity of the Prince's compassionate and unselfish character. Albert firmly believed he had been called to a higher station in life, from which he held the power to uplift and refine the condition of his fellow subjects. To realise this ambition, Albert the mistrusted foreigner, the interloper, was forced to tread a rocky path, strewn with obstacles of an institutional as well as a personal nature. One of the most formidable among the latter was Baroness Louise Lehzen.

Lehzen conformed in every respect to the caricature of a poor Lutheran pastor's daughter – artless, unworldly, a plain woman in every respect. But underneath this gormless facade, as Albert was shortly to find out, there lurked a deeply devious and scheming character. She was one of the Coburg clan, who rose to become governess and later the close confidant and companion of Queen Victoria. The severe, watchful Lehzen has been aptly described as 'a very soberly dressed parrot, with her sharp black eyes, bird-thin mouth…her glossy black head cocked on one side so that her sharp ears might catch any whisper'.[26] This stealthy and secretive woman, who rarely left the young Victoria's side, was not only frightening in her appearance – she was downright dangerous.

Lehzen had formed part of the future Duchess of Kent's entourage in Germany, and when the family moved to England in 1819, to strengthen the as yet unborn Victoria's claim to the throne, Lehzen was invited to accompany the Duchess and her husband Prince Edward Augustus as part of the household. Lehzen was appointed Victoria's governess, and quickly began to gain ascendancy over the Princess. When the dying William IV recognised Victoria as his heir, the King bolstered Lehzen's prominence by making her a Baroness of Hanover. With Victoria's ascendance to the throne, Lehzen was installed at Buckingham Palace as the Queen's unofficial private secretary, replacing her mother in influence and affection.

The arrival of Albert on the scene set Lehzen's antennae flailing about. She lost no time in intriguing against the Prince, fearful of losing her position of almost absolute control over Victoria's outlook on politics and personal matters. Albert possessed a gentle, compassionate soul, but he was by no means naïve or unwary of the challenges to his emerging authority at the Palace, a development much to his liking. For the Prince to make headway in winning over Victoria's mind, now that her heart was totally given to him, he would have to cleave the bind by which the Queen hung steadfastly to Lehzen's retrograde thinking. Melbourne found her repulsive, Stockmar was convinced she was a drunkard, and to Lytton Strachey she was a 'narrow, jealous, provincial' woman.[27] The task Albert set himself was no easy one: Lehzen was never to be found far from Victoria's side, even at official functions of the most solemn nature, such as the Coronation, where 'dearly beloved, angelic Lehzen'[28] occupied a place immediately above the royal box.

Lehzen's dominance was absolute: when the Princess was 13, the Duchess of Kent presented her daughter with a diary, with instructions that her governess be given access to her entries, a practice that persisted even after Victoria became Queen. Lehzen had control over most of Victoria's personal matters, even her finances, meaning that she had the power to approve or reject any of the Queen's (and consequently Albert's) spending. But the degree of her intimacy went beyond the remit of Personal Secretary. 'When she moved to Buckingham Palace, the Queen ordered there be a doorway made between her own room and that of Lehzen, intending to show everybody that she esteemed her old governess more highly than her mother,'[29] who was sent to live in apartments some way from her. This private doorway was kept even after the Queen's marriage. Lehzen was in every sense Victoria's 'yes' woman, always telling the Queen she was right – and indeed why not, since Victoria's opinions almost always faithfully reflected the teachings of her governess?

In a single morning, Lehzen turned from being a source of irritation to Albert, into a venomous back-stabber. In the final weeks of Victoria's pregnancy, Albert had all but stepped into the role of uncrowned king. Victoria had presented him with a treasured key to the red dispatch boxes that every day are delivered by a courtier of the royal household to the monarch for signature. One day Albert noticed that several of these boxes from the Foreign Office had failed to appear in the Queen's study. The missing boxes were eventually located – they had been waylaid by Lehzen, and were lying on her desk.

Albert was furious: this was the final straw. The incident opened his eyes to the reality that simply devising a scheme to have Lehzen sidelined would not do the trick – she would have to go. What brought about her eclipse from power, though it would require another two years finally to see her off, was the birth of Albert's first child, Victoria Adelaide, on 22 November 1840.

Victoria had dreaded her pregnancies: no more dancing, riding or girlish fun for this high-spirited, 21-year-old Queen. Vicky, as her first-born became known, was followed almost exactly a year later by their second child, the Prince of Wales, Albert Edward. To Victoria's dismay, seven more offspring were to follow, but what was she to do? The only contraceptive method available to her was abstinence, an alternative not at all to the couple's liking. Albert might have projected an image of prudery to the outside world, but this was far from the reality when in his wife's intimate company. He found his amorous life thoroughly enjoyable, while Victoria's sexual appetite was said to be voracious.

Lehzen's departure came as a consequence of Vicky's falling ill a few months after her christening in February 1841. The Baroness had placed the nursery in the hands of a Mrs Southey and the Royal Physician, Sir James Clark, who had already discredited himself as a practitioner in misdiagnoses in the Lady Hastings affair. Clark trivialised the child's rather serious illness as a minor colic, at which point Albert let loose with a ferocious colic of his own. In a note to Victoria, the Prince threatened to hold her responsible for their daughter's fate. He launched into a tirade against the incompetent Clark, accusing him of poisoning Vicky with calomel.[30] It would be on Victoria's head if the child died, he thundered.

It is not known what steps Victoria took to dismiss her guardian of nearly twenty years, though it would undoubtedly have involved a good deal of tears and hand-wringing. But in September 1842 Lehzen was gone, sent off with an annual pension of £800 to a town near Hanover, in which every wall of her small house was covered with portraits of the Queen.

That Victoria acknowledged Lehzen's departure had been for the best is made evident in the biography of Albert that she later had commissioned. 'A mistake…had been committed in not establishing the Prince from the first as Private Secretary of the Queen, and placing the internal arrangements of the Royal Household under his immediate control.' The official biographer says that investing Lehzen with these powers was inevitably 'to bring her into collision with the natural head of the household'.[31] One can be assured that Victoria had scrutinised every word of the text before granting it her royal approval.

The internal arrangements of the royal household alluded to in the official biography happened to be Albert's next target. Buckingham Palace before the Prince came on the scene was in a state of organisational chaos of the highest magnitude. The Palace was inundated with an army of servants in service to the Queen, in a classic case of too many cooks spoiling the broth: a multitude of staff working independently at cross-purposes to one another, and responsible to three different heads, namely the Lord Steward, the Lord Chamberlain and the Master of the Horse.[32] These were the three great officers of state, appointed anew with each change of government, and on the basis of sheer favouritism, without regard to qualifications for office. There was no uniformity of system or semblance of harmonious working between the various departments at the Palace. These dignitaries were responsible for all that concerned the interior of the buildings, while the exterior was the realm of the Office of Woods and Forests. This muddled arrangement led to a surreal state of affairs in which the function of cleaning the inside of the windows fell to the Lord Chamberlain's staff, who nonetheless lacked the authority to ensure that the outsides were clean as well, for this was the domain of Woods and Forests. Likewise, the Lord Steward laid the fires in the Palace which, as Albert constantly complained, were never sufficiently hot. The Lord Chamberlain's remit did not extend beyond lighting the fires. The latter officer was also in charge of providing the lamps, but it was the Lord Steward who was charged with cleaning, trimming and lighting them. Replacing a broken pane of glass often entailed a wait of months, given the need to put the request through a multitude of channels. There was no hierarchy in place to manage the Palace serving and attending staff, who tended to come and go as they pleased, for none of the three great officers kept a representative on the premises.

The silliness of the whole business might have struck a casual onlooker as a piece of British quaintness gone awry. Albert's orderly mind, however, was governed by the principle 'Wehn schon, den schon' ('If something is worth doing, it is worth doing well'). Hence the prevailing turmoil at Buckingham Palace left him rattled to the core. The trouble was that each of these three powerful offices employed people closely allied with friends and patrons of the major political parties. Sir Robert Peel, who had taken office in August 1841, was reluctant to antagonise forces that would inevitably rise against any attempt to reform a system of patronage enshrined in convention from time immemorial. They were not interested in having their authority challenged, much less by a German prince. Then again, Peel reasoned, a downgrading of these roles would render them less desirable to future occupants from the Lords.

Albert tactfully expressed his agreement that one should not tamper with such ancient institutions. Nevertheless, he asked Peel to help him introduce improvements to combat 'the existing and crying nuisances' caused by this clumsy and counterproductive system, or 'confusion', as he put it.[33] Stockmar then entered the fray, suggesting with the wise temperance acquired in his many years of treating with the royal household, that the changes should emanate from the officers of state themselves, by investing the Master of the Household with the authority to put the reforms into effect. It took Albert another three years of perseverance to bring about a logical system of management at Buckingham Palace. But persevere he did, and in the end, true to Stockmar's proposal, the Master of the Household was given absolute power over the Palace's whole internal operation. It was for Albert a triumph of Germanic centralisation and rational thinking. He even succeeded in putting an end to the wasteful habit of lighting the Palace candles only once, after which they were discarded or pinched by the servants.

On 25 April 1843 another Princess was added to the royal family. Alice, Victoria's second daughter and third child, kept up the Saxe-Coburg family tradition of reproducing itself with gusto, with the birth of seven children in ten years. Alice lived just long enough to see two of her children succumb to accident and illness, before dying herself of diphtheria in 1878, on the anniversary of her father's death, at the age of 35. This was a tragedy which Albert would not live to see, and it left Victoria shocked with grief. But Alice's birth coincided with an exceedingly happy time in the Prince's life. He was at last beginning to unfurl his artistic talent and high ideals over the country.

Flushed with his victory over the dreaded Lehzen and the success of his proposals for royal household reforms, Albert at this point was more determined than ever to bring the Crown closer to the people. An example of this effort to modernise the monarchy came in the aftermath of the disastrous war in Afghanistan. Soldiers were returning to India by the thousands from the empty victory achieved after the 1842 massacre of an entire army near Kabul. Prosecuting the Afghan war had increased the deficit in the Government's hard-pressed coffers to £5 million, forcing the Tories to bring in sweeping belt-tightening measures. Peel announced the reintroduction of a national income tax, which had been removed at the end of the Napoleonic Wars in 1815. This was set at seven pence in the pound for all incomes above £150 a year. When the Queen declared her intention to become a taxpayer, it didn't take much to spot the encouraging hand of Albert behind her decision. 'It was a surprise in the history of the relationship between the monarchy and the people, a hint that in future, monarchs might share the life of their subjects … that they might rule less through power and more through example.'[34]

Albert considered this a symbolic gesture, albeit one in accord with his grander vision of the modern monarchy. 'Modernise or Perish' could well have been the motto on the Prince's desk, a warning of the fate awaiting a European monarchy that turns its back on the people – and there were several examples across the Channel to bear out the validity of this maxim. The absolute monarchy was a doomed institution, a truth that royal despots, most strikingly in France, were to learn in the 1848 upheaval. Albert saw the writing on the wall, and he was eager to pass on his convictions to his family. The children were taught the principle that the Crown signifies responsibility as well as privilege, and that ministerial responsibility flows as a logical necessity from the monarch's dignity and accountability to Parliament. 'Make independence, not subservience, the essential of service,' he wrote in one of his letters of wise counsel to Vicky when she was German Empress, 'and you compel the Minister to keep his soul free towards the Sovereign, you ennoble his advice, you make him staunch and patriotic'.[35] Albert worked ceaselessly to make this the guiding principle of the modern monarchy, based on its concern for the well-being of the people.

Peel felt a sincere admiration for Albert, quickly realising his remarkable character and abilities. He saw that the Prince could be immensely useful to the nation. One of the first of the Tory Prime Minister's acts upon taking office was to make use of the Prince's talents in a way that would not provoke political controversy, for in the House as well as the shires, there still lurked powers that took a dim view of the Queen's husband, what's more a German, meddling in affairs of state. It was Peel's initiative to appoint a royal commission to promote the fine arts in Britain, and importantly to oversee the rebuilding of the Houses of Parliament. Peel suggested to Albert that he accept the chairmanship of the newly created commission, with a brief to find a way to use the reconstruction of the Palace of Westminster as a focal point to advance the public's appreciation of art.

Albert was 22, and had been living in England for less than two years when he abruptly found himself thrust into the task of overseeing the decoration of his adopted country's ancient seat of parliamentary democracy. The Prince threw himself into this project with his customary eagerness. One of his first steps was to appoint a select committee on the fine arts, whose report, after much debate, called for the House of Lords to be decorated with large fresco paintings. 'It was the Fine Arts Commission, under the chairmanship of Prince Albert, which between 1841 and 1861 masterminded the choice of subjects, artists and sculptors during this important period of patronage. The hand of Albert is very evident throughout.'[36] Experts were brought in from the School of Design, the Royal Academy, the Arundel Society and other organisations concerned with the arts. Given the chairman's personal preferences, it came as no surprise that the design they settled on was the modern German version of Raphaelesque Italian. Albert supported the view that Britain, a country he esteemed for its leadership in industry, should also place itself at the forefront of innovation in the arts, which in this case applied to fresco-painting technique. The Prince was determined to transplant this distinctly continental European school of art to London.

Until 1928, there stood in the garden of Buckingham Palace a small pavilion erected by Albert and decorated by several celebrated British painters of the day, including such prestigious names as Sir Edwin Landseer and Sir William Ross. The central, octagonal room of half-moon-shaped lunettes and the two walls of the central room were decorated with heroic scenes from John Milton and Sir Walter Scott, whose romantic tales of chivalry Albert and Victoria were most fond of reading to one another. Albert was satisfied that this work could be applied to the greater undertaking at Westminster, and in this sense the garden pavilion represented a forerunner of the first series of frescos that were to adorn the walls of Parliament.

Early in 1842 a competition was announced to select the best designs. An exhibition of 140 cartoons of the works submitted was held in July 1843, attracting up to thirty thousand visitors a day. The daily mob scene at the Houses of Parliament was a source of great satisfaction to the Prince and the Commission, for the crowds were made up largely of ordinary citizens, many of humble status who insisted on bringing infant children into the halls with them. These were 'collected in droves by the police and packed up in the vestibule of Westminster Hall to await collection by their parents'.[37] The Commission's secretary, Sir Charles Eastlake, with these underprivileged visitors in mind, had prepared a cheap edition of the exhibition catalogue. But he and the Prince were most gratified to see that it was precisely this poorer class of people who preferred the more expensive sixpenny version with quotations, which they diligently carried with them and scrutinised as they walked about the halls. Albert took Victoria on a personal viewing of the exhibition, which turned out to be his maiden triumph in improving public taste by raising the standard of design and technique.

Five years after the exhibition, the first four frescos were in place, and these, as well as the later ones, can still be appreciated today by visitors to the Palace of Westminster. In selecting the themes to be represented, the distinguished artist William Dyce,[38] one of those commissioned to decorate the walls of the House of Lords, recommended to Albert that he look back at British history. For the Queen's robing room, the subject agreed was the legend of King Arthur. Albert was responsible for the choice of fresco as the painting technique. This was considered at the time the noblest form of art, and therefore suited to the building. It was, however, a fatally flawed decision, as fresco is not suited to a damp northern climate, and particularly not for a building that sits on the River Thames. The artists voiced their frustration with the classic fresco technique of painting directly on wet plaster. The Irish painter Daniel Maclise begged Albert to allow him to paint in oil. Albert pondered this dilemma: he sent Maclise to Berlin to look at the German medium of using watercolour on a dry wall and a water-glass spray to fix it.[39] The Prince argued that this technique was better suited to withstand the ravages of the English climate, and to an extent it was.

When Maclise returned from Germany, Albert was frequently to be found in the Royal Gallery, observing the effect of water-glass as the work proceeded. The Prince took a decidedly hands-on approach to the project. He insisted that 'all organic substances, like oil and wood, ought to be eliminated, as too perishable for a monumental work...The oil, however flattened, would shine and be most disagreeable.'[40]

Some of the original frescos painted directly onto the walls have suffered some deterioration, and the only paintings that have come down to us in sound condition are those painted with water-glass facing.

Within a few years of the unveiling of the frescos, it was generally agreed, gauging by the multitudes that came to admire the newly decorated Houses of Parliament, that Albert had accomplished his ambition of raising public tastes in art, though the final work was not completed until after his death. His chairmanship of the Commission had served a dual purpose: the abundant schedule of meetings, the task of resolving conflicts of opinion and personalities and bringing about a consensus among the Commission members, all of this was an experience that served the Prince well when he came to chair the second royal commission, set up to plan the Great Exhibition of 1851.

Albert's satisfaction at having presided over such a consummate artistic enterprise was tragically marred in January 1844, when he received a letter from Stockmar telling him of his father's sudden death at the age of 60, after a few hours' illness. Stockmar had forewarned the Prince that Ernest's health was in decline and that he must be prepared for the worst. In spite of the Duke's profligate habits and the absence of an intimate relationship with his sons, Albert was deeply distressed by the tidings from Coburg. 'My heart impels me to vent my tears upon the bosom of a true and loving friend,' he replied to Stockmar. 'I have sustained a terrible loss, and can as yet scarcely believe it. Here we sit together, poor Mama (Ernest's sister the Duchess of Kent), Victoria and myself, and weep, with a great cold public around us, insensitive as stone.'[41]

The loss of his father in a sense marked a rite of passage for Albert. In early February he wrote again to Stockmar: 'A new epoch has commenced in my life, not indeed in action and aim, but in my emotional life. My youth, with all the recollections linked with it, has been buried with him around whom they centred.'[42] The message had been driven home for the first time that Albert's link to the Rosenau of his adolescence had been severed on the rainswept day he stepped out of St James's Palace as Victoria's husband. His life and his work were now in Britain, no longer in Germany. He remained in frequent contact with his brother, who had inherited the title Duke Ernest II of Saxe-Coburg and Gotha. But Ernest had married Princess Alexandrine of Baden two years previously, and though the union bore no children, he had a life and responsibilities of his own to look after. The two brothers' relationship henceforth in no way resembled the merry camaraderie they had shared in their student days or on their travels together. More often than not, Albert found himself firing off finger-wagging letters to Ernest, admonishing his roving eye and reckless spending habits.

Shortly after his father's death, the Prince embarked on a brief visit to Coburg during the Easter holiday to tidy up family affairs. It was his first separation from the Queen, and judging from the terms used to address her in the flood of letters that were dispatched at every stage of the journey, the Duke's passing had driven Albert closer to Victoria: 'My own darling' from Dover Harbour, 'Dear little one' from Ostend, and 'Dear, dear child' from Gotha, speak for themselves of the pain caused by this brief interlude separated from his wife and home.

Albert's solace in times of sadness or stress was his love affair with music. Music was his emotional outlet, more so as the passing years laid greater burdens on his shoulders as a voice of authority in matters of state and foreign policy, alongside his tireless work to improve living conditions. With his talents as a composer and organist, he saw in England an opportunity to raise public tastes and appreciation of classical music. Even before his arrival in his new country Albert noted with dissatisfaction what he considered to be a general lack of musical taste. The Prince's determination to take a clean broom to the Palace went beyond putting an end to the absurd protocols for cleaning windows, lighting fires and disposing of candles. His next step was to reorganise the Queen's band, which was composed entirely of wind instruments, as a string ensemble. Albert and Victoria's first Christmas together, in 1840, was celebrated at Windsor Castle with a concert of masterworks by such greats as Schubert, Beethoven, Mozart and Haydn. Two years later he invited his favourite composer, Felix Mendelssohn, to Buckingham Palace to entertain the royal couple with several of his *Lieder* and other compositions. That afternoon, Albert played one of his own chorales for the great composer, whose appearance was like that of some intense bird with flamboyant black plumage. Victoria joined in the festive occasion by singing one of Mendelssohn's own works, with Albert adding his own bass voice to the chorus. The Prince forged a lasting friendship with Mendelssohn, as he did with Richard Wagner, whose *Lohengrin* was first performed at Windsor Castle.

Mendelssohn provided his mother with an account of the visit to London, in which he describes the Prince's organ rendition of a chorale as having been played 'so charmingly, and clearly, and correctly, that it would have done credit to any professional'.[43] The German-born composer Sir Julius Benedict applauded Albert's love of Mendelssohn's work as a great stimulus to the appreciation of fine music in Britain, while the Prince himself came to compose nearly forty chorales, anthems, church hymns and other works, noteworthy among which was a piece entitled *L'Invocazione all' Armonia*, which was played at state concerts at Buckingham Palace and at the laying of the foundation stone of the Royal Albert Hall.

Music became a bond between Albert and the Queen. During the early years of their marriage they would steal moments from their official duties to play piano duets of Mozart and Beethoven symphonies, and later they would play on the piano that Albert had sent from Florence. They sang together under the tutorship of Victoria's teacher, and took part in private concerts: such occasions, as with their shared passion for sketching and etching, drawing them closer together.

The Prince took advantage of every opportunity to escape the smoke-choked atmosphere of London: a small-town boy by birth and upbringing, he revelled in the fresh, bracing air of his visits to the Highlands or the seaside, or even closer to home at Windsor. He and Victoria would occasionally retreat to the Royal Pavilion at Brighton with their children, attempting to flee the army of officialdom competing for the couple's attention. But with the extension of the railway to the south coast of England in 1841, Brighton had become a popular destination with day-trippers from London. It was becoming more difficult for Albert and Victoria to get away from the crowds clamouring for a glimpse of the royal couple out for a stroll along Brighton Pier. The town was in the midst of a building boom which, to Albert's annoyance, began to block the view of the sea from their residence. Brighton had moreover enjoyed the patronage of George IV, who set about building the Pavilion after his first visit in 1783. Like Windsor Castle, the ghosts of Victoria's Hanoverian predecessors, who had dragged the monarchy into disrepute, seemed to stalk the Pavilion's corridors.

The Prince was persuaded that to enjoy any semblance of privacy in their lives, he and Victoria would need to find some secluded, *gemütlich* place, far enough from London to discourage a daily onslaught of visitors, yet close enough to the capital to attend to any urgent business that might require their official presence. One evening, in conversation with Sir Robert Peel, Albert brought up the subject of finding a country haven offering undisturbed peace and quiet. Peel said that an acquaintance of his, Lady Isabella Blachford, might be willing to part with Osborne House, a small estate she possessed on the Isle of Wight. An island hideaway – it sounded like the ideal romantic refuge that Albert had in mind. He lost no time in paying a visit to Osborne, in March 1844, and on first sight he took the house on lease for a year.

By that time, Albert's assault on the royal household's chaotic operations had brought about considerable savings in Victoria's expenditures. In fact, he had saved enough to pay £200,000 to buy the house and grounds once the lease was up. The deal was executed in the name of the Crown, but it was Albert's initiative and the Prince's Secretary George Anson, who acted as agent for the purchase of some eight hundred acres of land, including 'the Manor, Bucket Coppice, Newbarn Farm and Barton Farm, in occupation of Lady Isabella Blachford held by scholars and clerks of Winchester College for term of twenty years'.[44]

It was apparent from the outset that what was to become a new royal residence was beyond *gemütlich* − 'diminutive' would be a more accurate description. Taking into account the expanding royal family (a fourth child, Alfred Ernest Albert, Duke of Edinburgh and of Saxe-Coburg and Gotha, had been born in August 1844, followed less than two years later by a third daughter, Helena Augusta) and, like it or not, the cavalcade of relatives, friends, courtiers and political visitors who were bound to turn up from time to time, Albert saw the need to enlarge Osborne. This left no recourse but to tear down the original house. The Prince had been told as much by the eminent builder and future Lord Mayor of London, Thomas Cubitt, whose architectural achievements − the houses of Bloomsbury, Belgravia and Pimlico − Albert greatly admired. 'Over the shoulders of the Cubitts (Thomas's brother Lewis was a structural engineer) Prince Albert designed Osborne House.'[45]

Albert and Victoria sailed to the Isle of Wight on their new steam yacht for a few brief holiday visits at the existing eighteenth-century, three-storey Georgian mansion before, in June 1845, laying the foundation stone for the new building. Albert and Cubitt, who both cut an elegant figure and shared a taste for dapper dress, quickly developed a coherent and congenial working rapport, which is why the Prince was later eager to delegate to Cubitt a hands-on role in the Great Exhibition of 1851. Albert provided the vision and exercised a strong influence on the house's design and construction in an Italian Renaissance palazzo style. The house was clad in the builder's Belgravia fashion, which conformed to the 'client's brief', while Albert busied himself in laying out the gardens, the drainage and the water supply systems. The laying out of the estate, gardens and woodlands provided a way for the Prince Consort to prove his knowledge of forestry and landscaping, an area in which previously at the more official royal residences he had been thwarted by the Commissioners of Woods and Forests. Below the gardens was a private beach, where the Queen kept her own private bathing machine. The Prince then turned his attention to the art collection, which was very much a manifestation of his own character. His interest in reviving fresco painting in Britain is vividly reflected in William Dyce's *Neptune Resigning the Empire* at the top of Osborne's main staircase. The abundance of naked bodies in the fresco gives the lie to Albert's reputation for prudery.

The Osborne estate was eventually extended to three times its original acreage. The entire house, pavilion and adjoining wings was completed by 1851, six years from the laying of the foundation stone. Cubitt was a rarity among builders, even in those days, in that he adhered faithfully to budget and timing.

> The Renaissance inspired architecture, with its Grand Corridor conceived as a sculpture gallery and marbled staircase hall in the manner of Raphael, was enhanced with highly decorated ceilings and rich polychromy. Certainly the young royal family's holiday home had little in common with comparable English houses.[46]

Victoria was delighted with what Albert had conceived and Cubitt executed, controversially using brick and stucco instead of conventional stone, in an unorthodox Italianate style with a strong Germanic influence and classical yet asymmetrical composition. Once the purchase was finished, Victoria wrote to Uncle Leopold to express her joy: 'It sounds so pleasant to have a place of one's own, quiet and retired, and free from all the Woods and Forests and other charming departments, which really are the plague of one's life.'[47] It was here that, half a century later, Victoria came to die, surrounded by three generations of her family. The bedroom in which the Queen breathed her last − surprisingly small, like the rest of Osborne's private chambers, so designed to achieve the cosiness she and Albert sought − is contemplated by more than two hundred thousand visitors to Osborne every year.

In 1853 a genuine wooden chalet was brought from Switzerland and erected two-thirds of a mile from the main house. What is today known as the Swiss Cottage was used to encourage the royal children to garden. Each child was given a rectangular plot in which to grow fruit, vegetables and flowers. They would then sell their produce to their father. The Prince used this as a way to teach the basics of economics. The children practised carpentry as well, and the princesses learnt cooking in a kitchen equipped with the most modern fittings.

In September 1842, Albert and Victoria set off on their first visit to Scotland. Neither had before been north of the border, and they made the journey with some trepidation, having heard alarming accounts of Chartist agitators spreading rebellion to the countryside. Manchester was eventually to see some of the worst violence, with disorderly mobs forcing their way into mills and factories, smashing machinery and threatening workers who stayed on the shop floor. Troops were deployed from London, and many people were killed and wounded in bloody clashes. Reports of violence having spread to Scotland, however, were wildly exaggerated, and Albert and the Queen were received with enthusiasm. The Prince spent some time visiting literary and scientific institutions and, according to Charles Anson, 'The people look upon him as the great patron of all arts and sciences.'[48]

Albert was completely taken by this first personal contact with Scotland. On his return to Windsor he wrote to the Duchess of Saxe-Coburg that the country is full of beauty 'of a severe and grand character, perfect for sports of all kinds, and the air remarkably pure and light in comparison with what we have here'.[49] Albert was also impressed by the 'honesty and sympathy'[50] of the people he met, with whom he felt a kinship through his avid readings of Sir Walter Scott.

Two years were to pass before Albert returned to Scotland. He looked forward to unwinding in the Highlands after a tense few months' diplomatic crisis with France over the arrest of the British consul in Tahiti, a confrontation that set both European powers on a war footing. After his brief sojourn at Blair Castle in Perthshire, Albert intensely regretted having to exchange the life of the 'bold deer-stalking mountaineer' for that of 'a courtier, to receive and entertain a King of France and play the part of a staid and astute diplomatist,'[51] as he lamented to Duchess Marie of Saxe-Coburg. This one line in his letter discloses much of Albert's uneasiness with the role that had been thrust upon him as Prince Consort. His largely self-imposed, it must be said, political vocation in the affairs of a foreign land never sat comfortably with him. Nor did he encounter a common ground with the easy-going English, who failed to respond to his love for cold theorising. In the Highlands, on the other hand, Albert encountered the genuine inner peace he sought, living close to nature, engaged in the pleasurable pursuits of tramping the wild heather and gorse-clad hills and invigorating his body and soul in the pristine Scottish air.

Albert's third visit to Scotland, which came after almost another two years had elapsed, was his last as a 'tourist'. The royal steamer *Victoria and Albert* carried a full complement of passengers when it sailed from Osborne on 11 August 1847, including the Queen, her two eldest children and an assortment of dukes, their wives, army officers and the usual array of courtiers and ship attendants. A groundswell was encountered as they pulled out towards the Atlantic, and two-thirds of the guests went scurrying below with seasickness. Albert, who was never noted for his sea legs, proudly stood his guard on this occasion due, he believed, to the advice of a fellow passenger, Admiral Sir Charles Napier, who prescribed a glass of port wine.

Five days into the voyage, the yacht was off the western coast of Scotland, at the little islands of Great and Little Cumbrae, where the Prince was told, to his amusement, that the clergyman prayed, 'Lord Almighty protect the inhabitants of Great Cumbrae and Little Cumbrae, and the neighbouring isles of Great Britain and Ireland.' Albert's thoughts were often drawn to Scotland's peaceful grandeur over the ensuing months and years, when his workaday life was assailed by the Sepoy Mutiny in India, war in China, turmoil in the provinces that make up modern Italy, civil strife in Hungary, anti-monarchist revolution in France and widespread civil unrest in the rest of Europe. The ceaseless consultations regarding the European crisis, the comings and goings of government officials at Windsor and Buckingham Palace, the reading of the daily red-box dispatches – the Prince could fairly be described as an unofficial member of every Cabinet.

As with Osborne, Albert and Victoria discovered their future Scottish retreat on the recommendation of a government minister. This time it was Peel's Foreign Secretary Lord Aberdeen, whose brother had owned the lease to Balmoral, a small castle in Deeside.

Sir Robert Gordon, Aberdeen's younger son, acquired the lease during 1830 and made major alterations to the castle, with baronial-style extensions. Gordon died in 1847, after which Victoria and Albert, upon visiting the property, acquired the remaining part of the lease. The royal physician, Sir James Clark, quack though he was, nevertheless put forth a sensible case for purchasing an estate on this site, whose sandy gravelly soil and location in the rain shadow of the western Highlands make it one of Scotland's driest regions. Albert was enchanted with the house, which was the successor to an ancient estate that had been built on the land in the late fourteenth century. Given the complexity of Scottish trust laws, the royal couple did not take possession as freehold owners until 1852, when the sale was completed for £32,000. As Albert was later to find out, the irony of having an isolated retreat in the Highlands was that ministers who came on official business were in closer contact with the Prince and Victoria in their Scottish hideaway than at any other of the royal residences.

Victoria disregarded these intrusions at her 'pretty little castle in the old Scottish style', and instead revelled in her walks across wooded hills, 'which reminded us very much of the Thüringerwald' of the Prince's homeland. 'All seemed to breathe freedom and peace, and to make one forget the world and its sad turmoils.'[52] Albert was absolutely in his element in the Highlands. On a visit to Balmoral, Greville remarked that the Prince and Victoria were like 'very small gentlefolks, small house, small rooms, small establishment. There are no soldiers, and the whole guard of the Sovereign and the whole Royal Family is a single policeman, who walks about the grounds to keep off impertinent intruders or improper characters.'[53] Every morning, the Prince would go out to shoot, return to luncheon with the Queen, and then dash out again for a walk or to ride. Victoria lived a very un-royal life, taking walks to the nearby cottages to chat and sit down with the women.

The fiercely independent, blunt Highlanders reminded Albert and Victoria of the Coburgers, so with this in mind the royal couple kept their presence discreet, avoiding grand shows of extravagance. 'The flavour of their life in the Balmoral retreat was like that of the small Germanic kingdoms of old fairy-stories, in which a king and queen, their sovereignty always recognised, are nonetheless on a carpet-slipper basis with their subjects.'[54]

Once the estate had passed into their hands as freeholders, Albert set about making plans for a larger house. The old castle was demolished and a new one put up on a site some three hundred yards from the original one. The Prince had a deer-stalker's familiarity with the surrounding hills, which allowed him to select the best location from his bird's-eye view of the area. When construction began in 1853, Albert would often model structures in the sand to instruct the builders on the type of design he wanted. And when the new house was completed in 1856, it was apparent that what he wanted was a dressed-stone castle, complete with Gothic turrets and decorative parapets, evocative of the cherished Rosenau of his youth. The Prince took an active role in laying out new grounds, planting conifers and putting up new farm buildings, which included a model dairy that was developed after his death. Albert's design for Balmoral left its mark on grand houses in Britain, America and continental Europe. 'The suburban mansions of Philadelphia after the Civil War, and the Chicagoans after the Fire, tended to emulate Balmoral, as they had tended towards Osborne half a generation earlier.'[55]

Once the house became habitable, Albert and Victoria journeyed to Scotland for a short holiday in their Highland retreat. The Queen was struck by the strangeness of the new castle, her 'dear Balmoral', remarking how 'strange, very strange, it seemed to me to drive past, indeed through the old house. An old shoe was thrown after us into the house, for good luck, when we entered the hall. The house is charming, the rooms delightful, the furniture, papers, everything perfection.'[56] Victoria called it a 'dear paradise', so much more as it was her 'dearest Albert's own creation, own work, own building, own laying out, as at Osborne'.[57] Albert was no less enchanted with their Scottish sanctuary. He wrote enthusiastically to his stepmother, 'We have withdrawn...into a complete mountain solitude, where one rarely sees a human face, where the snow already covers the mountain tops [this was in September], and the wild deer come creeping round the house.'[58]

The purchase of Balmoral was a milestone not only for the happiness of the royal couple – it had a more extensive impact on the nation as a whole. It would be a rude exaggeration to assert that Albert put Scotland on the map, but making Balmoral a royal residence, coupled with the Prince's influence on the castle's Scottish architectural design, definitely boosted the public's awareness of Highland culture and a land north of the border that was part of their heritage. Balmoral was decked out in tartans, and even visiting friends and relations from abroad would don the kilt, as did Albert himself. One historian mentions that 'the Scottishness of Balmoral helped to give the monarchy a truly British dimension for the first time.'[59] What is beyond dispute is that until the appearance of Balmoral, Scotland was virtually *terra incognita* to the political class in Westminster, as well as the overwhelming majority of the English people. Government affairs were not discussed outside England, and there was no cause for ministers to venture north of the border, if not for stag hunting. With the Court in residence at Balmoral, a steady stream of official visitors from London began to follow in the royal couple's wake, to the point that Albert reluctantly had a telegraph line installed at the castle. It was in fact at Balmoral, with the future leader of the Liberals Lord Granville in attendance, that in September 1855 Victoria received by telegraph one of the most momentous dispatches of her reign, with news of the fall of Sevastopol, which effectively ended the Crimean War. The remote Scottish Highlands had become one of the nerve centres of British imperial power.

3

The People's Prince

Albert was once more called upon to confront a challenge from the establishment powers: this time it was the cloistered, acutely xenophobic world of academia. The chancellorship of Cambridge University fell vacant on 12 February 1847 with the death of the Duke of Northumberland. The very next day the Master of Trinity, the most illustrious of the eight-hundred-year-old institution's colleges, approached Albert to try to persuade him to stand for election. This was an exciting opportunity for the Prince, offering the prospect of becoming a modernising influence on British education. Anson replied straight away that if the university's offer was unanimous, the Prince would have much pleasure in putting forward his candidacy.

Albert's concern was not so much the quality of education in Britain, rather its antiquated condition, which he regarded as totally out of touch with a modern nation's needs. The Prince had gone through his courses of higher education in Brussels and Bonn, where universities were not nearly so stringently under the thumb of the Church as was the case with Cambridge. He knew that as a reformer coming from outside, it was going to be an uphill struggle to bring about change in the statutes, structures and curricula that kept Cambridge, metaphorically speaking, rooted deep in the boggy soil of the Fens. All the university's senior dons were clergymen of the Church of England. For centuries they had been teaching, almost exclusively, classical subjects – divinity, law, and the like. To Albert's alarm, nowhere to be seen were professors of modern languages, economics, physics, all those disciplines he deemed essential for preparing young men to meet the challenges of mid-nineteenth-century life in Britain.

It was never going to be an easy contest, less so with the monarchy's prestige at stake. The university's conservative elements speedily put up a rival candidate in the person of Edward Herbert, the Earl of Powis, a Tory politician and Fellow of St John's, the great rival to Trinity. The Prince demurred – the unanimity he had asked for as a condition had not materialised. As far as he was concerned, his candidacy was withdrawn. But his supporters at Trinity were determined to take their campaign forward. This unleashed a battle between Trinity and St John's the ferocity of which lies beyond the comprehension of anyone who has not experienced academia's egomania at close quarters. Albert's official biographer described it with sardonic accuracy: 'The subsequent proceedings were conducted on both sides with the warmth and acerbity from which philosophic minds enjoy no exemption in contests of this kind.'[1] Thanks to the advent of the railway, members of the university as well as outsiders – Sir Robert Peel, Charles Darwin, William Makepeace Thackeray and Lord Alfred Tennyson among other notables – poured in from across the country in unprecedented numbers to cast their vote. The election brought a painfully close result: 953 votes for Albert, 837 for Powis. The university's Vice Chancellor rushed to the Palace with news of the outcome, expressing to Albert's Secretary his hope that the Prince would not refuse the honour of the chancellorship. Albert consulted Peel, who encouraged him to acquiesce and graciously accept his narrow victory. 'It is my first chance to do something in my own name for my adopted country,' Albert wrote to his brother.[2]

Thus it was that on 27 February the Prince informed the university that although he was not exactly delighted with the election that had been held 'without my sanctity ... I have resolved to accept the trust which the University is willing to confide to me.'[3] Albert had become the first foreigner to hold the position of Chancellor of Cambridge University, a post he retained for the rest of his life. In those 14 short years, while called upon to devote his talents and wisdom to myriad other spheres, Albert nevertheless found the time to bring about a 'spectacular revival of Cambridge University from medieval slumber to a world eminence it has never surrendered'.[4] These were very eventful years in the history of Britain's second-oldest university.[5] The Prince inspired the creation of a royal commission into university affairs, and this led to an Act of Parliament in 1856 which changed the constitution of the governing power. In a eulogy to Albert, the university's Regius Professor of Physics Sir George Paget spoke of the Prince's love of science and art, and how it was under his auspices that the Moral and Natural Science honours degrees were established. In keeping with Albert's belief that education should be placed within the reach of all, local examinations of students who were not members of the university were instituted in places throughout the country.

The changes Albert instituted at Cambridge were radical in nature and far-reaching in scope and, as was to be expected, not implemented without serious resistance from certain diehard ranks entrenched behind those unyielding Gothic battlements.[6] Those who had hoped that Albert's tenure would be of a ceremonial nature were in for a great disappointment. The Prince waded into the fray with his characteristic German thoroughness, demanding from the university's Vice Chancellor, Robert Phelps, a complete list of the subjects to be taught in the ensuing academic year in the different colleges, as well as the authors to be read, the subjects selected for competition and the prizes and lectures to be given by professors in each discipline. Albert wrote to the Prime Minister, Lord Russell, flabbergasted that the university failed to offer psychology, comparative physiology, metaphysics or political economy, subjects that to many bewildered dons would have sounded as alien as a modern foreign language, likewise absent from the curriculum. Phelps had placed himself without reservation in Albert's camp in the crusade to modernise the university. When he asked the Prince for advice on the gold medals to be awarded for the best English poem and for proficiency in Classics, Albert said the poem should be about Norse mythology, a suggestion bordering on heresy, while candidates for the Classics medal, he argued, should show expertise in philological criticism, an equally unheard-of speciality. 'This,' Albert reasoned, 'would encourage the young men rather to go deeper into the spirit and meaning of the classic languages and authors, than to learn appointed books by rote.' It was, to say the least, an astonishingly bold and forward-thinking proposal.

By early February 1848, Albert had persuaded the Senate, which remained the university's historic governing body until

1926, to put together a 'Syndic', or panel of distinguished academics, to consider the adoption of new subjects. Phelps cautioned the Prince to expect strong opposition to any alterations in the curriculum. But Albert was by now accustomed to conflicts on many battlefields, having stood up to even the cut-throat political world, and moreover he fully believed in his cause. It took two months to beat down the dissenters, but the result was that the syndicate ruled in favour of a reformed, modernised scheme of studies, to be put into effect in the Michaelmas term of 1850. *The Times* hailed Albert's reforms as a change that would open new professions to worthy young men, while the paper expressed its surprise that this had been accomplished 'without a long and arduous struggle'.[7] In the syndicate's ruling one could identify the hand of Albert in the list of subjects for bachelors' exams in 1850. Apart from the traditional biblical texts, it included revolutionary novelties like the third book of the *Odes* of Horace and four books of *Paley's Moral Philosophy*.

At the time of Albert's appointment to the Cambridge chancellorship, family life was starting to claim more of his time, or as Lytton Strachey wittily put it, 'The royal nurseries showed no sign of emptying.'[8] Victoria Adelaide, Albert's adored 'Vicky', was now seven, while her troublesome brother Edward Albert had reached his sixth year and was already showing signs of fleeing any form of mental exertion. The second daughter, Alice, had been born in 1843, and within the next three years, Alfred and Helena had been added to the family. Four more were to follow in the ensuing decade, namely the solitary Louise, Arthur the professional soldier, the haemophiliac Leopold, and lastly Beatrice, who was profoundly devoted to her mother, during the Queen's lifetime and afterwards.

Albert was acutely aware of the need for paternal guidance for children whose lives would be constantly exposed to public scrutiny. The press, to which Albert usually had a marked aversion, was growing ever more powerful, and correspondingly more intrusive to satisfy its readers' insatiable appetite for scandal. Stockmar's role in the Prince's life had been predominantly that of the educator – Albert was every bit the product of education, which is what made him what he was. This was often a bone of contention between the Prince and the Queen, who possessed not a fraction of her husband's refinement and knowledge. Albert criticised Victoria for her impatience and scolding ways with their children, though in fact the princes and princesses were awed by their father's Germanic reserve, which stood in sharp contrast to Victoria's more frivolous nature. Yet paradoxically she was much more the disciplinarian, while Albert got along on happier terms with the children, perhaps because they sensed that he genuinely adored them.

The Prince had sent urgently for Stockmar shortly before the birth of his first child, feeling the need to have the doctor, his mentor, by his and Victoria's side for the event. Stockmar's advice to the Prince was to take great care in choosing a nurse for the Princess Royal,[9] for, he said, a child's education 'begins the first day of his life and a lucky choice I regard as the greatest and finest gift we can bestow on the expected stranger'.[10] The blessings of education were never far from Albert's thoughts, so Stockmar was preaching to the converted when he reminded the Prince, in a letter concerning his second child Edward's upbringing, that he could 'never rate too highly the importance of the Prince of

Wales, or of his good education, for your own interests – political, moral, mental and material – are so intimately and inseparably bound up with those of the Prince'.[11]

Albert hardly needed to be reminded of the importance of educating children, or for that matter of the sorry state of schooling in Great Britain in his day. The Prince was a believer and collector of statistics, a science which he avidly supported. In a speech to the Conference of National Education, he revealed that more than half the five million children in England and Wales received no formal instruction whatsoever. He told the delegates it was their duty to work upon the minds and hearts of the parents 'to place before them the irreparable mischief which they inflict [on their children] by keeping from them the light of knowledge...that it is their duty to exert themselves for their children's education'.[12]

That in Europe's turbulent and fateful year of 1848 Albert managed to find a spare moment to bring about his historic reforms at Cambridge University or to devote time to his children's education was in itself an amazing feat.

Albert had been observing with unease the dark clouds gathering over the Continent, stretching from the Iberian Peninsula to the Balkans. In Portugal, the Prince's uncle, Ferdinand of Saxe-Coburg and Gotha had married Queen Maria II and now sat on the Lusitanian throne as Dom Pedro II. By 1846 a state of civil war existed between the royal couple's supporters and the radical constitutionalists. The state of political affairs was no less tumultuous in neighbouring Spain, which was in the throes of the Second Carlist War, Europe's last dynastic armed conflict. Insurrection had been brewing in Italy for nearly fifteen years, and now had come to a head, with outbreaks of civil disobedience foreshadowing two years of revolution. Greece had adopted a constitution in 1844 that established the principle of royal sovereignty, with the monarch as the decisive power of state. Once King Otto chose to disregard the constitutional provisions, his doom was sealed. As for France, the conditions of the working classes had steadily deteriorated under King Louis Philippe I. The build-up of anger and a worsening economic crisis in 1847 touched off republican riots that forced the monarch to abdicate and flee to England, where he was to live out his days.

'We can see the storm brewing,'[13] Albert wrote to Stockmar in late 1847, a few days before he sent another letter to Lord John Russell, the Prime Minister, outlining the European policy he believed right for Britain. Albert advised the Whig leader to follow an independent line, 'one based upon the principles of justice and moderation, and intelligible to all Europe'.[14] In terms of politics, the Prince's ties to continental Europe were a thing of the past. He espoused the view that Britain had acquired a start in liberty and prosperity over other nations. British popular institutions were more advanced, more perfected than those of countries like Austria, Spain or France, having been through stages of development that other monarchies were still to experience. 'England's mission, duty and interest is to put herself at the head of the diffusion of civilisation, and the attainment of liberty,' he said. Let Britain lead by example in this moment of European crisis, but not impose herself in a way that will generate ill feelings from other countries. The Government taking sides in the internal affairs of Greece, Spain and Portugal was, in Albert's judgement, quite the wrong course of action. 'The result proves that this deviation [from neutrality] cannot take place with impunity... and the general belief that we are disseminating disorder in these countries for selfish purposes.'[15] Albert's letter was shown to the Foreign Secretary Lord Palmerston and the Lord Privy Seal the Earl of Minto, both of whom agreed with its contents.

At home, the working-class movement known as Chartism, founded on six principles of a people's charter,[16] launched a campaign of public agitation in 1838, which for all practical purposes petered out within two years. Its death knell was brought about by an upsurge in economic prosperity, usually the most effective neutraliser of revolutionary zeal. In their heyday the Chartists drew support from those who had been hardest hit by a surge in food prices following a succession of bad harvests, as well as factory labourers whose wages had been cut due to a slump in manufacturing output. There were disturbances in London as late as 1848,[17] but by now the revival was confined mostly to Ireland, where a disastrous famine and an outbreak of lawlessness provided fertile territory for the revolutionaries. The last great Chartist march in the capital came in April 1848, when a petition with six million signatures, a significant number of which were found to be fake, was delivered to Parliament after a huge meeting on Kennington Common. The Duke of Wellington was brought in with several thousand troops, backed up by a large contingent of special constables, to confront the protestors, but the great show of force proved unnecessary and the day passed almost without incident. As Albert noted in a letter to Stockmar, 'We had our revolution yesterday, and it went up in smoke. The law was victorious. I hope this will make a good impression on the Continent. In Ireland things look still more serious.'[18] Reflecting on the riots that had taken place in various cities around the country, Albert knew there was a reason why people rebelled. He had studied conditions in heavy industries such as coal, steel and iron production, and found them terrible. Hence the Prince was shocked by the military force that had been deployed to put down the rioters. Such a heartless reaction was the wrong way to address workers' protests.

Queen Victoria had been sent to the Isle of Wight as a precautionary measure, in case Chartist violence were to reach the Palace. Shortly following the London demonstration, the Queen gave birth to her fourth daughter, Louise Caroline Alberta, who gave her third Christian name to the Canadian province.

There was little enthusiasm for insurrection in the rest of the country, and this was underpinned by a general indifference to the republican cause. In Scotland, the obvious breeding-ground for anti-English and anti-monarchist agitation, the Prince and Queen were extolled as deserving of the people's 'loyalty and attachment', and the throne as an institution 'which so marked a characteristic of the old Highland character'.[19] At the Royal Highland Society's meeting of 1848, the year of wholesale pandemonium across the Continent, the chairman proposed 'the health of Her Majesty and the Prince Consort...in the presence of such events as were at present agitating Europe to its very centre'. The British people, he added, lived 'in the tranquillity which they enjoyed under the reign of their beloved Queen, whose *limited monarchy* [author's italics] was the sure guarantee for the preservation of well ordered civil and religious liberty'.[20] His remarks were echoed by a chorus of 'Hear hear!'

The barricades were up on the Continent, and sovereigns who refused to release their grip on absolute power were soon to be out of a job, but in Britain it was business as usual for the monarchy. In those days of social convulsion in Europe, Albert and Victoria held an exhibition of their etchings, the Prince presided over a meeting of the Royal Agricultural Society in York, the royal couple reviewed the household troops, they sailed off to Scotland for a visit, and the Prince was the guest of honour at the annual banquet to celebrate the victory at Waterloo. Business as usual. The royal trips and engagements transpired in a climate of absolute serenity, evidence that the people themselves were at peace with this *limited monarchy* advanced by Albert, which, as he was to demonstrate by his works, strove to hold its subjects' best interests at heart.

It was in that troubled time, as well, that Albert chose to lay his egalitarian cards on the table. In May he delivered one of the boldest speeches of his career, regarded by the old guard as one of his most damnable as well. The picturesquely named Society for Improving the Condition of the Labouring Classes, formerly known by the no less quaint title Labourer's Friend Society, was established in 1844 with the Prince as its first president. This was one of numerous model-dwelling companies,[21] private enterprises in nineteenth-century Britain that sought to improve the condition of the working classes by providing them with decent living accommodation. Their operating principle was to build new homes from philanthropic investment that offered financial returns, a system that was given the name 'five per cent philanthropy'. The society's first urban project was completed in 1846 at Pentonville, North London, a group of blocks that reflected Albert's emphasis on utilitarian design, with particular attention to sanitation and ventilation.

At the 18 May meeting, the Prince spoke out passionately for that segment of British society 'which has most of the toil, and least of the enjoyments of this world'. He called upon 'influential persons who were wholly disinterested'[22] to come forward and act the part of friend to those in need. Albert had that day attended the opening ceremony of his Model Lodge in Kennington, South London, designed to the Prince's specifications by the society's honorary architect Henry Roberts. The houses were unusual in that hollow bricks were used for their construction, as it was believed that this would help keep the houses dry, warm, quiet and fire-resistant − as well as being 25 per cent cheaper than standard brickwork.

'Depend upon it,' Albert assured his audience, 'the interests of classes too often contrasted are identical, and it is only ignorance which prevents their uniting for each other's advantage'. This was food for thought for the affluent classes, who had been shaken from their complacency a few weeks previously by the overthrow of the Orléans monarchy in Paris. 'To dispel this ignorance,' Albert went on, 'to show how man can help man… ought to be the aim of every philanthropic person, but it is more particularly the duty of those who enjoy station, wealth and education'.[23] The speech brought a rousing ovation from the floor − Albert had established his credentials as royal champion of the poor.

Few areas of social welfare eluded the Prince's reformist zeal. After delivering his landmark speech on working-class housing, Albert gave an address to the Servants' Provident and Benevolent Society, attacking the lack of an adequate pension scheme for servants. The situation of people employed as servants in nineteenth-century Britain could only be characterised as one of extreme hardship. Albert was alarmed to learn that in London, the greater part of the population of the workhouse was made up of former domestic servants, and that 70 per cent of people from this occupation ended their days in workhouses or dependent on public charity for their survival. The Prince proposed a shake-up in the system by making available deferred annuities which would allow the poorer classes to receive part of their income later in life and provide a death benefit for their heirs. There existed in Britain no financial cushion for the poor once they ceased to draw a salary.[24] Albert argued that poverty alleviation was a necessary obligation, but he also perceived a higher duty: to prevent the poor from descending to pauperism in the first place. The Prince campaigned to allow those employed as servants to pay into annuities, to cover the lives of spouses and their survivors. Within days of the speech, contributions of £6693 5s 5d had been received from servants for the purchase of annuities, and a society was also formed expressly for the benefit of workers in the building trades.

Albert was deeply touched by a letter which reached him a few days after his speech. It was from a young servant, who signed his initials C.A. for fear of having his identity discovered by his employer. He described himself as a servant of good character, 'begging respectfully that he [Albert] would deign to accept the most humble and heartfelt thanks of a servant who can see the good effects that must ensue'. The anonymous writer assured the Prince that 'many more wish to express their humble feelings in this manner, but dare not.'[25]

It was not just the workers slaving away in mines or hellish steel and iron mills that touched Albert's emotions. He was equally incensed by the miserable life in London's sweatshops, such as the dreadful conditions the silk workers of Spitalfields were forced to endure. The majority were malnourished and chronically ill, and rarely left the shop floor, which is where they took their meagre meals and kept their children. Having witnessed their plight, the Prince organised a controversial ball in aid of the unemployed of this industry, at which guests were expected to be dressed in silk. Albert intended it as a gesture of solidarity, but the press saw it as royal paternalism of dubious taste, the event was savaged in the papers, and nothing of the sort was ever repeated.

Albert gradually gathered a group of collaborators to his cause, mostly prominent men in politics and wealthy industrialists. One of his close associates in these years was Lord Ashley, whom he had met as Chairman of the Society for Improving the Condition of the Labouring Classes. This aristocrat reformer had impressed the Prince with his spirited campaign in Parliament to ameliorate working conditions in industry. In 1842, Ashley had pushed through a bill prohibiting female and child labour in mines and collieries. Two years later he was responsible for another bill restricting factory labour and limiting working hours. The Tory MP in that same year formed the Ragged School Union, which in eight years expanded into a network of more than two hundred free schools for poor children.

Misguided charity balls aside, the Prince could never be accused of playing the role of armchair do-gooder. Taking a break from a visit to Peel's Drayton Manor estate (which the Prince had taken as his model for Balmoral) in November 1843, Albert went off on an impromptu visit to Birmingham. The city was Britain's Chartist stronghold and had in 1839 been the scene of violent rioting. Peel and Anson argued in vain to dissuade the

Prince from taking such a high risk, fearing the Chartist leaders, who included the city's Mayor, would take advantage of the occasion to unleash anti-monarchist demonstrations.

Anson later commented that it seemed the entire population of 280,000 had turned out on the day, but far from staging a protest the multitude had jammed the streets to cheer the Prince as he passed in his carriage. Albert inspected five of the city's factories, with the aim not only of observing working-class conditions, but also of acquainting himself with the city's metalworking, glass and weapons industries.

Albert spent a day at his desk in Buckingham Palace putting together a plan for alleviating the suffering of the working classes, which he outlined in a memorandum to his newly appointed Secretary Charles Phipps. He explained that the improvement of their condition could be achieved practically only in four ways. This plan listed the four points as education of the children with industrial training, improvement of working-class dwellings, the granting of allotments along with their housing, and the creation of savings banks and benevolent societies, if possible managed by the workers themselves. 'I shall never cease to promote these four objects wherever and whenever I can,' Albert vowed.[26]

There was nothing of a radical disposition in the Prince's fight for a better life for the working man. On the contrary, he had nothing but contempt for the revolutionary movements sweeping the Continent. Democratic excesses were a social evil, to his Teutonic way of thinking. And of course he had vested interests to look after, namely his wife's position. None of this detracted from his ideals of social justice and improvements, which could be achieved not by toppling the privileged classes, but rather by enlisting them to his cause. 'The unequal division of property, and the dangers of poverty and envy arising therefrom, is the principal evil,' Albert wrote to his brother as the dust began to settle on Europe's violent year of revolution. 'Means must necessarily be found, not for diminishing riches (as the communists wish), but to make facilities for the poor. But there is the rub. I believe this question will be first solved in England.'[27]

Albert's efforts to improve the lives of the impoverished stemmed in part from his deep-rooted Lutheran faith, in which good works have their true origin in God, and conversely failure to perform these works demonstrates an absence of faith. It must not be overlooked that though Albert converted to Anglicanism with marriage, the Prince had spent his entire youth under the shadow of Martin Luther, who three centuries before had lived and written in the great hilltop fortress overlooking Coburg. He remained a great admirer of Luther, and over the years in England his thoughts would frequently hark back to the reformer, as he compiled in his sketchbook a collection of drawings of Luther's confinement in the castle at Wartburg, the pulpit where he used to preach, and the cell he occupied at Wittenberg. The Prince remained an ardent believer all his life. Taking the sacrament, often with Victoria at his side, was for him a most solemn and personal occasion: he would make an effort to shun all contact with the public the evening before or the day on which he took it.

Albert believed the purpose of royalty to be 'the headship of philanthropy, a guidance and encouragement of the manifold efforts which our age is making towards a higher and purer life'.[28] The Prince's fascination with industrial advances, his striving to further the cause of science, his admiration of machinery and technological innovation were not inconsistent with his spirituality. On the contrary, these were tools for achieving the liberation of the oppressed.

Whatever charitable views were held by Victoria had been instilled and encouraged by her husband. The Prince passed on to his wife a sense of compassion devoid of doctrinaire prejudices, so that when it came to the religious education of Vicky, her first born, she made it clear that the child would be taught great reverence for God and religion, but not with a feeling of fear and trembling. 'The thoughts of death and an afterlife should not be represented in an alarming and forbidding view,' was the Queen's religious message to her children.[29]

Along with a deep-rooted Lutheran faith, the Prince retained all the attributes of his Germanic persona to the end of his days. He spoke German with Victoria, his last words on his deathbed were spoken in German, his most trusted advisers were German, his university education had been German, he was devoted to German art and music, and he was outraged to discover that his adopted countrymen held German literature in low regard. He felt a profound anxiety over the political state of his homeland, and the political turmoil that shook Europe's old order to its foundations in 1848 awakened in Albert an urgent awareness of Germany's uncertain future. The Prince was committed to building a strong German state out of the loose Confederation of principalities and ducal territories, headquartered in Frankfurt, that had been set up at the Congress of Vienna in 1815.

Albert was every inch the German nationalist, but it was never a case of divided loyalties. The Prince greatly admired Britain's system of constitutional monarchy − here was a model to be grafted onto a united German state, liberated from the yoke of Austrian tutelage.[30] There was an exigency in achieving this ambition. In 1848, the revolutionary fervour had spread even to tiny Gotha, and this raised Albert's patrician hackles: 'Such an outbreak of the people is always something dreadful,' he wrote to his brother on hearing the news of ransacking mobs in the streets, adding with flawless foresight, 'and what will have to be done now, will probably have to be done hurriedly and badly.'[31] He was right in assessing the outcome of the German uprisings. In Bavaria a new liberal government forced King Ludwig I to abdicate, Otto von Bismarck and other Prussian leaders were put on the defensive in Prussia, and King Frederick William IV was forced to yield to the crowds' demands. But far from bringing about a liberal and united German state, by 1852 the status quo had been restored throughout most of the Confederation and Germany was no closer to nationhood than it had been before the popular revolts.

As the dust began to settle on Europe's ravaged landscape, the Prince drew up a plan for a single, federal German state under Prussian leadership and an elected emperor, and excluding Austria.

In what years were left to the Prince, which numbered an ill-starred 13 but which were filled with good fortune and fulfilment, Albert was to realise his highest creative achievement and meet his most testing challenges as a statesman. The Great Exhibition of 1851 and the Crimean War lay ahead. The one stands as the most eminent of his endeavours, a stroke of genius that assured the Prince's prestige and took the British monarchy closer to the people than ever before in history. The latter developed into a ferocious power struggle with the mighty Lord Palmerston, from which Albert emerged the recognised statesman, having imposed his prerogative to speak out on affairs of state.

4

Hail, Britannia

In 1846, as tens of thousands of Irish families succumbed to the Great Potato Famine, Peel embarked on a politically risky campaign to repeal the Corn Laws, a draconian body of legislation that protected the landed gentry through the restriction of grain imports. Albert sensed this to be his moment to once more step forward to fight for the downtrodden, in defiance of the establishment patricians who never concealed their contempt for the German interloper. The Prince was genuinely astonished that educated, responsible men sitting in Westminster could attack Peel with such ferocity, a politician who, when all was said and done, strove to relieve the sufferings of British subjects. Albert held this to be one of the most momentous political initiatives undertaken by a British government. It was not enough to lend the monarchy's moral support: the Prince went down to the House to hear Peel's proposals, and did not take his eyes off the Prime Minister for the three hours it took him to deliver an impassioned appeal to abolish protective import tariffs on cheaper foreign corn.

The bill was passed, but it was a pyrrhic victory for Peel, and he knew it. On the very night that the Duke of Wellington persuaded the House of Lords to approve the repeal of the Corn Laws, Peel's Irish Coercion Bill was voted down in the Commons and four days later his ministry had fallen. Peel's resignation was as portentous an event for Albert as the loss of Melbourne had been for Victoria. But the political demise of his trusted friend catapulted the Prince into a role of political prominence. For it was Albert who facilitated the delicate business of the handover of power from Peel to his Whig successor Lord John Russell, the diminutive peer Albert held to be wanting in intellectual as well as physical stature.

Russell and the Marquis of Lansdowne, Lord President of the Council,[1] arrived at Windsor Castle on 16 December to be greeted by a remarkable sight. Victoria, who traditionally would receive her ministers on her own, stood in the reception chamber alongside her husband. The meaning was clear: Albert had stepped from behind the throne to emerge as a power in his own right. 'The Prince is become so identified with the Queen that they are one person…it is obvious that while she has the title he is really discharging the functions of the Sovereign.'[2] Describing the historic moment, Lytton Strachey proclaims, with his relish for grandiloquence, 'Albert had become, in effect, King of England.'[3]

Lehzen had been driven out, Melbourne languished in the political wilderness. Deprived of her mentors, Victoria had no choice but to seek shelter under her husband's wing, and Albert, if not King, was now at least the undisputed voice of royal authority. The Prince, at the age of 27, had become the acknowledged arbiter of power of the most powerful nation on Earth. Yet his crowning glory was yet to come, five years later, in the form of a colossal glass structure that set Albert squarely on a collision course with the British establishment. But it also confirmed him as the embodiment of almost everything we identify with the Victorian age.

What impulse spawned the defining work of his life? Was it his irrepressible passion for the advancement of science and modernity? Was Albert determined to sweep away the last pre-industrial vestiges of the eighteenth century, to give material expression to 'the new ideals and the new forces, so that they might stand revealed in visible glory before the eyes of an astonished world'?[4] Or was there something deeper, perhaps even darker, an unconscious resolve to show his landed gentry foes that he, not they, was the man of the hour, the spirit of England's future? In truth, there was no single motivation, but rather a convergence of forces that inspired his idea for a 'Great Exhibition of the Works of Industry of all Nations in 1851', a title devised by the Prince himself for an undertaking that came to epitomise the Victorian era.

As a child growing up in the unsophisticated environment of Coburg, Albert had been enthralled by the splendour of the Frankfurt Fairs, and in 1849 this memory served as a catalyst for a similar but infinitely more ambitious project. The Prince's enthusiasm was further fired by his friend Henry Cole, the Assistant Keeper of the Public Records. He was a remarkably versatile man who shared with Albert an ability to take on a multitude of activities: from author of successful children's books, musical composer and organiser of the British national archives, to publisher of the first commercial Christmas card, campaigner for the standard-gauge railway track and creator of the 'penny post'. Cole had just returned from Paris, where he attended the splendidly named Exposition Nationale des produits de l'industrie agricole et manufacturière de la Deuxième République. Cole was summoned to Buckingham Palace on 30 June 1849, along with Francis Fuller and John Scott Russell, both prominent figures of the Royal Society of Arts. This was to be the historic meeting to settle the details of a grand project, one that in fact had been circulating in the public domain for weeks. Albert's thoughts had been focused on this idea for the past year, and now was the moment to give formal expression to this ambitious undertaking. Cole, 11 years the Prince's senior, but still a vigorous 41, had already put together under Albert's patronage a successful Exhibition of Art Manufactures two years earlier, and had put on enlarged versions of the show in the period leading up to the 1849 meeting at Buckingham Palace. Albert was determined to make this a gathering of loyal friends, people he could rely on to fight his corner in the inevitable conflict with his antagonists of the establishment. Hence the fourth guest was Thomas Cubitt, the Prince's trusted co-creator of Osborne House and future guarantor of the Great Exhibition. Cole argued over tea in favour of a British exhibition to surpass what he had admired in Paris, a project to exalt the nation's achievements in commerce and industry, coinciding with the dawn of the Second Industrial Revolution and Britain's gift to the world of steam-powered ships and railways. As Fuller and Scott looked on in admiration of the two young men's enthusiasm, the ideas for an exhibition in two years' time began to flow. Albert threw his full weight behind the scheme, but being a foreigner at heart, the Prince's imagination was not constrained by his adopted country's embedded xenophobia. An exhibition, by all means, but with an added dimension. The

Great Exhibition of 1851 must be international in scope, and let it be a bold venture, setting aside fully half the floorspace for foreign exhibitors.

Even as his guests pulled up at the Palace gates in their broughams, Albert's Teutonic mind had been bubbling with meticulous plans for the Exhibition. He envisaged dividing the exhibits into four sectors: raw materials, machinery and mechanical inventions, manufactures, and sculpture and plastic art. For the Prince, these four categories would combine to offer the world a celebration of all that is noble and progressive in mankind's endeavours, from 'the natural productions on which human industry is employed' to the 'taste and skill displayed in such application of human history'.[5] Next there was the issue that would inevitably become the stickiest point of all, namely where the hall for this Exhibition was to be erected. The Government had offered Somerset House or, if deemed more suitable, a site under Crown ownership.[6] Yes, Albert declared, of course the royal family would be delighted to host such an event. And what could be a more appropriate venue than Hyde Park, the London icon that had belonged to the city since before the Norman conquest? Albert pointed out on a map a plot of vacant ground on the south side of the park, between what is now the bustling shopping thoroughfare of Knightsbridge and the genteel Rotten Row, adjacent to the Serpentine. Hyde Park appealed greatly to the egalitarian Prince, for it had served as a common recreation area for more than two centuries since Charles I had abolished the royal hunting preserve by declaring the park open to the general public.

The Royal Commission, which had been set up in 1850, fixed 1 May 1851 for the opening ceremony. This left little more than a year to raise the necessary funding, obtain site approval, design the building, dispatch invitations across the globe, negotiate with exhibitors, organise their product displays and deal with a multitude of lesser tasks, from setting entry fees and providing accommodation for visitors from outside London and abroad, to installing toilet facilities for the many thousands of visitors expected daily. All this, in 22 months from conception – a mere nine months, in fact, from start of building work to the grand opening day. What an achievement! All the more so, one is tempted to argue, when contemplating this same city's struggle to prepare for the 2012 Olympic Games, with seven years' lead time and the attendant advantages of twenty-first-century engineering and construction technology. Not only the construction of the building itself, but the transportation and arrangement of more than a hundred thousand exhibits, constituted a major logistical problem. The historian Robert Rhodes James was right in asserting that 'The establishment of the Great Exhibition, from Cole's discussion with Albert in June 1849, to its realisation on 1 May 1851, was the story of surmounting problems that most sensible people considered insurmountable.'[7]

Cole's energy and creative power were to prove an invaluable support to Albert, who assumed the presidency of the Royal Commission, and whose task was to manage this vast undertaking. Yet there can be no doubt that the concept had been occupying the Prince's thoughts for some time. This was 'a project long thought over and matured in his [Albert's] own mind before it was communicated to anyone'.

It was a superb moment to conceive a Great Exhibition in celebration of British grandeur. Industry reigned supreme, as the swift movement of goods across the country became a reality with the opening of the first direct rail link between London and Edinburgh. In India, the Sikhs had been dealt a crushing blow on the battlefield, and the ensuing annexation of the Punjab took the Empire right up to the borders of Central Asia. Victoria reigned supreme among European monarchs, and as a tribute to her magnificence the fabled Koh-i-Noor diamond taken by the British from the Lahore Treasury, was presented to the Queen and it now adorns the crown of England. The populist revolutions that had shaken the foundations of Europe in the previous year, and which in France had brought down the monarchy of Louis Philippe, passed virtually unnoticed in British society. In England, constitutional monarchy went about its business, unchallenged in all quarters, and Britain luxuriated in self-confidence. The Empire's dominions extended to every continent, and Albert felt totally sanguine about inviting the world to display its competing products in London. The Prince was a precursor of the free-enterprise spirit, though it would not be long before the voices of xenophobia, some of which rose to quite a hysterical pitch, were to make themselves heard.

A commissioners' meeting broke up late on a summer afternoon, with Cole handed the role of what in today's jargon would be designated the 'marketing man', at a remuneration of £800 per year. He was dispatched on a European tour to persuade foreign governments to promote their countries' goods in London. Albert's thoughts were now focused on a marketing exercise of his own. The Prince was due to announce the Exhibition's formal launch at the Mansion House banquet on 21 March 1850, in the presence of 'Her Majesty's Minister's, Foreign Ambassadors and the Mayors of 180 towns'.[8] The prospect of this 'make-or-break' affair aroused all his horrors of public discourse, more so on this occasion, which would place at stake the Crown's reputation and credibility. In the end, the ordeal Albert had dreaded was acknowledged to be a tremendous success. The Prince laid before his exalted audience his inspirational vision of enterprise and progress, speaking in terms that today would be recognised as a tribute to globalisation: the rapidly vanishing distances between nations, the increasing knowledge of other nations' languages, the communication of thought with the 'rapidity of lightning'. 'Gentlemen,' he concluded, 'the Exhibition of 1851 is to give us a true test and a living picture of the point of development at which the whole of mankind has arrived in this great task, and a new starting point from which all nations will be able to direct their further exertions.'[9]

The groundwork for that occasion had been laid two months earlier, when in January 1850 the full Royal Commission was announced at the same venue, the residence of the Lord Mayor, to 'a highly respectable meeting of the merchants, bankers and traders of the City of London'.[10] The Prime Minister Lord Russell[11] rose from his plush chair in the Great Egyptian Hall and made it clear that he stood firmly behind Albert's, and hence the Commission's, decision to cancel a funding contract with City financiers Messrs Munday & Co. Russell concurred that if this were to take the form of a popular enterprise, the money must be raised from public subscription. In distancing the Government from any funding commitments, Russell neatly ring-fenced Downing Street against the potential fallout of the Great Exhibition ending up a financial disaster. That night, the Great Exhibition was praised to the skies by all the dignitaries in attendance, the Royal Commission's visionary undertaking was lauded as a tribute to British ingenuity and pluck, the banqueting hall reverberated with cries of 'Hear, hear!' and when the cigars were extinguished, the last drops of brandy drained and the hansom cabs summoned to the gates of the Georgian mansion, Albert and his colleagues found themselves truly left on a limb.

But not for long. The indefatigable Cole soon came rushing back breathlessly from his European tour 'with ardour undimmed, and with reports of considerable enthusiasm, interest and solid pledges of support. Five thousand influential persons had agreed to act as promoters [of the Exhibition].'[12] To Albert's immense relief and joy, there was even better news to follow. Within three months of the Mansion House meeting, money was pouring in from commoners across the land. The Prince would have been deeply touched to receive from one James Randle, Parish Constable of Braintree, Essex, a humble contribution of one shilling to support the Great Exhibition. 'It is all I can afford, as I am a working man with a wife and four children, but always ready to do good work.' Randle suggests to Albert that

> if our great men could induce the working classes to give one shilling a family to be placed with your large subscriptions, you would be able to carry out the great work which has been begun by your Royal Highness, in a manner becoming a great nation like ours, presided over by a good and gracious Queen.[13]

At a meeting in Bradford's Hope and Anchor Inn, a 'money club' was established 'for the purposes of accumulating the funds to enable the members to visit the Exhibition…in £5 shares to be paid by monthly subscriptions'. This represented a considerable burden for any wage earner in those days, and the initiative was to be followed by 'similar clubs to be commenced at various inns in the town and neighbourhood'.[14] From the clerks and workmen of Messrs Winfield and Son in Birmingham came a donation of £14. The workmen in the employ of Messrs Holmes of Derby subscribed, 'without solicitation', the sum of £5 6s 3d. The employees of Messrs Gott in Leeds pledged £78 11s 10d, with another £11 3s coming from the firm of John Walker. A Provident Society was formed in Northampton 'to enable the working classes to visit the Exhibition by the payment of weekly subscriptions', while the staff at Oxford University Press subscribed upwards of £18.[15]

The great outpouring of enthusiasm from factory floors, shipyards, coal mines and working men's clubs left those with deeper pockets little moral alternative but to shoulder the burden along with the humbler classes. Charles Dickens himself took time out from his monthly serialisation of *David Copperfield* to serve on a committee that was set up 'for the purpose of communicating with the working classes on the subject of the Exhibition'. The Queen had from the outset declared her unflinching support for Albert's dream. The Crown would accordingly fund the venture to the tune of £1000. An identical amount was pledged by the Rothschilds, more modest contributions came from prominent parliamentarians and business leaders, while the Duke of Wellington, in his eighty-first year and as ever the most revered man in the kingdom, agreed to be a subscriber to the Exhibition and 'promote it in every way which it may occur to him that he can be of service'.[16]

Having tactfully drawn the Prince away from his initial proposal to erect the Exhibition Hall in Leicester Square, the Commissioners now confronted the formidable labour of winning Parliament's approval for the Hyde Park site. But first, the project needed a home – 800,000 square feet of floorspace was envisaged – to be selected from the 245 architectural designs submitted. Which among the piles of boxes sitting in the Commission's London offices contained the most suitable blueprint, how long would it take to build, at what cost, and which of these could guarantee the Commission's assurances to its many sceptics and detractors, that this was to be a temporary structure, easily disassembled soon after the 15 October closing ceremony?

After spending weeks sifting through the stacks of plans presented by this multitude of architects, the Commissioners realised to their dismay that only two of all the designs submitted even remotely fulfilled their criteria for an acceptable structure. Yet even these were brick and mortar monstrosities that would require many months of construction, with dubious consideration given to their eventual dismantlement.

It was at this distressing juncture that one of Britain's most talented garden designers, Joseph Paxton, stepped from his railway carriage at London's Euston Station to attend a meeting of the newly established Midland Railway, in which he happened to hold a directorship. Paxton had a prodigious green thumb: at the age of 20 he had been given the job of Head Gardener at the Duke of Devonshire's sprawling Chatsworth estate. On receiving his appointment, Paxton had travelled from his native Bedfordshire on the Chesterfield coach, arriving at Chatsworth well before dawn, where he proceeded to clamber over the kitchen-garden wall and sit down to breakfast with the housekeeper, whose niece he later married – all this before he had had occasion to meet his new employer the bachelor Duke, who was away on a visit to Russia. At Chatsworth, Paxton created what is still considered one of the country's finest landscape gardens. He also presented the Duke with a mammoth cast-iron glasshouse dubbed the 'Stove', which at that time was the largest glass-enclosed building in the world.

Paxton wore several hats during his career, and it was one of these that had brought him up to London for a meeting with the Midland Railway's director, John Ellis, an MP, who was extremely interested in Paxton's mention of a possible design for the Exhibition Hall, a structure which Paxton was confident would comply with the Commission's specifications. His most singular work at Chatsworth was the Victoria Regia House, built to accommodate and cultivate the Victoria Regia lily, a spectacular species with leaves that extend up to ten feet in diameter, discovered in British Guyana and sent to Kew in 1836. Contrary to expectations, the only seed in Paxton's possession flowered to enormous proportions in his vast greenhouse.[17] The concept of the Great Hall was modelled on this revolutionary conservatory, to which Paxton had applied his genius for working with glass. The original design, which was said to have been sketched during a railway board meeting, envisaged a structure covering 16 acres, three times the length of St Paul's Cathedral, with 293,655 panes of glass, more than 4500 tons of iron and 24 miles of guttering. This bold and revolutionary building was to become one of the engineering marvels of the nineteenth century. Nothing like it had ever been attempted, and the very concept of this gargantuan glass-enclosed structure inspired Luddites across the land to pronounce on its folly. Some feared the great mass of working-class people and foreigners packed together under one roof would bring a second visitation of the plague. Sir John Airey, the Astronomer Royal, upon examining the plans, gave his solemn assurances that with the first gale the structure would collapse in a heap of splintered glass and twisted beams, probably killing everyone inside. In the end, none of these dire events came to pass, and the Crystal Palace saw more than six million visitors through its doors, safely and in good health.

The sketch was sent to the contractors Fox and Henderson on 22 June, and a fortnight later it was published in the *Illustrated London News*. The design was subsequently sent to the Commission, where it was received with great enthusiasm and relief, and only one significant modification: the central transept was to rise to a height of 108 feet to accommodate several elm trees, in response to an outcry from the Exhibition's critics, who demanded that they be saved from felling. Paxton's original drawing is on display today in the Victoria and Albert Museum.

Resentment had been brewing for months in Parliament's most reactionary recesses over the Great Exhibition. On 19 March 1851, Lord Brougham, the designer of the four-wheeled, horse-drawn carriage that bears his name, rose in the House to deliver an attack on the Commission's plan to erect the Exhibition Hall in Hyde Park. His tirade strikes one as somewhat out of character for a man of his intellectual stature, as founder of the *Edinburgh Review*, Chancellor of the Exchequer and Fellow of the Royal Society. Yet few could have foreseen the outburst of passion this project was to rouse − certainly not Albert, who was in a state of anguish over the attacks. Brougham trusted that 'no such erection would be allowed...in the lungs of London'. He suggested, on the other hand, Victoria Park in London's downtrodden East End as 'a fitter locality'. A jibe at the flood of working-class support for the project? Brougham's blimpish remarks were swiftly challenged by the Earl of Carlisle, who reasoned that as the planning application had been duly lodged with the Government and the projected building sanctioned by the sovereign, there should be no justification for throwing obstacles in its way. 'Besides,' Carlisle added sardonically, 'I do not see why their Lordships should be more tender of the aristocratic lungs of one portion of the metropolis than to those of the densely-populated district around Victoria Park.'[18]

One of the most ludicrous characters ever to occupy the back benches of the Commons was Charles de Laet Waldo Sibthorp, the longstanding MP for Lincoln, popularly known as 'Colonel Sibthorp', a man who took British xenophobia to new heights. One of the most consistent politicians of his day, Sibthorp could be faithfully relied upon to bellow a hearty 'Humbug!' at any piece of legislation that might bring about an improvement in mankind's lot. Sibthorp lacked any affection, or indeed respect, for Albert, and when an increase in the Prince's annuity to £50,000 was being debated in the Commons in 1841, the dyspeptic Sibthorp staunchly opposed the motion on the grounds that £30,000 was quite enough 'pocket money' for a foreign Prince.[19] On the issue of Paxton's Crystal Palace, as it had now been dubbed by *Punch*, Sibthorp publicly prayed to God to destroy it with hail or lightning, in curious contrast to the Colonel's alleged concern for the lives of his fellow citizens on the new steam railways – he was certain they would all fall victim to wholesale slaughter from 'this degrading form of transport'. *The Times* reported that Sibthorp detested the Exhibition for every possible reason, including the extreme protectionist objection to anything that might introduce foreign goods to the English market. 'The Exhibition,' he was quoted as stating in the House, 'is the greatest trash, the greatest fraud, the greatest imposition ever to be palmed upon the people of this country. The object of its promoters is to introduce amongst us foreign stuff of every description – live and dead stock – without regard to quantity or quality.'[20]

The Times, whose editorial policy on many of the great social issues of the day was firmly embedded in the blimpish camp, came out braying for the Commission's blood over the 'profanation of Hyde Park'. The paper carried on churning out its vitriol even as Parliament voted to sanction the Hyde Park site. Now it was the foreign bogeyman who would be descending in hordes on London's placid streets to cause horrific episodes, such as that witnessed in Paris in 1814, 'when the termination of a twenty years' contest had concentrated the warriors and the gazers of the world in the streets of the French capital'. The reader is invited to shudder at the spectre of similar events taking place in London: 'Asiatic carols issuing from sheepskin tents, grotesque costumes and barbarous clamours … a motley assemblage' as 'from Piccadilly to St Paul's there pours one continuous stream of bearded visages, pleasantly diversified by peculiarities of cheekbone and headgear'. Curiously enough, in the midst of this frenzied rant the paper correctly called attention to one melancholy fact, which was that 'twice as many Frenchmen would be landed in England as Napoleon ever intended to bring here. The Grand Army was never likely to have exceeded 150,000 on the shores of Kent,' where as nearly 300,000 French citizens (female and adolescent non-combatants among them, it must be said) had applied for passports to visit the Exhibition.[21] The peaceful citizens of London, however, could sleep soundly in their beds, for Lord Palmerston had already raised strong objections to French guards visiting the Exhibition bringing side arms into

England. The Foreign Secretary insisted they 'leave their swords on the French side of the Channel'.

Albert was fully aware that the semi-deranged prophesies and malicious rumours were intended to frighten the public. But after the Exhibition's successful inauguration day, during which 25,000 visitors passed through the vast Hall without incident, Albert remained dismayed by the barrage of condemnation that surged from his detractors. A letter to King Frederick William of Prussia reflects the anguish of a man struggling to make his voice heard above the forces of ignorance.

> Mathematicians have calculated that the Crystal Palace will blow down…engineers, that the galleries would crash in and destroy the visitors. Political economists have prophesied a scarcity of food in London…doctors, that owing to so many races coming into contact with each other, the Black Death of the Middle Ages would make its appearance, moralists, that England would be infected by all the scourges of the civilised world and uncivilised world.[22]

In spite of his many virtues, Albert lacked the one quality that more often than not sees the English through times of adversity. The Prince never quite managed to acquire a sense of irony. He was incapable of appreciating the ridiculous quality of these political and newspaper assaults on his cherished project. It was in these moments of anguish that the Prince would turn to the spiritual confidant of his youth. 'The Exhibition is now attacked furiously in *The Times*, and the House of Commons is going to drive us out of the Park,' he wrote to Stockmar on 28 June 1850. 'There is immense excitement on the subject. If we are driven out of the Park, the work is ruined. Never was anything so foolish.' And five days later he again turned to the Baron.

I cannot conceal from you that we are on the point of having to abandon the Exhibition altogether. We have announced our intention to do so, if on the day the vast building ought to be begun the site is taken from us…It is to come to the vote tomorrow, and the public is inflamed by the newspapers to madness.[23]

Within days of dispatching his letter of distress, Albert had cause to turn once again to his old friend Stockmar, this time with news of an event which, apart from intensifying the pain caused by the Exhibition affray, plunged the nation into a state of shock. In the early hours of 29 June Sir Robert Peel had left the Commons, exhausted after an all-night debate on the Don Pacifico affair. This was a classic piece of Palmerstonian gunboat diplomacy, in which the Foreign Secretary had sent the Royal Navy to blockade Athens in reprisal for a racist attack on David 'Don' Pacifico, a Portuguese Jew who by virtue of having been born in Gibraltar held British citizenship. Peel, Albert's closest friend and adviser for many years, left Buckingham Palace later that day following an Exhibition Commission meeting where he vociferously proclaimed his support for the Hyde Park site. Peel mounted his horse for a leisurely ride through St James's Park to clear his head, returning by way of Constitution Hill. On his way back, a bystander spotted Peel's horse acting nervously and tried to shout a warning that it was about to bolt − but too late. Peel was thrown from his mount, and died in great agony three days later, aged 62, due to a clavicular fracture rupturing blood vessels.

Albert was shattered by the tragedy: 'Dear Stockmar, You will mourn with us deeply, for you know the extent of our loss, and valued our friend as we did.'[24] Stockmar could well appreciate the impact of Peel's untimely death, for the Baron had been a close friend of the Tory leader for more than thirty years. The Queen's anxiety was no less acute. She wrote to the King of Prussia the day following Peel's death, 'This is one of the hardest blows of Fate which could have fallen on us and on the country. You knew the great man, and understood how to appreciate his merit. His value is now becoming clear even to his opponents.'[25] Yet more sadness was to follow. On 9 July, the day of Peel's funeral, Victoria had cause to exclaim to Leopold, 'We live in the midst of sorrow and death!' Her uncle, the Duke of Cambridge, Viceroy of Hanover, had died. 'I still saw him yesterday morning at one, but he did not see me, and today I saw him lifeless and cold.'[26]

The debates on the Great Exhibition site that were held in both Houses of Parliament on 4 July 1850 saw the Opposition defeated by a large majority − Hyde Park it was to be. It is reasonable to speculate that Peel's untimely death may have been a contributing factor to the outcome.

> It is impossible to say how much of the vote of the House of Commons may have been influenced by its being known that the voice of its most distinguished member, now silent, would have been the first to be raised in support of the appropriation of the space in Hyde Park to the purpose...In the other House, the hostile motions were withdrawn.[27]

It is interesting to follow the editorial policy of *The Times*, the country's most influential paper of the day, which lost no time in denouncing the coming 'profanation' of Hyde Park. The morning after the vote, the paper came out with an editorial expressing its 'deep regret' at the outcome. 'For nearly two years the inhabitants and visitors of London are to be virtually driven from Hyde Park...as multitudes from the continent of Europe and the provinces flock to visit the monstrous Exhibition.'[28]

Curious indeed that once it became manifest that the 'monstrous Exhibition' had in fact become a raging success, with virtually no breach of public order or well-being, *The Times* quickly began to sing a much chirpier tune.

The Commissioners had their mandate – it was time to push ahead with the construction and logistics of providing space to some 14,000 exhibitors, of whom nearly half would be arriving from abroad. The building was nearly two thousand feet long and more than four hundred in width, with 19 acres of floor-space under 900,000 square feet of glass – made, in larger panes than ever before, by Chance Brothers of Birmingham – not including the 217,100 square feet of galleries. This was an area four times that of St Peter's in Rome, with a total enclosed volume of 33 million cubic feet. Paxton's Crystal Palace was an almost unbelievably intrepid venture: nothing on this scale had been attempted before. Building materials included 550 tons of wrought iron, 3500 tons of cast iron and 600,000 feet of wooden planking to walk on. The latter served their purpose in an experiment carried out to demonstrate the building's stability and safety. There were fears that a large throng of people shuffling about inside the building could trigger vibrations that would bring the entire structure crashing down, in fulfilment of Colonel Sibthorp's furious ravings for divine retribution. To put this to the test, three hundred workmen on the site were sent through the Hall to walk about and jump simultaneously into the air. Even more of a strain was placed on the structure when a detachment of the army's sapper and miners were drafted in to tramp across the entire floorspace. To Paxton's delight, the maximum girder movement was found to be a quarter of an inch, hardly a cause for concern.

By the autumn of 1850, Fox and Henderson had spent more than £50,000 on building works and the firm still had not secured from the Commissioners more than a pledge of future payment. The firm's rapidly submitted tender estimated the cost at £150,000, to be reduced to £79,800 if they could have the materials after demolition. There was much discussion over advances and guarantees of payment, and inevitably the word got out that the Commission was bankrupt. This was not true, but it created enough uncertainty to complicate further the job of fundraising. Then there were the endless logistical problems that crept into Albert's sleep. The elms that had been spared from felling were found to host a huge number of sparrows − what could be done to prevent them fouling the exhibits, not to mention the visitors? When Victoria brought this to the Duke of Wellington's attention, he famously replied, 'Sparrow hawks, Ma'am!' Fortunately the flock of sparrows was chased from the Hall before the opening day. Albert insisted on being involved in every detail of the Exhibition's planning and execution, even down to the debate over the catering contract, which the Prince awarded to Messrs Schweppes for £5000. On the more precarious issue of funding, Fox and Henderson took the pressure off the Commission's parlous financial situation by reassuring Albert that his word was sufficient guarantee of payment.

The work progressed apace, and as each beam was raised and each glass pane fitted into place, London began to experience a knock-on effect from the preparations for the Great Exhibition.

Victoria Street was opened, ploughing a path through Westminster's worst slum. The Marble Arch was moved from the Palace grounds to anchor the north-east (Speakers') corner of Hyde Park. Trafalgar Square was finally completed…Little populated areas around new railway junctions underwent building booms…Kensington, abutting Hyde Park to the west, became citified and in Knightsbridge…a tea merchant, Charles Harrod, opened a grocery.[29]

The city was undergoing a massive regeneration, its physiognomy taking the form of what we today recognise as central London.

There was no doubt that Albert was suffering the strains of shouldering, day after day, the relentless demands of the Exhibition: speech-making, negotiations with contractors, suppliers, foreign dignitaries, plus the increasingly difficult task of obtaining the funding required to see his dream through to fruition. The Prince was not endowed with a particularly robust constitution, and this was noted with alarm by those of his immediate entourage, including the Queen. Lord Granville of the Board of Trade, who took a prominent part in the Exhibition, made mention of Albert's crucial stewardship of the project. In a conversation with the Prince's Secretary at Buckingham Palace, he said that 'Albert appears to be the only person who has considered the subject [of the Exhibition] both as a whole and in its details. The whole thing would fall to pieces, if he left it to itself.'[30] Even before Albert delivered his key Mansion House speech in March 1850, Victoria had confided her anxiety to Stockmar, in a letter from Windsor. 'The Prince's sleep is as bad as ever, and he looks very ill of an evening…He *must* be set right before we go to London, or God knows how ill he may get.'[31] Albert was aware of his precarious state of health. 'Just at present I am more dead than alive,' he wrote to his grandmother, the Dowager Duchess of Saxe-Coburg.[32]

Albert's life might have conformed to a statesman's normal routine had the Great Exhibition been the only issue absorbing his thoughts. But many other affairs at the time, of a political and personal nature, were making enormous demands on his energies. In June 1850, the Prince was badly shaken by the attack – mentioned earlier – on the Queen by former army officer Robert Pate, who leapt out of the crowd as the Queen left Cambridge House and struck her repeatedly with a cane. Victoria had not yet fully recovered from the birth of her third son, Arthur, a month earlier, on the Duke of Wellington's eighty-first birthday. Her bonnet deflected the full impact of the blows and this saved her from serious injuries, but the assault left bruises on her forehead. When Pate, reputedly 'a man of good family', was brought to trial, no motive for the attack could be established. The usual plea of insanity failed, and Pate was sentenced to seven years' penal transportation to the colonies. Victoria's confidant Uncle Leopold learnt of the incident in a letter from Buckingham Palace. 'I have not suffered except from my head, which is still very tender, the blow having been extremely violent, and the brass end of the stick fell on my head so as to make a considerable noise.'[33]

It was around this time that Albert was thrust into an awkward position by the elderly Duke of Wellington, the Prince's truest of friends and the one person he would be horrified of offending. The Duke, now in his eighty-second year, knew that his end was not far off. He had, in fact, just two more years to live. Yet his mind remained sharp, and he had decided it was time to appoint a successor as Commander-in-Chief. The frail old soldier braced himself against the blustery spring chill to travel to Windsor to deliver a proposal, that Albert eventually be appointed his successor as head of the armed forces. No matter that the Prince lacked any military experience, the Duke was seeking a respected figurehead capable of commanding the General Staff's respect. This was Wellington's rationale, although he later revealed the real motive behind his plan: to ensure that command of the army remained under the Crown (as it does today) and not, as he feared, fall into the hands of an ever more power-hungry Parliament. Albert wanted no part of it, and he summoned all the tact he could muster to put forth his objections. 'Suppose there was to be serious rioting, as there nearly had been in 1848, it would be the Commander-in-Chief's duty to quell it – but how could the Queen's husband shed the blood of the Queen's subjects without imperilling her throne?'[34]

After Wellington's departure, the Prince took his courage in both hands and wrote an official rejection to the Duke. It would be insensitive, to say the least, to tell the most celebrated military hero in British history that the Prince had no interest in taking on military duties. Albert couched his letter in well-crafted logic, explaining that such a role would interfere with his position as the Queen's Consort. It would be wrong, the Prince argued, to pursue any powers for himself. He must make his position entirely a part of the Queen's, hence it would be inconsistent for the Prince Consort to undertake the leadership of a crucial branch of public service. 'I am afraid, therefore, that I must discard the tempting idea of being placed in command of the British Army.'[35] Albert's reasoning was flawless, notwithstanding the fact, well known of course to the Duke, that the Prince had for years past exercised the real power behind the throne. Nevertheless, Wellington graciously acknowledged Albert's refusal, and when the Duke died two years later, the job of Commander-in-Chief went to

Viscount Hardinge, who was charged with responsibility for the direction of the Crimean War.

Albert's relationship with the Duke of Wellington was one of deep mutual regard, from the day of the Prince's marriage, to the Duke's death in 1852. But there was another, utterly exasperating, public figure who threw Albert's life into turmoil and tried his patience to the limit during those difficult days of planning for the Exhibition.

In a political career that spanned nearly sixty years – from Lord of the Admiralty in 1807 to his death in office as Prime Minister in 1865 – Henry John Temple, later Lord Palmerston, succeeded in annoying more people, at home and abroad, than any British politician before or since. 'Palmerston personified the bombastic self-confidence of Britain as the only world power.' He was simultaneously 'an aristocrat, a reformer, a free-trader, an internationalist and a chauvinist'.[36] As Foreign Secretary, a post Palmerston particularly cherished, his policies were largely responsible for the creation of an independent Belgium at the expense of the Netherlands in 1830, which did little to endear him to the citizens of the low countries, and he also advocated the suppression of revolutions in Portugal and Spain two years later. Palmerston outraged the Persians in 1838 by disembarking British troops on their soil to persuade the Shah to break off a military alliance with Russia which threatened Afghan and ultimately Indian security, while the Greeks were incensed over his blockade of the port of Piraeus in the celebrated Don Pacifico incident. The supreme nineteenth-century meddler in other countries' affairs, Palmerston generated widespread indignation in Poland, Denmark, Switzerland and Italy, and for good measure raised the hackles of Abraham

Lincoln's Unionist government in Washington with his support for the secessionist Confederacy.

Palmerston acted impulsively and, more often than not, without consultation. He blithely offended any foreign power that displeased him, as well as his colleagues in government and even his sovereign – who had cause to write a dozen letters expressing her displeasure with her minister – by his overt friendliness to the European revolutionaries of 1848 and his unofficial approval of the coup d'état of Louis Napoleon in 1851, three years after the abdication of France's last king, Louis Philippe I. That said, Palmerston's diplomacy, though reckless, domineering and deployed with a lofty indifference to the opinions of his detractors, more often than not advanced British prestige overseas.

On matters of foreign policy, Albert counted himself squarely in the anti-Palmerston camp. Theirs was a chalk and cheese relationship, particularly with regard to Europe. Palmerston would today sit comfortably at the table of Britain's most intransigent 'Eurosceptics'. For him, continental politics were to be judged solely on the basis of their usefulness to British interests. The Prince was a passionate believer in Europe and an ardent supporter, unsurprisingly, of German unity, along with the desirability of constitutional monarchy and other causes that clashed with Palmerston's views, which were premised exclusively on what stood to benefit Britain. 'In short, each misunderstood and underestimated the other.'[37]

Albert's exhaustion, brought about by the endless attacks on the Exhibition and the pressing need to get on with the job, had reduced the 32-year-old Prince to a man at least ten years older in appearance, with a receding hairline, a premature paunch straining at his waistcoat and a weary, almost glassy expression in his eyes. This state of mental and physical fatigue put a severe strain on his humour, leaving him little disposed to tolerate Palmerston's disregard of royal opinion. Albert vented his anger in a letter to Lord Russell, in which he acknowledged Palmerston as an able politician with 'large views', but stating that there was no doubting his preference for expediency – a man of 'easy temper, no very high standard of honour and not a grain of moral feeling'.[38]

Victoria wanted Palmerston out, and she said as much: 'The Queen must say she is afraid that she will have no peace of mind and there will be no end of troubles as long as Lord Palmerston is at the head of the Foreign Office.'[39]

The abyss that separated Albert from Palmerston over all matters European was the real bone of contention between these two antagonistic titans. The Prince had looked on with horror when in 1848 populist uprisings rampaged through the streets of France, Sweden, Belgium, Poland and elsewhere, while the crafty Palmerston saw these events through a much different prism. The waves of civil disorder represented an opportunity to be exploited to Britain's benefit, strengthening the country's position among her weakened, strife-torn neighbours. 'Palmerston wanted a swift resumption of diplomatic relations with the French Republic. He supported the Danes over Schleswig-Holstein,[40] the Italians against the Austrians and the Hungarians against the Russians, in total contradiction to Albert's views.'[41]

The Prince condemned Palmerston as the key stumbling block to a well-ordered relationship between the Crown and Government in executing affairs of state. Stepping out of the spotlight, as befitted his position as Consort, the Prince wrote a disparaging memorandum on Victoria's much-disliked Foreign Secretary. 'The fact that the Queen distrusted Lord Palmerston (a reference to Palmerston's failing to consult Victoria over official correspondence) was a serious impediment to the carrying on of the Government.'[42] Albert then goes on to set out the scheme that had been hatched between himself and Lord Russell to have Palmerston ousted from the Foreign Office. The Prince had earlier managed to persuade Victoria that despite Stockmar's urging to the contrary, she did not have the constitutional right to dismiss one of her ministers. Nor was appointing Palmerston Leader of the House of Commons, a possibility that had been quietly mooted, deemed an acceptable solution. Albert recoiled at the prospect of Palmerston using that platform to destabilise Russell, force a general election and capitalise on his own popularity with the masses to be returned as Prime Minister.

Russell, acting under intense pressure from Buckingham Palace, at last mustered the courage to dismiss his obstinate Foreign Secretary. The pretext was Palmerston's unofficial conversation with the French Ambassador Count Walewski, in which the Foreign Secretary unofficially expressed his approval of Louis Napoleon's coup d'état. This took place on 2 December 1851: a fortnight later Palmerston was dismissed. Russell wrote to him on 17 December stating bluntly, 'I am sorry to say I think matters have now become so serious that the conduct of foreign affairs can no longer be left in your hands.'[43] Russell's case was flawed in that he and several of his Cabinet members had manifested similar opinions to the same ambassador at nearly the same time. 'The theory was that approval from the Foreign Secretary to a French Government representative meant a great deal more than from other members of Government.'[44] On hearing the news of Palmerston's ouster, the Austrian statesman Prince Felix zu Schwarzenberg gave a ball. At that time there was a doggerel rhyme making the rounds of Vienna, which must have been music to Albert and Victoria's ears:

Hat der Teufel einen Sohn,
So ist der sicher Palmerston
(If the Devil had a son,
Who could it be but Palmerston!)

Palmerston's retaliation, which he called 'tit for tat for Johnny Russell', was not long in coming: within a few weeks the irrepressible Palmerston had brought down the Russell ministry in an amendment to the Militia Bill, and he later found himself once more in the Cabinet, this time as Home Secretary in the Whig–Conservative coalition under Lord Aberdeen, the recognised leader of the Peelites.

There was to be no abatement in the feud with Palmerston, the despised defender of the dreaded republican cataclysm which Albert imagined would sweep away civilised Europe. But it was time to put aside these time-consuming political wrangles and get on with the final preparations for the Great Exhibition – the 1 May opening date was drawing alarmingly near. The anxiety caused by a prolonged political crisis over a number of stormy issues, in particular parliamentary reform, protectionism versus free trade and the 'papal aggression'[45] affair had added greatly to the stress of Victoria and Albert's life in London. The Queen felt grave concerns, and with much justification, at Albert's precarious state of health. The bouts of painful stomach cramps that were to make his life a misery in later years were now beginning to manifest themselves. Victoria was, with some difficulty, able to persuade Albert to snatch a few days' rest in the bracing environment of their Osborne retreat, where the Prince had not long before completed a major work of landscaping, remodelling the valley that slopes from the house towards the sea. He spent nearly a fortnight in early March planting rhododendrons and other plants in the gardens, striving to divert his mind from the hectic days that lay ahead in London. Once back in the capital, Albert threw himself night and day into the Exhibition's opening arrangements.

The great building had been completed and given over to the Commissioners at the start of the year. Among its most passionate admirers was the novelist William Makepeace Thackeray, who laid aside his acerbic pen to produce an epic of hyperbole, which the Prince kept among his private records of the Exhibition:

> But yesterday a naked sod,
> The dandies sneered from Rotten Row,
> And cantered o'er it to and fro;
> And see, 'tis done!
> As though 'twere by a wizard's rod,
> A blazing arch of lucid glass
> Leaps like a fountain from the grass
> To meet the sun![46]

At 32, Albert stood on the threshold of achieving a visionary triumph. In doing so, he had confounded such obdurate critics as Lord Brougham, who advised Albert, as Consort, not to take any initiatives whatsoever, lest he leave himself exposed to public ridicule. The indomitable Sibthorp was still not to be silenced: during a Commons debate shortly before the Exhibition inauguration he leapt from his seat to alert the House to a most distressing development: 'No less than one thousand five-hundred foreigners have been disembarked in this country yesterday, many of whom, no doubt, had been surveying the ground where this exhibition was to take place, and looking after matters with a view to their own interests.'[47]

By mid-February the Crystal Palace was near enough to completion to begin receiving the more than one hundred thousand exhibits that would soon cause amazement and dazzle the millions of visitors, some of whom had already ordered their season passes (three guineas for men, two for ladies), others of whom would be purchasing tickets on the door, at prices ranging from one pound down to two shillings and sixpence for the working classes, the price of a couple of pints of beer. The eastern portion of the building, nearest to Hyde Park Corner, housed the foreign exhibits, and at the western end displayed those from Britain and the Empire – valued in total at nearly £3 million, a vast sum at the time. From India, the jewel in the imperial crown, came sumptuous silks and damasks, ebony furniture, intricate sculptures in ivory, delicate lapidary works of agate, jasper and cornelians, martial arms of all descriptions. From each province came some specimen of its industry and art. 'They will form no insignificant addition even to the grand spectacle which will be presented, and many of the rude machines of the natives will be found to be as remarkable for their ingenuity as the more perfect contrivances of European artificers.'[48] The world was treated to the dazzling sight of the Queen's Koh-i-Noor diamond, an array of technological innovations, from the mechanical wonders of the electromagnetic telegraph device to the prototype of the modern calculator, marine engines, hydraulic presses and great pieces of steam machinery. The French collection was heralded as one of the most attractive and extensive in the Exhibition. The total number of French exhibitors was around 1750, and their floorspace was second only to the British, with two large courts displaying tapestry, machinery, arms and instruments. The United States was proudly present, with Singer's sewing machines, Colt's revolvers and McCormick's reapers representing American manufacturing ingenuity. One sensational exhibit that attracted large crowds to the American sector was the new-style 'bloomer'.

> Three ladies, attired according to the Bloomer fashion…made their appearance in the large open space to the west of the Crystal Palace. They appeared to be persons of some station in society, and bore with considerable good humour the taunts which were freely directed against them.[49]

These were the same ladies of Alabama high society who had put on a similar show at home and caused 'quiet a sensation among our quiet citizens. In fact, we never saw a place more effectively stirred up.' One of them, a Miss Julia Mortimer, pranced down the gangplank of a schooner recently docked from Europe, attired in a scarlet bodice and white linen cambric pantaloons, tipped with lace, and 'fastened around her small ankles with fancy ribbons, which gave her little feet an exquisite appearance'.[50] Belgium and Austria were there with furniture, carpets and machinery, while Russia showed off her malachite doors, vases and ornaments. In all, seventeen thousand exhibitors entrusted their wealth, their skill, their industry and their enterprise to the guardianship of some fifty policemen, armed with nothing more than wooden batons. Day after day and night after night passed, and no added force was called in to protect the wealth deposited within these glass walls. Albert could truly take pride in his labour, for one

Albert's Coat of Arms. Courtesy of the College of Arms.

clockwise from top left Albert, Victoria, Prince Leopold, Lord Melbourne, Lord Palmerston, Sir Robert Peel, the Duke of Wellington. Portraits by Moussa Saleh.

Schloss Rosenau, near Coburg, Albert's childhood home.

Coburg, Albert's home town. From the author's collection.

Ehrenburg Palace, Coburg, the city residence of the Coburg dukes. Albert's father, Ernest I, substantially remodelled the palace.

Albert and his elder brother Ernest as children c. 1831, attributed to Sebastian Eckhardt. Courtesy of the Royal Collection.

Baron Stockmar, from the portrait by John Partridge.

The Wedding of Albert and Victoria, 1840, by Sir George Hayter. Courtesy of the Royal Collection.

Prince Albert in 1842, by Francis Xaver Winterhalter. Courtesy of the Royal Collection.

Albert and Victoria dancing. Artist unknown, reproduced from *Victoria and Albert* by Hector Bolitho (1938).

Albert and Victoria sledging. Artist unknown, reproduced from *The Prince Consort and his Brother* by Hector Bolitho (1933).

above The royal family at Carn Lochan. From the picture by James Stephenson, after Carl Haag.

right 'The Queen and Prince Albert at Home', a cartoon from 1843.

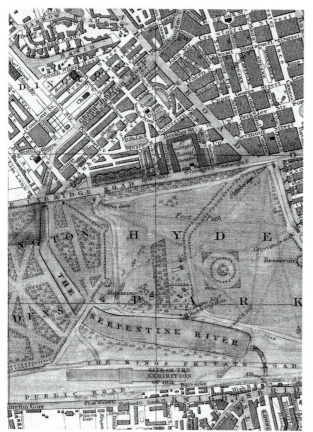

left A map of Hyde Park, London, showing the location of the 1851 Great Exhibition.

below The facade of the original Crystal Palace in Hyde Park, London.

Balmoral Castle, purchased by Victoria and Albert in 1852.

The new Osborne House. Purchased by Victoria and Albert in 1845, it was subsequently redesigned by Prince Albert in Italianate style.

The royal family at Osborne House, 1857. Courtesy of the Royal Collection.

right Prince Albert in later life: a carte de visite. Both Albert and Victoria were fascinated by the new technology of photography.

below The death of Albert, by Oakley under the pseudonym Le Port. Courtesy of the Wellcome Library/Wellcome Images.

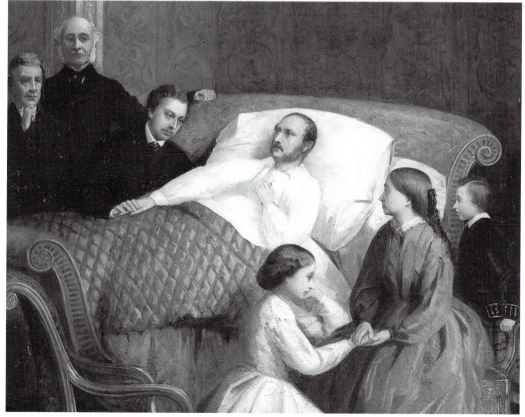

The Albert Memorial in Kensington Gardens, London. Courtesy of Nick Smith.

A statue of Prince Albert in his home town of Coburg. From the author's collection.

would be hard pressed to find another country in which such an exhibition could have taken place under these conditions, in absolute peace and without incident.

The Prince spent the final hectic days in the run up to 1 May in a flurry of activity, rushing from the worksite to oversee construction progress and make arrangements for exhibitor space, to meetings with the Commissioners, finalising last-minute details for the grand opening ceremony. Victoria herself came eight times to witness the works, and the Duke of Wellington was also a frequent visitor, overseeing security matters and exhorting the builders not to slacken the pace. Albert was at this time firing off letters of encouragement to members of the European nobility, many of whom were loath to attend, fearing attack by exiled revolutionaries. This caused the Prince extreme frustration, as evidenced in his letter to King Frederick William of Prussia. 'As regards England, I can only assure Your Majesty that we fear neither risings nor murderous attacks, and that, although many political refugees from every country live and perhaps conspire here, they behave peaceably.'[51] In the end, the pusillanimity of these unloved princes kept most of them at home.

Then came the glorious day. On 1 May, London awoke to a fine drizzle under ominous thunderclouds that threatened an even more dismal afternoon. But just before the appointed hour of one o'clock, as if by divine intervention, the clouds rolled aside to reveal a radiant blue sky over Hyde Park. Public expectation had been roused from the earliest hour, as was reported in *The Times*, which had already embarked on a *volte face* over the Exhibition: 'The arteries of the great city, surcharged with life, beat full and strong under the pressure of a great and hitherto unknown excitement. Never before was so vast a multitude collected together within the memory of man.' The paper's insightful correspondent did not fail to observe that this multitude was composed not only of Londoners: 'Strange-looking foreigners passed along in the stream ... Every variety of beard, moustache, hat, coat and trouser was permitted for the day.' The paper reported the opening day as 'a sight the like of which has never happened before, and which, in the nature of things, can never be repeated'.[52]

Victoria was beside herself with joy. She recounted the event to Uncle Leopold in a flurry of girlish exhilaration. 'I wish you could have witnessed the 1st of May 1851, the *greatest* day in our history, the most *beautiful* and *touching* spectacle ever seen, and the triumph of my beloved Albert.' It was for her a 'fairy scene', touched with 'devotional feelings', the '*happiest, proudest* day of my life, and I can think of nothing else'. Best of all, Albert's months of anguish, his overwork and apprehensions, they had been worth every moment. 'Albert's dearest name is immortalised with this great conception.'[53]

On that morning, the Commissioners assembled at half past eleven in the Exhibition transept, some in full dress, others in evening attire. The Archbishop of Canterbury, the Cabinet, the great officers of state and foreign dignitaries took their places on the platform. The Queen and Albert arrived at noon, at which moment a choir of six hundred voices struck up 'God Save the Queen'. This was followed by a short report on the Commission's proceedings read out by Albert to his wife. There were more speeches, more tributes, as the throng of thousands pressed at the gates to catch a glimpse of the royal couple. But before opening the Hall there was still to come a prayer by the Archbishop of Canterbury, invoking God's blessing on the undertaking, ending with a rendition by the choir of Handel's 'Hallelujah Chorus'.

The royal procession was formed for a march west and east, to either end of the Hall, so that all the invited guests might see their sovereign and her consort. Finally, it was time for Victoria to proclaim 'The Exhibition is opened', at which there came a crash of chords from the organ, a flourish of trumpets and a firing of a salute from the banks of the Serpentine.[54] It all went off without a hitch, apart from one curious incident in which a Chinese mandarin, apparently an ordinary visitor, made his way slowly round the great fountain and bowed low before the Queen. When the Royal cortège was formed for a formal tour of the Exhibition, it was discovered that the diplomatic corps had no Chinese representative, so the celestial interloper was impounded and made to march in the rear of the ambassadors, which he did with supreme steadiness and gravity.

By any measure, Albert's Great Exhibition of 1851 was an unqualified triumph. This was the judgement of the great figures of the day, as well as the six million ordinary folk who in the course of five months passed through the Crystal Palace gates. Charlotte Brontë visited the Exhibition on five occasions, and pronounced it 'splendid'. Gustave Flaubert was another enthusiast, and even Dickens returned twice after the day of his private tour. The Commission's creditors were no less delighted with the Exhibition's commercial success. The Commissioners were able to report a revenue of £500,000, a truly huge fortune in 1851, more than enough to pay off the contractors, workers and suppliers of a host of goods and services. Moreover, the Exhibition had cleared a healthy £186,437 profit. As agreed (after a minor contretemps with Paxton, who wanted to make it a permanent feature of Hyde Park), the building was taken down and re-erected at Sydenham in 1854, in an area of South

London that came to be known as Crystal Palace. One would today search in vain for any remnants of the magnificent structure, which in 1936 was totally destroyed by fire. But during its 82-year reincarnation the Crystal Palace, 'as a permanent exhibition and pleasure-garden combined, became even more of a wonder than it had been in Hyde Park'.[55]

Albert and Victoria travelled to Balmoral in early October, where the Prince threw himself ardently into deer-stalking, and strove to slow the hectic pace of the past two years. On the return journey to London, where Albert was officially to close the Exhibition, an alarmed Victoria confided to her diary on 10 October, 'From one o'clock in the morning Albert was very unwell − very sick and wretched.'[56] Entries concerning the Prince's health from this time onwards were to appear with greater frequency in the Queen's diaries and letters. The greatest victory of Albert's life, achieved through many months of exhausting toil, struggling against his many powerful enemies in government and the press, had been won at a price.

5

'King to all intents and purposes'

When the Exhibition closed on 15 October 1851, Albert the mistrusted, the resented foreigner, suddenly found himself elevated to a pedestal and glorified as a national hero. Even the political and social diarist, Charles Greville,[1] who was notoriously sparing in his praise for his contemporaries, was moved to proclaim, 'He [Albert] is King to all intents and purposes.'[2] Greville had expected the Exhibition to collapse in a bedlam of working-class jostling and chaos, but was instead inspired to observe graciously, 'the masses and their behaviour...all so orderly and good-humoured. The success of everything was complete.'[3]

The Exhibition had indeed been a resounding success, and the Government agreed to match the profit of nearly £190,000,[4] to underwrite future endeavours. Albert and Victoria left for Osborne in early August after paying their last official visit to the Crystal Palace. The royal couple's holiday was ostensibly taken to escape the hectic routine to which Albert had been subjected in the many months of planning and executing his grand undertaking. In fact, the Prince was by now so consumed with enthusiasm – and the onset of severe stomach cramps that were later to take an ominous turn – that he straight away set his mind to the question of how best to dispose of this handsome surplus. He ruled out any notion of turning the Crystal Palace into a public promenade, museum or winter garden – it had been agreed that the structure was to be dismantled, and come down it must. Yet had not the Exhibition focused the world's attention on the remarkable progress achieved in industry and the arts? Here then was an opportunity to reaffirm Britain's greatness on a permanent basis, not just for five months. Albert sat pensively in his study by the sea and penned a memorandum on how to fulfil this ambition: 'If I am asked what I would do with the surplus, I would propose the following scheme,' he wrote on 10 August. The plan that began to take shape in his mind eventually led to the creation of a cultural development, jokingly dubbed at the outset 'Albertopolis', which has endowed London with what is arguably the world's foremost complex of art and science museums, attracting more than nine million visitors a year. 'I am assured that from twenty-five to thirty acres of ground, nearly opposite the Crystal Palace…are to be purchased at this moment for about £50,000. I would buy that ground, and place on it four institutions.' Albert envisaged on this site four structures housing the four great sections of the Exhibition: raw materials, machinery, manufacturing and plastic art. 'I would devote these institutions to the furtherance of the industrial pursuits of all nations in these four divisions.'[5]

Instead of limiting the project solely to exhibiting what his adopted country had to offer the world, the Prince saw Britain 'taking the initiative and pointing the direction in which all other nations should move'.[6] Albert was too much the passionate internationalist to confine his vision to one nation's achievements, not even those of the Exhibition's host country. The Prince's global views were manifested in his Mansion House speech of 1850, when he proclaimed to an audience composed of men with a decidedly less cosmopolitan disposition,

> The distances which separated the different nations and parts of the globe are rapidly vanishing before the achievements of modern invention, and we can traverse them with incredible ease... thought is communicated with the rapidity, and even the power, of lightning. On the other hand, the great principle of division of labour, which may be called the moving power of civilization, is being extended to all branches of science, industry and art.[7]

The Exhibition, Albert announced, was to give 'a true test and a living picture of the point of development at which the whole of mankind has arrived in this great task'.[8] The project itself was evidence that the Prince had brought with him from Germany in 1840 a strong sense not only of the unity of culture, but also of the public's right to direct contact with it.

The Royal Commission eventually acquired an area of some eighty-seven acres on a neglected, semi-derelict site that was to become South Kensington, now one of London's most fashionable neighbourhoods. The purchase was motivated by the Prince, as the Commission's president, in order to provide a site 'for institutions that would further the general aims of the Exhibition and extend the influence of Science and Art upon Productive Industry'.[9] Some of this land is still the Commission's freehold property. One could hardly have drawn on a more distinguished body of public figures to promote this scheme, including such luminaries as Lords Russell and Derby, Gladstone and Disraeli. It was acknowledged, however, that the Prince himself remained the Commission's driving force until his death ten years later. Lady Eastlake, the wife of one of the Commissioners, wrote in her obituary of Albert that 'his powers of debate had been particularly in evidence at meetings of the Commission, where he came into contact with the most practised orators of the day, in debate of no insignificant character, and always maintained his part with conspicuous ability'.[10]

Albert knew that it was his will alone that had driven the Exhibition forward against its many formidable obstacles, and that to him were due the plaudits of its success. Yet unlike some of the Commissioners, who engaged in an unseemly scramble for honours, the Prince sought no self-aggrandisement as a reward for his work. Albert categorically rejected a proposal by the Lord Mayor of London to commemorate his achievement by erecting a statue of the Prince in Hyde Park. He exclaimed with characteristic good humour that such a tribute would disrupt his quiet rides in the park. Seeing his own face staring at him from what would almost certainly be 'an artistic monstrosity, like most of our monuments,' he remarked, would make him 'permanently ridiculed and laughed at in effigy'.[11]

The creation of South Kensington, that wonderfully 'un-English complex of museums, scientific institutions, colleges of music and art, part university and part polytechnic',[12] in its neo-Gothic splendour, stands as Albert's crowning life achievement as well as his most splendid gift to Britain. The three great museums clustered about Exhibition Road, along with the Royal Albert Hall, the Royal Geographical Society, the Royal College of Art, the Royal College of Music and Imperial College are commonly referred to as a legacy of the Victorian age. This is accurate inasmuch as the collective project evolved mainly during Queen Victoria's long reign. But it is beyond question that the complex is Albertine in conception and execution, and it is to the Prince Consort that the nation is indebted for bequeathing it this cultural treasure.

In developing his dream to establish an educational centre for the general public, Albert relied heavily on his friend, the gnomish, bewhiskered Henry (later Sir Henry) Cole, the most active of the Prince's assistants. Several months after the closure of the Great Exhibition, the Prince set up the Department of Practical Art under the Board of Trade, a body that was intended to improve standards of art and design education in Britain, particularly with reference to their applicability to industry. Cole, along with Lyon Playfair, who by then had also secured his knighthood, were appointed joint secretaries of the organisation that in 1856 was redesignated the Department of Science and Art, and was shifted to South Kensington to oversee the development of the scheme. In his new role, Cole was later responsible for moving what was then the Museum of Oriental Art to the Commission's newly acquired land.

The first building to be inaugurated on the site was the South Kensington Museum, which opened its doors to the public in 1857. The original structure resembled a set of corrugated ironclad boilers, hence the nickname 'Brompton boilers'. The building housed a collection of primarily industrial and decorative arts, and was in several ways quite an advanced concept in museum design, being the world's first to provide visitors with refreshment facilities and to offer late-night openings, thanks to the introduction of gas lighting. Cole brought in this innovation 'to ascertain practically what hours are most convenient to the working classes'.[13] In the 1880s the South Kensington Museum's collections underwent a major expansion with the acquisition of the contents of the Patent Office Museum and the establishment of a Science Library, which remains a valuable research facility for the academic world and the general public. But its real importance was as a forerunner, jointly with the Museum of Oriental Art, of the future Victoria and Albert Museum, or V&A as it is popularly known. In her last official public appearance, in May 1899, Queen Victoria laid the foundation stone and decreed that the new building should be named the Victoria and Albert Museum. A decade later, after the official opening of the new South Kensington buildings, the arts collections were assembled under the roof of the V&A, while the science and engineering collections were separated to be housed across the road in the Science Museum, known by that name since 1885.

Albert was not destined to live to see the opening of the Natural History Museum, with its displays of some seventy million life and earth-science specimens, whose ornate terracotta facade dominates Cromwell Road. The museum was built on a plot of land occupied by the Great London Exposition of 1862, as it was designated, a follow-up international fair that sought to capitalise on the success of the 1851 Exhibition. The 1862 Exposition attracted a similar number of visitors, but in financial terms it ranked as a poor cousin to its predecessor, making a profit of only £790. The Natural History Museum that replaced it was inaugurated in 1881, 20 years after the Prince's death.

There is a sad irony in the statue of Charles Darwin that sits in the main hall in tribute to the Prince's much admired contemporary, and likewise in the museum's Darwin Centre that was designed as a new home for the collection of tens of millions of preserved specimens. One of Albert's perennial regrets was his failure to secure a knighthood for Darwin, who ranked high among his most admired men of science. It was the Bishop of Oxford who persuaded Victoria that a knighthood for the man who espoused the theory of evolution would have negative repercussions on the sovereign as Defender of the Faith.

Albert's orderly Germanic mind had always envisaged the creation of an all-encompassing complex of museums and cultural institutions, centralised in a single location − an objective he came close to achieving. His project even called for the transfer of the National Gallery to a prominent position in South Kensington, in order to enhance and complete the unprecedented collection of art being assembled at the site. The Government was for a time inclined to support this proposal to shift the gallery from Trafalgar Square, a location considered inadequate for such a world-class art collection. The Earl of Aberdeen's Whig and Peelite coalition had gone so far as to commission a report on possible new sites for the gallery, and they came close to purchasing the land, but these plans were swept aside by weightier affairs, namely the management of the Crimean War that led to the downfall of the Aberdeen ministry. This was a great disappointment to the Prince, who observed with dismay that the proposed site on the south side of Kensington Gore adjoining Hyde Park was kept vacant for the remaining nine years of his life. Albert would surely have read with a blush the name inscribed across the facade of the structure that later came to occupy this empty plot of land: the Royal Albert Hall, built on the spot where the Prince had originally hoped to relocate the National Gallery. The idea for the name was, of course, chosen by Albert's widowed queen.

Still overshadowed by a dark cloud of mourning, Queen Victoria laid the foundation stone on 20 May 1867, surprising the thousands assembled by attaching the words Royal Albert to (what was meant to be called) the Hall for the Arts and Sciences, an addition that of course had to remain.[14]

The Prince's memory is enshrined in a mammoth frieze on the building's exterior, bearing an inscription that proclaims the hall's dedication to the advancement of the arts and science 'in the fulfilment of the intention of Albert Prince Consort'.

Apart from the South Kensington scheme itself, one of the Royal Commission's most enduring gifts to the nation is the system of bursaries, scholarships and research fellowships made available to applicants from the 54 Commonwealth member states. Taking their inspiration from the memory of Albert and his reverence for furthering human knowledge of the arts and science, in 1891 the Commissioners began using their resources to finance higher scientific and artistic education, chiefly in the form of scholarships. The idea of endowing grants had been on the Commissioners' minds once the great building projects were completed, hence it was decided to support research and studies with funds derived from an annual revenue.

> The purpose of furthering thereby the training of Captains of Industry was declared in the [Commission's] Eighth Report of 1911, and the denial henceforward of funds for buildings at South Kensington reiterated. In that year they established in its present form the British School at Rome and the associated Rome Scholarships in the fine arts, which they continue to support.[15]

Albert could justifiably derive a great deal of personal satisfaction from the cultural and social advancements he and the Commission had brought about thanks to the Exhibition's resounding success. Yet this was also a time of grieving for lost friends, as well as mounting concern over the shadows casting their dark pall across Europe.

Lord Melbourne was three years in his grave when the Exhibition closed its doors for the last time, and his disappearance had brought immense unhappiness to Albert. This was partly in sympathy with Victoria's deep and lingering grief for the death of her mentor, but also in recognition of the loss of a dedicated social reformer who had three times served as Prime Minister. Shortly thereafter, the Queen Consort Adelaide of Saxe-Meiningen, Victoria's aunt, died after a long period of illnesses. Victoria, who never forgot her aunt's kindness to her, remembered her at the christening of her first-born child, Victoria Adelaide Mary Louisa. Adelaide's death was followed by that of Lord George Bentinck, to whom Albert paid tribute despite the Conservative politician having been instrumental, along with Disraeli, in unseating Peel over the Corn Laws. Then in August 1850 it was the turn of the exiled Louis Philippe, and within a few months of his passing that of his daughter the Belgian Queen Louise.

In October 1849 the Prince had been dealt the most brutal shock of all with the loss of George Anson, whom Albert had frequently employed on diplomatic missions. In his ten years of service, Anson had become a faithful friend, as much to Victoria as to the Prince, since he had been appointed on Melbourne's advice. Lady Sarah Lyttelton, governess to the Prince of Wales, told of Anson's sudden collapse with symptoms of what he had described as a mild cold. He never recovered consciousness, and was gone within two hours, tragically at the age of 37, and more likely than not after having suffered a stroke. She describes the

Prince and Queen 'in floods of tears', and of Albert, four days later, she says, 'The Prince's face is still so sad and pale and grave, I can't forget it.'[16]

A much heavier blow, an event that stunned the entire nation as well as Albert, was the death of the Duke of Wellington in September 1852, at a moment that found the Prince fully engrossed in his plans for the South Kensington development. Albert and Victoria had been luxuriating in the late summer wildness of Scotland by the side of Loch Dhu when one of their Highland gillies arrived with a letter from the Prince's secretary Colonel Charles Phipps bearing the news of Wellington's death. Albert had the day before seen a late-edition report of the event, and had treated it with some scepticism. 'Although you said that the intelligence it transmitted had every appearance of being true,' he replied to Phipps, 'we did not believe it, as *The Sun* is not a very creditable authority and a sixth edition looked more like a last attempt to sell the stock on hand of an old paper in the streets.'[17] Once Albert had accepted the report's veracity, his first words were, 'What the country has lost in him, what we personally have lost, it is almost impossible to estimate.'[18]

The hero of Waterloo was in many ways a father figure for Albert, without a shadow of a doubt a man of far deeper integrity and strength of character than the Prince's philandering biological father. Albert took to heart the words of his mentor Stockmar, who had sent a letter of condolences in which he extolled Arthur Wellesley as a man of destiny. The Prince needed no encouragement to seek to follow in Wellington's footsteps. Here was a giant of a figure to take as a model, and Albert was making every effort to mould his own life in accordance with the old Duke's adherence to duty above all other considerations.

Wellington, the nation's first soldier, who had invited Albert to succeed him as Commander-in-Chief, had stood by Peel in his hour of need, and was godfather to the Prince's son Arthur, born on the Duke's eighty-first birthday and bearing his name. Wellington, an ally to the young, insecure foreign Consort, recognising early on the Prince's qualities and basic goodness. Wellington, a legend in his own time, the man who remained aloof from party politics, looked up to by all, an exemplary life devoted to service and duty, and in every respect a figure for Albert to emulate.

The Great Exhibition had brought Albert respect and glory, yet his triumph was shortlived. The Aberdeen ministry that succeeded Russell's in December 1852 saw Palmerston reinstated in the Cabinet, albeit ostensibly, from Albert's point of view, with the less threatening portfolio of Home Secretary. It could be said that the political changes of the past year, since the close of the Exhibition, had seen the Prince's will prevail. But these happy changes turned out to be the precursor of much darker events. On a national level, Britain found herself facing imminent war with Russia over territories of the terminally ill Ottoman Empire.

It was never conceivable that Palmerston would accept a position on the sidelines at a time when great issues of state were at stake. In January 1853, Tsar Nicholas I dispatched troops to occupy Wallachia and Moldavia, two Turkish principalities in the Balkans, the perennial cauldron of European conflict. In November of that year, Russian warships annihilated in one fierce hour-and-a-half battle a fleet of seven Turkish frigates anchored in the harbour of Sinope, a seaport in northern Anatolia.[19] The press in Britain stood behind Turkey as the innocent victim of imperial Russia's brutal expansionism, and public opinion dutifully fell in line with the headline version of events. The war cries came as most distressing news to Albert, who had espoused the cause of peace, and if at all possible an entente with the Tsar. This stood in sharp opposition to Palmerston's belligerence towards Russia, a power whose territorial ambitions he had resisted and successfully countered in Afghanistan in 1838. Albert was up against a formidably skilled adversary. By March 1854 it was no longer a question of war or peace: Britain and France had already opened hostilities with Russia. Throughout these months Palmerston kept up his determined attack on the Tsar, and when it was revealed that Britain's armed forces were woefully ill-prepared to wage a foreign war, Aberdeen lost the confidence of his Cabinet, and in February 1855 Palmerston, at the age of 70, once more took possession of 10 Downing Street.

It was at this point that Albert was drawn into the treacherous waters of European politics. The consequences were to prove disastrous. The Prince considered it senseless for Britain (and France) to maintain a permanent presence in the Black Sea for the sole purpose of keeping a watchful eye on Russian naval movements. To his thinking, this was not the way to guarantee European political stability. He made known his view that such a strategy would be interpreted as a provocation to Tsar Nicholas I and his successor Alexander II. A question mark hung over the neutrality of Austria and Prussia, two states which in the public eye were close to the Prince's heart by virtue of his German origins. Albert had urged the Government to form a coalition of Western powers, including Prussia and Austria – though Prussia, for one, lacked any urgent strategic interests to defend in the Balkans – to deter Russia from waging war, but his plan was dashed when Britain and France sent fleets to the Dardanelles in 1853. Albert still hoped to persuade the two Germanic states to join the Anglo-French alliance, but his efforts fell on deaf ears.

In the midst of this gathering European turmoil, Albert found himself embroiled in the most sinister attack the British royal family had ever had to tolerate. On 8 January 1854, Greville penned a furious entry in his diary: 'It only shows how much malignity there is amongst the masses, which a profligate and impudent mendacity can stir up.'[20] This damning comment was motivated by an unforeseen and wholly unjustified deluge of journalistic vitriol against the Prince. Fleet Street had launched a concerted attack on Albert, the nation's erstwhile man of the hour, accusing him of a raft of offences, from meddling in foreign affairs to conspiring with foreign governments to the detriment of British interests. It was a collective jamboree of abuse of the sort not unheard of in our own time, with each paper striving to outdo its rivals in sensationalist 'revelations' of a public figure's alleged misdemeanours. Albert was charged with favouring neutral Austria and belligerent Russia, while conniving to undermine Britain's French ally. The Prince had conspired to have Palmerston removed from office the previous year, the headlines shrieked, without mentioning Palmerston's hand in spreading these calumnies. Was there not a foreigner in the highest position whose hostility to Palmerston was unconcealed and known to all? The onslaught went on day after day, for weeks on end, as if a pack of half-starved wolves had been turned loose at the gates of Buckingham Palace. 'For many weeks these accusations filled the whole of the Press,' wrote Strachey.

Repeated at public meetings, elaborated in private talk, they flew over the country, growing every moment more extreme and more improbable. While respectable newspapers thundered out their grave invectives, halfpenny broadsides, hawked through the streets of London, re-echoed in doggerel vulgarity the same sentiments and the same suspicions.[21]

Albert had his own thoughts on where the campaign of defamation had originated. He suspected the Tory protectionists who resented his friendship with Peel and the success of the Exhibition. The 'stupidity', in Albert's words, of the Lord Mayor of London in wishing to erect a monument to the Prince could also have contributed to inflame public resentment. Then too, there were hostile elements in the army, in particular Lord Raglan, who never forgave Albert for passing him over for the post of Commander-in-Chief.[22]

Though deeply hurt by this outpouring of abuse, Albert kept a calm head and almost made light of the affair, albeit with an obvious twinge of frustration, in a letter to his brother Ernest. 'The Emperor of Russia now reigns in England, it is said, and that he telegraphs to Gotha, you to Brussels and Uncle Leopold to me. And I influence Victoria.' Nonetheless, the stiff upper lip prevailed at Windsor Castle: 'We are all well,' he says in the same letter. 'We skate a good deal, and this gives the children much pleasure.'[23]

The Prince's dignified silence throughout only served to reinforce the general opinion that the German Consort was indeed covering up his seditious activities. He did complain to Stockmar about the assault, as it continued with uninterrupted violence. 'There is no kind of treason to the country of which they say I have not been guilty. All this must be borne tranquilly until the meeting of Parliament on the 31st [January] when Aberdeen and John Russell are prepared to undertake my defence.'[24]

At one point the word spread that Albert had been impeached for high treason and was committed to the Tower of London. There was even a rumour that Victoria had been arrested and imprisoned with her husband. One morning, Greville's 'malignant masses' gathered in their thousands outside the Tower to catch a glimpse of their sovereigns being marched past in manacles. In keeping with his inherent morose character, Albert might have kept his sentiments bottled up inside himself, but Victoria was shocked by the way the public allowed themselves to be duped by these ridiculous newspaper stories. 'In attacking the Prince,' she wrote to Lord Aberdeen, 'who is one and the same with the Queen herself, the throne is assailed…she little expected that any portion of her subjects would thus requite the unceasing labours of the Prince.'[25]

Then, with the swiftness of a cloud of locusts vanishing beyond the horizon, it was ended. Parliament met, as scheduled, on 31 January, and in its inaugural session the authoritative voices of Lords Russell and Aberdeen were heard demanding an end to the defamatory campaign, while in the lower house the highly respected former Home Secretary Spencer Walpole spoke out in support of the Prince. Albert's right to express his political opinions and likewise to support the Queen by giving advice in all matters of state was upheld by these speakers as well as by the legal authority of the Chief Justice Lord Campbell. Russell's defence of Albert brought thunderous cheers in the House, and this from a man whose views often differed sharply from those of the Prince. After listening to the speech, Albert was moved to write to King Leopold, 'Nothing could have been more clear, complete and dignified than his [Lord Russell's] words.'[26]

Albert greeted his vindication with a mixture of relief and bitterness, the latter brought on by the hypocrisy of the press, which by now had performed its traditional *volte face*.

'The *Herald*,' the Prince tells Stockmar, as the Tory organ, is distressed at Ministers having brought before Parliament circumstances, which from the sacredness of private life, and from the fact of the individual being by the Constitution removed *beyond* discussion, 'ought not to have been mentioned'. Not bad this, when for six consecutive weeks this journal had slandered and outraged this individual and his private life without intermission.[27]

Once the Prince was assured that the dust was about to settle on this dismal affair, he sat down to spill out his heart at great length to Stockmar. The letter is one of the documents most revealing of Albert's intrinsic unhappiness and disappointment with the reception he had received from his adopted fellow countrymen. The letter is somewhat suffused with sanctimony and self-pity of a sort that would have found little favour with buttoned-up 'Victorian' Britain. But his feelings are genuine, and come from a man who spared no effort to make himself a benefactor of society and defender of worthy causes, and who asked no more than to be accepted.

When I first came over here, I was met by this want of knowledge and unwillingness to give a thought to the position of this luckless personage. Peel cut down my income, Wellington refused me my rank, the Royal Family cried out against the foreign interloper, the Whigs in office were only inclined to concede me just as much space as I could stand upon... As I kept quiet and caused no scandal, all went well, no one has troubled himself about me and my doings…Now when the present journalistic controversies have brought to light the fact that I have for years taken an active interest in all political matters, the public…fancied itself betrayed, because it felt it had been self-deceived.

Everyone who has been able to express or surmise any ill of me has conscientiously contributed his faggot to burn the heretic, and I may say with pride, that not the veriest tittle of a reproach can be brought against me with truth.[28]

The Crimean War followed hard on the heels of this painful episode, and has been described as the 'darkest and most difficult period' of Albert's life.[29] The character-assassination campaign of a few weeks' duration paled into insignificance compared with a great European conflagration that claimed more than half a million lives, including that of some 22,000 British troops, who succumbed to battle wounds but above all to disease. If the Prince's right to express his political opinion and give advice in all matters of state had been confirmed by both Houses of Parliament, Albert was no less determined to exercise that prerogative.

Albert's intellectual preferences lay decidedly more in the arts and applied sciences than in military affairs: in 1853 he had accepted the ceremonial colonelcy of the Grenadier Guards, whose ranks would from time to time pass before him in review, and that was the closest the Prince came to commanding a brigade in the field. As an armchair strategist, however, he displayed an acute insight into the basic realities of the Crimean conflict. 'Russia is not to be conquered,' he wrote to his brother Ernest, 'but financially she can be ruined. The one and a half million troops they keep will be a great help in this affair. If only we could take Sevastopol!'[30] The prescience of the Prince's masterplan was to be proven when Britain and her French ally deployed precisely these two tactics, namely economic blockade and the conquest of this key port city, to bring the war to a successful conclusion. The Prince's unwitting accomplice in facilitating this plan of action was the veteran Russian Foreign Minister Count Karl Nesselrode. He effectively sealed Russia's fate, advising the Tsar against sending a fleet to the Bosphorus and a land force through the Balkans to close the straits. This was a fatal mistake, since such a tactic would have stretched the European allies to a point that might have tipped the balance in Russia's favour. Nesselrode instead advised his master to adopt a purely defensive strategy that confined the fighting, in the end, to the battle for Sevastopol, after which Nesselrode announced his wish to retire.

Albert was in great distress over what he perceived to be the country's lack of preparedness for a conflict that was to change the face of modern warfare, with the emergence of such innovations as trench fighting and the replacement of sail with the ironclad, steam-powered warship. A month later Albert once again confided his concerns to his brother: 'We have much trouble with the Ministry. Aberdeen still lives in 1814, Lord John in 1830, Palmerston in 1848. Parliament and the Press have suddenly become born generals.'[31]

An alarming report produced less than three years previously by the War Office had come to Albert's attention. It laid bare Britain's lack of preparation to defend itself against an invader, much less fight a war in foreign lands.[32]

We have on our side, in our present condition, no land force in the country... nor a possibility of raising one. The relative condition of our military strength would be the cause of very great and well founded alarm on the breaking out of a war, when the eyes of the public would be suddenly opened to these facts. Between the years 1818 and 1844 every military establishment was reduced to the lowest ebb.[33]

The Prince had always taken an interest in the country's military establishment and specific practices which he considered obsolete or counterproductive to the task of modernising the army. On two of these issues − officers settling their quarrels with duels and the purchase of commissions − Albert found himself at odds with the Duke of Wellington. The Iron Duke was rather indifferent to the subject of duelling. Oddly enough, Albert, coming as he did from a culture in which the accepted way of settling offences to one's honour was with sabres or pistols, nonetheless felt disgust at a system comparable to primitive tribal blood vendettas. Wellington had given attention to the subject, but when the Prince sought his assistance he found the Duke frustratingly unsupportive. Wellington believed that only public opinion and not legislation could put an end to the practice. Albert was not about to let the matter rest, and he persuaded the Cabinet to take up the matter. The result was an amendment to the Articles of War, which in 1844 introduced a system of 'apology and redress'. From that time duelling was so discredited that it became practically extinct.

Wellington's rather quaint view of the longstanding practice of purchasing commissions was that gentlemen of affluence who could afford to and desired to buy their way into the officer corps, thus gaining high rank quickly, would help ensure the army's loyalty, because these were men with a stake in the country.[34] He maintained that this tradition set the British army apart from mercenary forces, thus safeguarding its status as subservient to civil authority. For Albert, the soldiery amounted to a loose grouping of regiments that only paid lip service to being part of the Queen's army. The Prince considered the purchase of commissions – a tradition which he noted had been stopped in Austria in 1803 – a gross abuse that allowed inexperienced officers to buy their way into the army over the heads of seasoned commanders. Albert petitioned the Government to take action, and in 1855 an official inquiry commented unfavourably on this institution, which was finally abolished in 1871 as part of the overall armed forces reform programme.

Even as the battle raged at Sevastopol, Albert's thoughts were focused on the post-war reorganisation of the army. Early in 1855, Albert drafted a lengthy memorandum to Lord Aberdeen which in later years was to have a profound effect on the shape of Britain's land forces. While extolling the victories the army had so far achieved over the Russians, placing the force 'before the world as pre-eminent in fighting qualities, discipline and obedience', there remained a deeply embedded flaw in the country's military system. 'I hazard the opinion that our army, as at present organised, can hardly be called an army at all, but a mere aggregate of battalions of infantry, with some regiments of cavalry, and an artillery regiment.' The inherent deficiency in the army's structure, as Albert put it, was that 'We have nothing but distinct battalions.' Granted, these were 'admirable' fighting units, but there was nothing beyond this old-fashioned established military order. 'We have, in consequence, no generals trained and practised in the duties of that rank…no general staff or staff corps…no field commissariat, no field army department, no ambulance corps, no baggage train…'[35] In short, nothing remotely resembling the large standing armies of continental Europe, which were organised under a unified command structure – certainly nothing that could be matched against the army of neighbouring France, the perennial potential enemy poised in the wings. Albert was absolutely correct – in the nineteenth century, the British 'army' was composed of up to 153 loosely connected regiments whose colonels would typically identify more closely with his regimental colours than with the national flag. This is even reflected in the lack of the title 'royal' before the army's name. Unlike the Royal Navy, and later the Royal Air Force, the army was not raised in the monarch's name.

Albert saw an alternative to this confusing hotchpotch of disparate fighting units. The remedy lay in giving the British army 'permanently' the organisation which every other European army enjoyed, that of brigades and divisions. Britain, he argued, should move towards this system, and he devised a detailed plan to reorganise the army's 103 battalions of infantry into 34 brigades, and these into 17 divisions. The existing 23 regiments of cavalry would be amalgamated into eight brigades. Under this scheme, each of the 17 divisions would have its proper compliment of artillery permanently attached to it. Albert also insisted on the need for weekly reports from the field commanders, to keep the Government informed not only of progress on the battlefield, but of the number of serviceable guns, how the troops were secured against weather, the level of stores and the number of horses. This plan was endorsed by the War Office, and Lord Raglan was required to furnish the information in weekly dispatches.

The memorandum was sent to Lord Aberdeen on 14 January 1855, and it received an enthusiastic reception from the Cabinet. But it was left to another ministry to deal with the Prince's proposals, for ten days later the Aberdeen administration had ceased to exist, and the man charged with overseeing the conclusion of the Crimean War was none other than Lord Palmerston.

Unlike Albert, who threw himself body and soul into defending the Turks, Aberdeen had taken a lukewarm and fatefully unpopular position on entering into war with Russia. Worse, once it became evident that the scandalous inefficiency of the War Office was causing more deaths from sickness than battlefield action, public indignation grew apace. A public inquiry was launched in January 1855, and less than a month later Aberdeen resigned.

Albert was not to see his plan gradually incorporated into the army's structure, for it wasn't until seven years after his death, in the period between 1868 and 1874, and mainly under the Disraeli ministry, that the changes undertaken by Secretary of State for War Edward Cardwell began to give the army its modern shape and defined its regimental system.

A visit to the Belgian army camp at Beverloo during his 1835 European tour had made a lasting impression on the 16-year-old Albert. The sight of well-disciplined troops conducting manoeuvres and mock battles, equipped with the accoutrements of modern warfare, was pure delight to his young eyes. As early as 1847, Albert had written to the Duke of Wellington proposing a provisional training camp for the army, necessarily with a railway link for the swift movement of troops to the coastal defences. The idea met with a cool reception from the Commander-in-Chief, mainly on the grounds of the costs that such an undertaking would entail. But the Beverloo experience remained ingrained in Albert's memory, and in

1852, when from across the Channel the sabre-rattling of the Emperor Louis Napoleon was heard, Wellington's successor Lord Hardinge gave in to the Prince's appeals and agreed to acquire a few acres of flat ground in Chobham, Surrey, to serve as a training camp.

'Almost overnight, Albert had become an enthusiastic army man: one wall of his study was covered with maps of the Black Sea and the Crimea...and he scrutinised them until he knew the whole area like the back of his hand.'[36]

The Prince was not satisfied with the temporary facility set up at Cobham – he was convinced of the army's need for a long-term headquarters. He went back to the Government and pleaded passionately for the purchase of a 3000-acre tract of heathland around Aldershot, the garrison town that is today home to the British army, to be set aside as a permanent base. Albert was closely involved with the development of Aldershot, and shortly after the Crimean War ended, he established and endowed the Prince Consort's Library, which is still a major research and education facility. The Prince paid for the building out of his own pocket, at a cost of more than £4000. In 1859, Albert wrote to the Secretary of State for War, stating his wish to present a thousand books from his personal collection to the officers at Aldershot. Work on the library began in September 1859, and the building was officially opened a year later. The library was founded to contribute to the education of soldiers in the British army, and it now stands as one of the country's foremost facilities specialising in the provision of information on current military topics, political subjects and international relations in support of operations, intelligence, training and education in the armed forces.[37]

With the growing inevitability of an imminent clash with Russia, Albert sensed he was backing the right horse by siding with the hawks. Even Victoria remarked that the war, with the formal opening of hostilities still two months away, was 'popular beyond belief'. Her husband's intuition did not fail him. 'By one of the supreme ironies of Prince Albert's life, the one result of the war was the breaking of the links between Austria and Russia which led to the unification of Germany and the liberation of Italy,'[38] though he was not to live to see his two objectives achieved.

The Crimean War was on the face of it a conflict motivated by religion. The Tsar's pretext for moving troops into Moldavia and Wallachia was to defend the Orthodox Christian communities in those principalities against Muslim domination. In reality, the conflict was part of a long-running feud between the major European powers for influence over territories of the declining Ottoman Empire. Lord Aberdeen's Government interpreted the Tsar's aggression as a deliberate tactic to expand Russian power in Asia, hence the decision in July 1853 to dispatch Royal Navy gunboats to the Dardanelles, where they were joined by a French fleet. Buttressed by the navies of the two most powerful nations in Europe, the Ottomans declared war on Russia in October of that year, scoring a few victories before the Sinope disaster a month later. By that time it was quite clear that the two allied powers saw the situation as beyond any hope of a diplomatic settlement. Even when Nicholas I abandoned the Balkan territories to 'neutral' Austria, thus removing the original grounds for war, Britain and France continued to press their attacks. The Tsar was offered a four-point peace treaty which, almost as a foregone conclusion, he rejected at the outset as unacceptable, and that was when hostilities began in earnest.

The first serious naval action took place when the British fleet bombarded and came very close to obliterating the port of Odessa. Flushed with what seemed certain victory, and with no resistance in sight, in September 1854 the allied expeditionary force set sail for the Crimea. Sevastopol came under siege, and it was at this strategic port city that the Russians scuttled their warships to mount a shore-battery defence, while the British and French kept up the naval bombardment.

It was by now evident that the war's make-or-break objective would be Sevastopol, home of Russia's Black Sea fleet and the vital gateway to the Mediterranean. The combined French and British forces unleashed an all-out offensive against the city, making the siege one of the bloodiest actions of the war. In the final attack, the French lost 7567 officers and men, including five generals killed and four wounded. The British were less badly mauled, with losses amounting to 2271 officers and men, and only three generals wounded. This was small beer compared with Russian casualties on the last day of fighting, which amounted to 12,913 killed and wounded, with two senior generals among the casualties. The Russians displayed their customary ability to absorb appalling losses: it is estimated that perhaps as many as one hundred thousand died in the battle for Sevastopol. On 11 September 1855, the Russians burnt the remaining ships of their Black Sea fleet, and with this action the siege was effectively brought to an end. The stranglehold imposed by the sea blockade, along with the loss of Sevastopol spelt the beginning of the end. Five months later, in February 1856, the Congress of Paris established peace terms at a tremendous disadvantage to the Tsar, for the protocol greatly diminished the naval threat that Russia posed to the Ottomans. Moreover, all the signatories pledged to respect the independence and territorial integrity of the Ottoman Empire.

Albert's most memorable legacy in the aftermath of the Crimean War was the creation of the Victoria Cross, which could rightly be called the 'Albert Cross', for it was the Prince's proposal that a new medal be awarded 'for valour in the face of the enemy'. This was in keeping with Albert's European outlook on all things military, for it did not escape his notice that Britain was the only great power lacking an award that did not discriminate against class or rank, to wit France's Légion d'Honneur or the Netherlands' Order of William. The Prince therefore stipulated in a memorandum that if approved, the award should be open to all ranks. The first medals, which were designed by Albert himself, were struck on 4 March 1856. Under the Prince's guidance, Victoria vetoed the suggestion that the award be called the Military Order of Victoria, and instead suggested the less pretentious name Victoria Cross.[39]

The Victoria Cross, or VC, remains the highest military decoration awarded for valour to members of the armed forces of Britain and the Commonwealth countries, and previously to British Empire territories. It takes precedence over all other orders, decorations and medals. Of the soldiers who were awarded a Victoria Cross for their acts of heroism in the Crimean War, two are listed as 'German citizens'. Albert's most hard-fought initiative of the war was to gain passage of the Foreign Enlistment Bill, a battle in which he found himself supported by the unlikeliest of allies: Lord Palmerston. With the Prince's influence, Palmerston pushed the bill through, though not without vehement opposition and cries of 'immoral' and 'degrading' from some of the House's leading members. The law authorised the immediate enlistment of ten thousand foreign soldiers, to be drilled in Britain and sent off to fight in the Crimea. Albert was delighted to see thousands of his young countrymen enlisting in the Royal German Legion, instead of joining the many who were at that time emigrating to America to seek their fortunes. The bill's passage highlighted the woeful lack of trained manpower at home with which to prosecute the war, a situation that had been foreseen by Albert, who also prevailed on the Government to create a reserve force of nearly thirty thousand men in addition to the German recruits. The Prince reminded the Government that Napoleon always had reserves stationed between the army in the field and the home depots, without which the Grande Armée could not have carried on. In this case, troops were sent to Malta, thereby shortening the deployment time for the Crimean theatre.

On 5 December 1855, the Prince went to Shorncliffe on the Kentish coast personally to present the colours to two regiments of German recruits embarking for the Crimea to be attached to Lord Raglan.

The first distribution of the Victoria Cross took place in Hyde Park on 26 June 1857, before a throng of a hundred thousand spectators, including twelve thousand British and foreign dignitaries and four thousand troops on the parade ground. Victoria appeared on horseback, dressed in a scarlet jacket with a black skirt, accompanied by Albert and Prince Frederick William of Prussia. The Queen pinned the cross on the tunic of each of the men brought before her, and as the men withdrew the Prince bent with a gesture of marked respect.

It was an especially proud moment for Albert, and not only for having promoted the creation of the new military distinction. Only the day before the event, Albert's title Prince Consort had been legally defined and he had become a member of the British royal family. Until then he had held no official rank, and had even been denied a British peerage in that same year. In contrast with the humiliating episode of nearly 19 years previously, the conferring of the title of Prince Consort was authorised without opposition, at the Queen's personal request. Victoria had fought hard to have the title conferred on her husband – her impetuous nature flared up over this issue, and at one point she even threatened to abdicate if the Government failed to acknowledge Albert's official status, 'leaving the country to choose another ruler after their own heart's content'.[40] She got her way, and no longer would Victoria appear before her subjects in ambiguous circumstances alongside a foreign husband. 'No one can object to the distinction which is thus conferred on the husband of the Queen after seventeen years of married life,' *The Times* conceded. But the paper was quite out of step with popular sentiments when it reminded its readers rather sneeringly that the title 'gives no authority at home, but assures him a higher position abroad, for he will meet royal families with the status of a British Prince'.[41]

Exactly one year after the Congress of Paris put an end to hostilities in the Crimea, Albert once again had cause to lament the fact that Britain's armed forces were in no fit state to conduct an overseas campaign. The occasion was the Sepoy Rebellion that erupted in Meerut in 1857. The Mutiny was a complex affair, and cannot be attributed exclusively to the Indian troops' fear of an alleged plot to convert them forcibly to Christianity, nor to the often-cited belief among soldiers that cartridges were coated with pig or cow grease, substances unclean to Muslims and sacred to Hindus, respectively. There were several other factors that sparked the rebellion, from the well-founded concern of Indian princes over further territorial annexations by the East India Company, to the more fanciful belief that the centenary of the Battle of Plassey, which began British dominion, would witness the end of British rule in India. The protracted siege of Lucknow, followed by the massacre at Cawnpore and finally the fall of Delhi demonstrated just how unprepared the East India Company's army was to deal with the uprising, as well as the urgent need for reform.

Albert anticipated with unerring foresight a 'severe and bloody' rebellion, since the European troops deployed in India were few in number and scattered over the whole country.

> The confidence of the public in the Indian army…has proved to be utterly mistaken, and now we shall, no doubt, have recourse to a rational military system. Whether the [East India] Company will maintain its position is somewhat doubtful. What causes a thrill of horror is the thought of…the acts of vengeance of the English soldiery.[42]

The Prince was right on all counts. British casualties amounted to more than 4500 killed and wounded, including civilians, in the engagements at Lucknow and Delhi alone. In percentage terms, the casualty rate was higher at the storming of Delhi than at the siege of Sevastopol. The number of sepoy mutineers and non-combatants killed in those 14 months of carnage is almost impossible to calculate with accuracy, but there is no doubt it far exceeded British losses. Egged on by a bloodthirsty press at home, the 'acts of vengeance' Albert so feared were carried out with terrible swiftness. It was reported that in the battle for Delhi, all people found within the city's walls when the British troops entered were bayoneted on the spot. The executions of convicted mutineers and sympathisers were so widespread that entire swathes of forest were covered with corpses hanging from branches, while many more were subjected to the grim parade-ground death of being blown from the mouth of a cannon.

The army reforms Albert had advocated were eventually brought into being in the wake of the Sepoy Mutiny. His orderly Germanic mind recoiled in horror at the ramshackle system of 'perpetual counteraction and conflicting authorities'. He fumed to Stockmar of the absurd quasi-sovereignty exercised by the commanders-in-chief of the different Indian presidencies,[43] each with its independent army and

> a state of discipline in the local European troops characterised as disgraceful by some of the most competent judges on the spot, and nothing but jealously and animosity between the different services...The great principles on which the efficiency of the military force in any country, and under any circumstances, must depend, are *simplicity, unity and steadiness of system, and unity of command* [Albert's emphasis].[44]

Under the restructuring, the old Bengal army almost completely vanished from the order of battle. Gone were all ten of the Bengal light cavalry regiments, Indian artillery was replaced by British units, and the native contingents in general were watered down, with more troops recruited from among the Sikhs and Gurkhas, whose loyalty was above reproach. The ratio of British to Indian soldiers was increased, and it was these post-rebellion changes that formed the basis of the military organisation of

British India until the early twentieth century. Albert's doubts concerning the East India Company's future were vindicated in 1874, when it was formally dissolved and India was thereafter directly governed by the Crown.

In 1876, Victoria was proclaimed Empress of India,[45] a title that may have stuck in the throats of Indian nationalists, yet as the Queen herself pointed out, at the stroke of a pen this act put nearly three hundred million Indians 'on an equality with the subjects of the British Crown, and the prosperity following in the train of civilisation'.[46]

Even during the terrible days of the Rebellion, Albert's thoughts never strayed far from his lifelong concern for the plight of the labouring poor. The Prince shunned the blinkered existence of the privileged echelons of British society, be they the nobility, the landed gentry or the emerging industrialist class. He was not alone in his resolve to better the working man's condition, which in most instances at that time was unenviable in the extreme. The Industrial Revolution sent people streaming into London, the world's foremost commercial city, as well as to the urban manufacturing centres of the north. At the time of the Battle of Waterloo, in 1815, London was already the largest city in Europe. Within less than fifty years, it had undergone a population explosion, taking the number of inhabitants to 3.2 million, while half a century after that the numbers had once again doubled. Large houses in the capital were converted into flats, in which it was common for several families to be crammed together in hideous living conditions.

The misery of these poor souls touched the consciences of some, and one of these philanthropically minded men, John M. Clabon, had published a pamphlet in 1857 entitled *Leisure-Houses for the Labourer*. Clabon's plan was to create working-class premises that would replicate the appeal and companionship of the pub, without the drawbacks of immoderate drinking. When the pamphlet came to Albert's notice, Clabon was invited to Buckingham Palace, where he arrived one chilly November evening to meet the Prince. Albert greeted him in a drawing-room, 'standing with his back to the fire, his hands behind him in true English fashion'.[47]

The Prince listened attentively to Clabon's scheme to coax the working classes into seeking self-improvement through lectures and courses – but first it would be necessary to provide them with a congenial place of entertainment. This was a fine idea, Albert interjected, but it must be a strictly commercial, self-financing venture and not a government-funded project. The Prince enthusiastically envisaged these clubs growing into a network of 'reformed pubs', and here came to the fore Albert's ever-present Europeanist perspective. He stressed that wives and families be encouraged to attend these clubs, thereby removing their stigma as men-only hard-drinking places. There was to be no distinction of creed, but membership must be restricted to labourers. 'The lower classes,' Albert told Clabon, 'would always feel a restraint in the presence of the higher classes.'[48] Their location must always be in the middle of working-class housing, for Albert reasoned that the poor would not be willing to travel far after a long day's work. Thus was laid the groundwork for Britain's working men's clubs, a classic Victorian institution that lives on to this day.

The Prince was at this time also made aware of the plight of London's ballast heavers,[49] whose existence differed little from that of Russian serfs. These dock workers, who numbered around four hundred in the mid-1850s, petitioned Albert to take up their cause: living as indentured servants, the men were expected to load as much as a hundred tons of ballast in the course of a working day. In return, they were obliged by ship owners, who contracted with a local publican to provide their lodgings, to obtain their meat, groceries and beer from the contractor. When the ballast heavers sent a deputation to lay their case before Albert, the Prince petitioned the Government to put a stop to this abusive system and allow the men to work independently of the contractors. It was truly an act of emancipation, which two years after Albert's death inspired the ballast heavers to present a memorial tribute to Victoria, a document that could have flowed from the pen of the Prince's contemporary Charles Dickens.

> Before he came to our rescue, we could only get work through a body of riverside publicans and middlemen who made us drink before they would give us a job, made us drink while at it, and kept us waiting for our wages and drinking after we had done our work, so that we could only take half our wages home to our families...through a drunkard's hand.
>
> We tried hard to get out of this accursed system...but we got no real help till we sent an appeal to your late Royal Consort. He could put himself down from the throne he shared [sic.] to the wretched home of us poor men, and could feel what we and our wives and children were suffering...At once our wrongs were redressed and the system that had ruined us swept away.[50]

In the last years of his life, Albert's prestige, social and political influence soared to their loftiest heights. He had indeed, as Greville remarked, become King in all but name, and the monarch was among the first to acknowledge her husband's greatness.

Tomorrow is the eighteenth anniversary of my blessed marriage,' she wrote to Uncle Leopold, 'which has brought such universal blessings on this country' and Europe! For *what* has not my beloved and perfect Albert done? Raised monarchy to the *highest* pinnacle of *respect*, and rendered it *popular* beyond what it *ever* was in this country! [Victoria's emphasis].[51]

Palmerston and Foreign Secretary Lord Clarendon praised the Prince's enlightened counsel during the Crimean War and Sepoy Rebellion. Albert had set in train a host of reforms that were to have a sweeping impact on Britain's civil and military society, most of which he was not to live to see. The Emperor Louis Napoleon acclaimed him an inspiration to do good in the world. Even the ballast heavers had created the title 'Albert the Good', out of gratitude for the man who had lifted them out of their pitiable servitude. Esteemed and acclaimed by the vast majority of the people, Albert's personal life was anything but a bed of roses.

Bertie became a nagging disappointment, a source of anxiety that undoubtedly aggravated the stomach cramps and general fatigue that were slowly undermining Albert's health. The Prince could not reconcile himself to the stark reality that his son, the heir to the throne, was not a particularly intelligent person, nor one who would ever come up to the elevated standard set by his father. Albert believed that Bertie's 'shyness and timidity' was a child's way of covering up for his backwardness. Yet the Prince deeply regretted his son's lack of interest in most things. 'In Bertie it goes astonishingly deep,' he wrote to his cousin Princess Augusta of Prussia, 'and hangs together with his want of knowledge, for in most things he is noticeably backward, and the lack of development, which physically is visible in him, is even greater on the mental side.'[52]

The Prince of Wales showed little comprehension of the great burden that would one day be placed on his shoulders as King of England. Bertie shared his father's interest in clothes, but little else. Bertie was packed off on a visit to his sister in Germany in the hope that an early marriage and fatherhood might instil in him some sense of responsibility. Albert made inquiries about eligible young ladies, with the help of Leopold, who had once drawn up a list of seven marriageable European princesses for his great-nephew. The first woman the Prince had in mind was the Princess of Saxe-Meiningen, but alas it was not to be, for on his return to London all Bertie could talk about was 'balls, reviews, the success of his investiture of the Order of the Golden Fleece…and what a good fellow Fritz (Prince Frederick William) was for getting him made an honorary colonel in the Prussian Guards, so he could wear the uniform at a parade'.[53]

It was Vicky who eventually engineered her brother's marriage. The Princess Royal had come into contact with Princess Alexandra of Schleswig-Holstein, daughter to the heir of the Danish throne. Vicky wrote enthusiastically to her father about the princess, and Albert, with great trust in his daughter's judgement, placed Alexandra at the top of the list, in spite of his misgivings about the union. The Prince was desperately eager to see his wayward son become a family man, but he was extremely cautious in this matter given his pro-Prussian and consequently anti-Danish views on German unification. Nevertheless, the wedding took place at Windsor Castle in March 1863, more than a year after Albert's death.

A much weightier cross for Albert to bear than Bertie's frivolity was his agonising separation from Vicky. Albert's letters to his daughter at this time dealt largely with mundane matters concerning household management, the need to set aside for the unforeseen, to maintain a rational judgement in all things, not to criticise others too harshly, to strive after the tranquillity that brings health of mind and soul – all the values that characterised Albert's own life. The Prince's underlying feelings were of a far more complex nature, typical of someone who always strove to conceal his emotions. On the day Vicky departed England, Albert could hardly hold back his own tears when his sobbing daughter embraced the father she so adored in farewell. Soon afterwards, Albert's letters took on the quality of a bereavement, filled with expressions such as 'void', 'your absence' and 'abide henceforth in my heart'. Albert never recovered from the loss of his daughter's presence, and it was this, more than any other single event, that hastened the onset of his fatal illness three years after Vicky's departure.

6

'Weary and out of heart'

War with Russia, military insurrection in India, and now the menace of invasion by Britain's former Crimean ally France. The year 1858 opened under a heavy threat of renewed military action, and Albert, who longed to devote his time to family and cultural interests, was not to be relieved of his role of Albert the statesman. In August of the previous year the Prince and the Queen, along with six of their children, had embarked on an official visit to Cherbourg. The Prince was deeply mistrustful of French ambitions, and he considered England's troublesome neighbour a destabilising force in Europe. Stockmar was always the confidant of these intimate personal feelings, and it was to his mentor that Albert wrote, 'The French were taught by the experiences of 1813, '14 and '15 to keep quiet, and to this Europe owes forty years of peace.'[1] During the war of Italian unification fought between Napoleon III and the Austrian Empire, a letter to William Prince Regent of Prussia left little doubt regarding his scepticism, or where his sympathies lay: 'If France is victorious, I see no rest or security for Europe for the next twenty years.'[2]

Albert found good grounds for his fears of French naval superiority the moment the royal yacht *Victoria and Albert* docked in the harbour. He was struck by the massive fortifications under construction at the French naval base, which lies only seventy miles from the English coast. 'Cherbourg is a gigantic work that gives me grave cause for reflection,' the Prince confided to Stockmar. 'The works at Alderney by way of counter-defence look childish.'[3] Even Victoria could not fail to be unnerved by the sprawl of the French garrison and England's resultant vulnerability to invasion. 'It makes me very unhappy to see what is done here, and how well protected the works are, for the forts and the breakwater (which is treble the size of the Plymouth one) are extremely well defended.'[4]

The cause for apprehension literally exploded early in the new year. On 14 January, the French Emperor Napoleon III and his wife Eugénie were the victims of an assassination attempt as they rode in their carriage to the theatre to see Rossini's *William Tell*. The would-be assassin was Felice Orsini, an Italian republican, who accused Napoleon III of being the chief obstacle to his country's independence. Albert's brother Ernest happened to be staying in Paris at the time, a stopover on his way to London to attend Vicky's wedding. He arrived at Buckingham Palace that same night to relay the news of the bombing to the Prince, who was deeply shocked to learn of the triple blasts that had left ten dead and more than a hundred and fifty wounded. There was worse to come: Orsini was captured and executed (the royal couple bravely carried on to the theatre to appear in their box, the Empress still wearing her blood-spattered frock) but it later emerged that the bomb plot had involved a British connection. Before the attack on Napoleon, Orsini had visited Britain, where he persuaded gunsmith Joseph Taylor to make him six copies of a bomb of the Italian nationalist's own design. Relations between the British and French royal courts went into a tailspin once it became known that the prototype had been tested in England with the complicity of a French exile, one Dr Simon Bernard, a resident of Bayswater. When the case came to trial, Orsini's accomplice was acquitted by an English jury on a technicality, upon which the French press began to fire one furious broadside after another at 'perfidious Albion', accusing the British Government of having taken a hand in the plot.

The French attacks brought the predictable uproar: it never required much provocation for the public to give vent to their Francophobia, and even in the Crimean War the Anglo-French alliance was always an uneasy partnership. In London a tumultuous crowd of twenty thousand poured into Hyde Park shouting 'Down with the French!' Albert warned Palmerston that in such a heated environment there was a real danger the French might take advantage of their naval dominance to stage an attack on England from their Cherbourg base. At the same time, he confided to Vicky his worries for political stability between the two countries.

> The outcry against England is quite absurd and begins to provoke excessive indignation here. The Government will, under the circumstances, have trouble in carrying through Parliament, which met yesterday [2 February] a suitable measure for the punishment of conspiracy to assassinate.[5]

Once again, the Prince's ability to anticipate political outcomes proved accurate. Albert considered Palmerston's introduction of the Conspiracy to Murder Bill at best a useful means of defusing tensions between the countries. He therefore threw his support behind the Prime Minister, though in his heart he held out little hope for its passage through Parliament. Under existing English law, conspiracy to murder was classified as a misdemeanour. Palmerston's proposed modification, which it was hoped would quell the outrage in France that by now was infecting sectors of the military, would elevate this offence to a felony. The Conservatives initially gave Palmerston their backing, but in the second reading the Government was defeated and the Prime Minister tendered his resignation to the Queen. There was great indignation in the House as well as a general public condemnation of what was alleged to be an attempt to legislate in deference to the wishes of France. Public meetings were organised across the country to protest against 'the surrender of English liberties at the discretion of a foreign power', and these gatherings were enthusiastically reported in *The Times*.[6] Albert could only hang his head in despair.

So Palmerston was out, but as usual, not for long. Albert had been delighted when in 1851 he had persuaded Russell to remove this thorn in the royal side from the Foreign Office. In the ensuing years, the Prince and his antagonist had come not only to tolerate one another, but to forge a relationship of mutual understanding. Palmerston's return to office was therefore not such a bitter pill to swallow as it had been in 1855 when he had taken over from the discredited Aberdeen ministry at the height of the Crimean War. The 1859 general election was the first to be contested by the Liberal Party, a name unofficially adopted to cover the alliance of Whigs, Peelites, Radicals and the Irish brigade who had previously voted against the Derby administration in the House of Commons.

The election failed to produce a clear majority for Lord Derby's Conservatives, with some of the Whigs, led by Palmerston, holding their majority in the House of Commons. The Queen asked Lord Granville, a Liberal, to form a government. But nothing could be agreed without taking into account the all-powerful Palmerston, who refused to serve under Granville, the veteran Foreign Secretary. Russell, for his part, equally would have nothing to do with a Liberal-led ministry. Victoria knew full well that in these circumstances the final choice would have to be made between the two most powerful contenders, Russell and Palmerston. 'They had both served her long and faithfully, and Her Majesty felt it to be an invidious task to select one of the two.'[7] Victoria's comments regarding Palmerston bespoke improved relations with Albert as well as the Queen.[8] By this time, no memorandum or official correspondence would have been dispatched from the Palace without Albert's explicit seal of approval, if indeed it had not been personally framed by the Prince himself. Cabinet ministers would routinely communicate directly with Albert, who was widely accepted as the Queen's unofficial private secretary, even when the correspondence dealt with confidential matters of state.[9]

There was little question as to how the leadership bottleneck was to be overcome: on 12 June 1859, Victoria wrote to Lord Derby saying that after Granville's fruitless attempt to form a government, she had now charged Lord Palmerston with the task. So to Palmerston, at 75, was entrusted the job of putting together a strong and durable Cabinet, an undertaking he masterfully accomplished (keeping it together until his death six years later) by bringing in Russell as Foreign Secretary, while

Gladstone was appointed Chancellor of the Exchequer, a post he had held for three years under Aberdeen. Albert praised the new Government as 'the strongest that was ever formed, so far as the individual talent of its members is concerned'.[10] At the same time, he perceived the ministry to be sharply divided over policy towards the forces contending for supremacy in Italy. This posed a worrying state of affairs, with war about to break out in a matter of weeks.

Palmerston was unreservedly anti-Austrian and pro-Napoleon. Foreign Secretary Lord Russell's sentiments were hostile towards the French but strongly in favour of the Italian cause, as were Gladstone's. The rest of the Cabinet, including Secretary for War Sidney Herbert, stood behind the Austrians and opposed France, while the rest were neutral. 'We look forward to pleasant times in store for us!' Albert wrote to Prince William of Prussia.[11]

Palmerston took office in June 1859. One month later the cause of Italian unification, which had so nearly cost the French Emperor his life, dragged Europe into another conflagration. The Austrian Emperor Franz Joseph I was determined to hold on to his Italian possessions. He was opposed by a confederacy of France and Sardinia, two royal houses that had been brought together by the marriage of Princess Clothilde of Sardinia with a cousin of Napoleon III.

Palmerston's diplomatic strategy in the conflict that followed was to support a strong, independent northern Italian state, which to his thinking would pose no threat to British interests. This was always his overriding criterion, and in this case, even with the incorporation of Genoa and Venice and their two seaports, he remained confident Britain would be safe from aggression. Palmerston's reasoning was that these ports could easily be blockaded and Italy's commercial sea routes cut off by British squadrons, which would give the Italians pause for thought before embarking on any adventurism. After the war Palmerston remained suspicious of Louis Napoleon's territorial designs, and he proposed a tripartite alliance with Austria and Prussia to counter any such moves by France.

But what of Albert, whose Germanic blood and wariness of French military power, one might assume, would naturally drive him into the Austrian camp? In fact his feelings were shaped not so much by an active support of Austria's territorial claims as his dislike of Louis Napoleon, a ruler who to Albert's mind was 'a born and bred conspirator'.[12]

The French Emperor was looking to enlist a powerful ally to his cause, but as an alliance with England 'means maintenance of public law and treaties, and progress in civilisation, it has been most irksome to him... Now he has got Russia, and is longing for revenge against Europe.'[13] Albert was not taken in by Russia's peace rhetoric – on the contrary, he was convinced that Tsar Alexander II represented an instrumental force in the shaping of French policy. His suspicion was confirmed in a report from the British Ambassador in Paris, disclosing Russia's offer, in the event of war, to place an army at Russia's border to hold Austria and Prussia in check, thus giving France a free hand in the Italian campaign.

Before the conflict broke out, the Prince's sympathies veered towards Austria, not on emotional grounds of kinship with a Germanic race, but rather on the very English principle that he believed the country to be within her legal right. That view held until 21 April 1859, shortly before the French marched troops into Sardinia, when Albert (and popular sentiment throughout Britain) turned against Austria for having laid down an ultimatum to Sardinia to disarm. Now Franz Joseph was depicted as the aggressor, for his 'tremendous mistake...and Austria is once more the oppressor of Italy...At one stroke, the [Austrian] Emperor has turned public opinion here against Austria,' the Prince wrote to King Leopold.[14]

Once war was declared, Albert's thoughts immediately rose above any form of partisanship: his concern was for Britain and the country's security, which he held to be the only sound basis of any national policy. If war was threatening Britain's coast, it was now solely a matter of 'self-interest, of which the highest factor is self-preservation. This is the only possible motive at great moments, and does not deny either morality or nobility,' he told the Prince Regent of Prussia.[15]

The Government was at work to establish a volunteer force for protection against the contingency of a French invasion. Albert took an active role in this initiative, despite certain misgivings about disciplinary problems with such a force and its trustworthiness and potential for causing disorder in peacetime. The Prince submitted his plan for organising the corps to the Cabinet, which adopted his suggestions to the letter, and on 25 May 1859 the Volunteer Corps Code was issued to the Lord Lieutenants.[16] This measure laid the groundwork for what nearly fifty years later was to become Britain's Territorial Army, an amalgamation of the existing Volunteer Force, the Militia and the Yeomanry.

Austria's invasion of Piedmont was the spark that provoked the French Emperor into deploying what he portrayed as an army of liberation dispatched to Italy to drive out the Austrian aggressors. The French sent 132,000 soldiers, half the country's army, and they were joined by a 74,000-strong Sardinian force. The Austrians had the advantage of numbers, with 242,000 infantry and cavalry troops in the field, yet in less than a year Franz Joseph's forces were humiliated in five set-piece defeats.

The menace of a more widespread German entry into the war, and the potential for the creation of an overly strong state of Piedmont, induced Louis Napoleon to sign a separate peace with Austria, which in July 1859 resulted in the Treaty of Villafranca. Under this preliminary peace accord, Parma, Modena, Tuscany and the Papal Legations were annexed by Sardinia, while France ceded Milan to Piedmont. The peace conditions foresaw that the dukes of Tuscany, Parma and Modena, who had been expelled by revolutionaries, would be reinstated in their dukedoms. In the carve-up, the Emperor Napoleon was awarded Savoy and Nice as a consolation prize. These two territories opted for annexation by France in a plebiscite the following year. An armistice was signed in August, and in November 1859 an agreement negotiated in Zurich brought definitive peace, marking the beginning of the process of Italian unification. The handover of Savoy and Nice was, however, vehemently opposed by the Italian freedom fighter Giuseppe Garibaldi, a native of Nice, who took a force of one thousand volunteers to Sicily in May 1860 to lead an uprising. This action was shortly to bring about the final creation of the Italian state.

Albert was overjoyed to see peace restored to Europe, though he was less pleased with the armistice terms, which he thought had not provided in strong enough language for Italian independence. His general feeling was one of disappointment that so heavy a price had been paid for so little purpose. 'The Confederation with the Pope at its head sounds like a bad joke,' he remarked to a friend.[17] Palmerston was totally dismayed at Austria having retained a foothold in its former territories, and he laid down a demand that the French Emperor grant full independence to Italy without delay, or be stigmatised as a betrayer of the Italian people. Albert was content to see French troops return to their barracks, thus lifting the immediate threat of invasion, and at the same time relieving Britain of the trouble of having to make war preparations. The country's increased outlay on naval and military defences in that period had obliged Gladstone almost to double the rate of income tax from five pence to nine pence in the pound for incomes above £150 a year.

Leaving aside his many other duties, the Prince's political involvement in three wars in the period 1853 to 1859 had taken its toll on his already debilitated health. In August 1859, he was struck down by a renewed attack of stomach cramps, which he correctly ascribed to worry about political affairs. There was to be no relief in his daily work pressures. His speaking engagements ranged from presenting new colours to the 13th Light Infantry ('Prince Albert's Own') to addressing a meeting of the British Association for the Advancement of Science. He continued to deal with the red leather dispatch boxes[18] and meet with ministers to offer his views on affairs of state. There was no respite, even on 26 August, the Prince's birthday. If ever there was an unwelcome guest on such an occasion, it was Palmerston, who turned up at Osborne venting his anger over the Italian settlement. Two months later, on a visit to Bertie at Oxford, Albert caught a chill that obliged him to take to his bed for two days, a thing he had never done since his marriage, except during an attack of measles. Albert then complained of having suffered gastric pains for a fortnight, with violent cramps in the pit of his stomach.

Stockmar was 72 and broken in health, almost unable to take pen in hand. Yet he wrote to advise Albert, perhaps somewhat naively, to slow the pace. Stockmar would have sunk even deeper into gloom had he known that his protégé was now working on plans for a second Exhibition. The event was planned for 1861, but on the outbreak of war in Italy the date was pushed back a year. The Prince's success with the Great Exhibition had inspired imitators around the country, such as the 1853 Exhibition of Art-Industry in Dublin and another in Manchester in 1857. This time, Albert's chosen site was the new Natural History Museum in South Kensington. He threw himself into the project with his characteristic great energy, chairing committee meetings and carrying out an extensive correspondence with fellow planners. Victoria, distraught over Albert's frail condition, had tried to prevent the Prince from embarking on this project. Her journal entries at that time are filled with concerns for her husband's health. She went so far as to ask Lord Granville, President of the Council, to do all in his power to discourage the Prince from this undertaking, but to no avail. Despite Albert's efforts, or more probably because of the additional weight this placed on his workload, the Prince did not live to see the project through to completion. The Exhibition was inaugurated on 1 May, and over the course of six months it attracted nearly as many visitors as had its predecessor in 1851. But the opening ceremonies were not attended by the Queen or any members of the royal family.

In January 1859 Albert's thoughts were absorbed by the war fever spreading across Europe, as well as developments on the home front, where Parliament was engaged in an acrimonious debate over electoral reform aimed at broadening the voting franchise. The Prince described his state in the early days of

January as 'weary and out of heart',[19] yet an hour after writing these words a telegram arrived from Berlin with tidings that at once dispelled all his anxiety over war and politics. Albert, at the age of 40, had become a grandfather. It had been a difficult delivery that caused the Princess Royal much suffering, and for a time her infant son's life hung in the balance.[20] But once the crisis had passed, the church bells began to peal across Berlin and people poured into the streets to hail 'Die Engländerin' ('the Englishwoman'), as she was often known, and the birth of her son, the future Kaiser William II, Germany's last emperor.

On the morning of 25 July of the following year, Albert and Victoria's breakfast at Osborne was interrupted by another telegram, this one bringing news of a second royal birth. Vicky had just been delivered of a daughter, Charlotte, and this time mother and daughter were both doing splendidly. Queen Victoria's first child was well on her way to matching her mother's productivity – she was to give birth to nine children in all. In a surge of elation, Albert immediately dashed off a letter to his daughter in Berlin. 'Only two words of hearty joy can I offer to the newly made mother, and these come from an overflowing heart. The little daughter is a kindly gift from heaven that will, as I trust, procure for you many a happy hour in the days to come.'[21]

One of Albert's dwindling sources of joy in the final years was the visits and letters he received from his adored Vicky. The Princess Royal's first visit to England following her marriage was in May 1859, a little more than a year after her tearful departure from Gravesend. She had come to attend the Queen's fortieth birthday celebration, but the family reunion at Osborne turned out to be a cheerless event, overshadowed by the sudden illness of Victoria's mother, the Duchess of Kent.[22] The Duchess lingered in poor health for almost two more years, before dying in March 1861. In spite of all that had transpired during the years of their estrangement, Victoria was much affected by her mother's death. This was for the Queen the start of her *annus horribilis* that would end with the loss of Albert. After this brief visit, Vicky returned to England with her husband Frederick William on 9 November, this time to celebrate her brother Bertie's birthday.

A visit to his birthplace had long been in the back of Albert's mind. His last visit to Coburg had taken place in May 1858, to see his beloved valley for the first time in 13 years. It was a frustrating journey, for Vicky had badly sprained her ankle and was unable to travel. Albert noted in his diary that he felt himself an utter stranger in Coburg after an absence of so many years. He returned to England within a fortnight, tired and disappointed.

He and the Queen then followed up with a trip together to Germany in August 1858, this time with the assurance of spending a few days with Vicky and their son-in-law Prince Frederick William. But on this occasion Coburg was not on the agenda. It was an uneventful journey confined mainly to Potsdam, outside Berlin, though there were a couple of unforeseen twists along the way. On 12 August, an ashen-faced Albert staggered into Victoria's room in their host Prince Hohenzollern's home, a telegram in hand. It informed him that his valet Cart, who had been in his service for nearly thirty years, had suddenly died of a heart attack. The Prince was inconsolable at the loss of his servant, and noted in his journal that he spent the entire day in tears. The next morning Albert and Victoria had set off on the train, passing through Hamm in Westphalia on their way to Berlin. From the window they were greeted with a spectral sight at the station, for there stood Baroness Lehzen, quietly waving a handkerchief. The vision of the Queen's former governess, combined with the ninety-degree heat in the railway carriage, left the royal couple staring in astonished silence.

On the afternoon of 22 September 1860, the Queen's carriage rolled out of the gates of Buckingham Palace, bearing Victoria, the Prince and their daughter Princess Alice on the first stage of what would be Albert's final journey to his birthplace. It was as if a voice of forewarning had tried to set Albert against making the trip: shortly before he was to set off, the Prince was struck down by a bout of cramps, made worse by flu-like symptoms and a general malaise. Those who later saw him on his arrival in Germany were shocked by the appearance of a paunchy and stooped man looking in his sixties.

The first set of ill tidings reached Albert on board the train from Antwerp. It was a telegram from his brother Ernest: the Prince's stepmother, the Dowager Duchess Marie of Saxe-Coburg and Gotha, had fallen gravely ill, and her death was expected at any moment. Despite Ernest's entreaties to put off the visit, Albert instead carried on in all haste, and at Verviers, close to the German border, he found another telegram waiting for him. 'Mama Marie', as he called her, had died in the early hours of 24 September.

It was by no means a jovial onward journey to Germany, at least not until Albert reached Frankfurt, where his spirits were lifted at the sight of Vicky and Fritz, waiting with a band of honour at the steps of the Hôtel d'Angleterre. The scene was one of tearful rejoicing, tempered by bereavement for the Dowager Duchess. Vicky and her mother wore long black veils over pointed bonnets at the funeral ceremony, at which 'Jerusalem' was sung and which, as Albert described the day, plunged Gotha into mourning.

Albert's mood of melancholy was not helped by his meeting with Stockmar, whom he found in a debilitated state and seriously showing the signs of his 73 years. Nor was his mood lifted by an accident he suffered while out riding on the visit. The Queen was returning from Coburg and her first meeting with her grandson. The horses of the Prince's carriage bolted, and he only escaped serious injury by jumping into the road.

The Prince nevertheless made an effort to put the sadness of his visit, as well as the injuries of his carriage mishap, out of his mind, noting in a letter to the Duchess of Kent that his 'Coburg is prettier than ever, and the weather hitherto has been unusually propitious... Your great-grandson [William] is a very pretty, clever child – a compound of both parents, just as it should be.'[23]

Albert held his last meeting with Stockmar on 8 October, and after returning sorrowfully to his room he and Victoria made their final preparations for the next morning's return to London. The royal travellers were met at Mainz, near Frankfurt, by the Prince Regent of Prussia, and over a late breakfast arrangements were discreetly discussed for a visit to Britain by Louis of Hesse, a minor German royal and the nephew of Grand Duke Louis III of the same state. Vicky had taken a hand in searching for suitable candidates for their third child, the 17-year-old Alice. Her shortlist included William, Prince of Orange, and Prince Albert of Prussia, cousin to Vicky's husband Frederick. The Prince of Orange was soon put out of the picture – he had fallen hopelessly in love with a Catholic archduchess. Alice had been given a quick look at him, and she turned up her nose at his candidacy. The Prussian Prince Albert was likewise snubbed. Louis's trip to London, ostensibly to attend the Ascot races, was in reality planned to give the young nobleman and Alice a chance to get to know one another ahead of a much-hoped-for engagement. It worked: Alice, a somewhat plain girl, to her mother's eye, was persuaded to accept the proposal of the prince, himself of a somewhat rustic-looking appearance.

The stopover at Mainz coincided with an incident which created an atmosphere of bad blood between Britain and Prussia. At this time some British politicians and newspapers were voicing alarm over attempts by the main German dukedoms to expand their territorial influence and suppress liberal ideas in a reactionary way. The sensitivity that had developed, especially within the British–Prussian relationship, was illustrated in the rather trivial but poignant Macdonald scandal. A Captain Macdonald, who was travelling through Germany, tried to occupy a row of seats in a Prussian railway carriage by distributing his vast amount of luggage across them. He refused to take any of it away when the ticket collector appeared, and the ensuing quarrel between the two men ended violently. 'Macdonald was arrested for attacking the ticket collector and, after a highly publicised trial, jailed for a couple of days. British and German papers covered the incident by calling each other's countrymen arrogant and dangerous.'[24]

Victoria acknowledged Prussia's right to be angry, arguing quite reasonably that British subjects had the same obligation as anyone else to observe the laws of the country in which they travel. Albert tried to brush the incident aside, but it clearly placed him in a sensitive position, with his German countrymen ready to pounce if he were openly to express sympathy with the British officer, while taking the German side would inevitably leave him open to attack by the British press and possibly even cast him in a bad light with the army. On arriving in London, the Prince was alarmed to find Palmerston in a furious state, having 'written a memorandum, in which he represents that unless the [German] judge is at once cashiered and punished, and reparation made to Captain Macdonald, he will break off diplomatic relations with Prussia'.[25] It was also particularly unhelpful, and a factor that further inflamed Palmerston's wrath, that at Macdonald's trial the German public prosecutor had denounced the behaviour of the English abroad as rude, impudent and boorish. The episode fortunately died a natural death, thus putting a line through Palmerston's thoughts of sending the gunboats up the Rhine. A less fortunate development, however, was that the incident became one of the causes of the dislike and suspicion with which the Princess Royal came to be regarded by a section of the Prussian people.

In the last complete year of Albert's life, the Prince continued to work indefatigably, and always under the shadow of death. Though by his own admission, in a letter to Vicky, he had never witnessed a person's final moments of life, the year 1860 brought a surfeit of funerals of people with whom he had shared a close friendship, most notably that of his trusted and loyal minister Lord Aberdeen. The former Prime Minister's death affected him deeply, for he had been one of Albert's few allies in politics, a man with whom the Prince could easily sympathise, as a victim of Palmerstonian aggression. On a happier note, on 30 November Albert and Victoria were able to agree the engagement of Alice to Prince Louis of Hesse, after giving him a studious look over at Windsor Castle. Albert had summoned Louis to his room, and after giving his blessing to the marriage he called for his daughter and the Queen to discuss a date for the ceremony. It was decided to set this two years hence, when the Princess would have reached her nineteenth birthday. The marriage was officially announced on 30 April 1861.

On 5 December, a few days after the meeting with his future son-in-law, Albert was again made miserable by violent stomach cramps and bouts of shivering. The attacks were coming on with increasing frequency, yet until now the Prince was able to recover quickly enough to allay the anxieties of his inner circle in London, with the exception of the Queen. As for those abroad, Stockmar was, as ever, Albert's trusted counsellor, but Vicky was now also taken into his confidence. He confided to his daughter, by way of excuse for failing to convey immediately the news of her younger sister's engagement, that in this latest attack he had found himself 'too miserable to be able to hold my pen'.[26]

Albert was obliged to remain indoors for four days during his recovery, yet he kept actively at work. He generally rose at seven, breakfasted and went to his sitting-room to sit by the fire – unlike Victoria and despite his German blood, the Prince always had a healthy dislike of cold, draughty houses. One of his most daunting tasks was to keep up with the huge volume of correspondence that arrived each day, and, as unofficial monarch, one might dare to venture, draft Victoria's replies to Cabinet questions on matters of state.

Albert's chief worry was France's growing superiority as a naval force, and with this in mind, he fired off a memorandum in point-blank terms to Foreign Secretary Russell, describing the situation as 'a perfect disgrace...that we can do no more than hobble after the French'.[27] Albert received first-hand intelligence on the Royal Navy's relative weakness in the four years of the Second Opium War, a campaign waged jointly by Anglo-French forces which ended in June 1860 with the capitulation of the Qing Dynasty. Such was the weight the Prince's voice carried in Whitehall that within hours a reply was delivered from the Duke of Somerset, First Lord of the Admiralty, promising active measures to increase the number of ironclads.

The run-up to Christmas brought some of the worst weather on record[28] but also brighter news from Bertie, who was touring the other side of the Atlantic. It had been his father's idea to send his difficult son on a visit to Canada and the United States in July. Bertie was beginning to display signs of enjoying intellectual as well as physical activities, and Albert felt he could now be presented in public in a semi-official capacity. The Prince of Wales had achieved adequate exam results at Oxford, and had formed lifelong friendships with prominent scholars, but had also developed habits which his parents found less pleasant, such as an addiction to smoking and an obsession with blood sports. If nothing else, these pastimes would stand him in good stead with the landed aristocracy.

Sending the Prince of Wales off to North America was a bold move, for in these 'classless' societies a member of the European royalty was not likely to encounter much of an enthusiastic welcome. But in Washington and New York Bertie's unaffected, almost rough-edged character, which set him a world apart from the popular image of the English toff, proved an asset. Victoria was overjoyed to receive a letter from the US President James Buchanan extolling Bertie's dignity, frankness and affability, qualities that amply compensated for a lack of intellectual enquiry.

Bertie's ship docked at Plymouth on 15 November 1860, and he made straight for London, where that same evening found him regaling his parents with tales of his North American adventures. The visit had been chaperoned by the Duke of Newcastle, who successfully kept his impetuous charge on a tight lead to avoid any embarrassing banana skins. There was only one close call, and that took place in Toronto, when a deputation of Orangemen had tried to trick Bertie into passing under arches decorated with their political mottoes.

The Bertie saga fell quiet for a spell, much to the relief of his father, who, even with only the most threadbare signs of progress, never abandoned his hopes for a satisfactory outcome to the Prince of Wales's education. Albert held a genuine affection for Bertie, and often enjoyed sharing in his son's manly outdoor activities. There was a memorable Highland excursion which took the family up Ben Muich Dhui, at 4297 feet one of the highest mountains in Scotland. Victoria and Alice rode part of the way on horseback, but then turned back when the track became too steep,[29] while Albert and Bertie carried on to the summit, chatting avidly along the way. One of her gillies said to Victoria, referring to Bertie, that day 'in simple Highland phrase, "It's very pleasant to walk with a person who is always content."'[30] But there can be little doubt that a considerable number of Bertie's faults stemmed from the fact that Victoria, on the contrary, regarded her son with disapproval verging on scorn. Not long before that outing to the Highlands, Victoria confided her feelings towards Bertie in a letter to his sister Vicky: 'Bertie continues such an anxiety...He is improving very decidedly – but oh! It is the improvement of such a poor or still more idle intellect.'[31]

Albert's last Christmas was a time for celebration in the political sphere. Hostilities in China were brought to a successful conclusion, with Britain acquiring Kowloon, next to Hong Kong, and the legalisation of the opium trade. For a few days, the

Prince was able to banish the affairs of state and indulge himself in the simple pleasures of his family. Albert was not the first to introduce the Christmas tree into Britain – one was erected at Windsor by Queen Charlotte, the German-born wife of George III, for a party she held on Christmas Day 1800 – but it was the Prince who popularised the custom and made it an integral part of British tradition. Albert wrote to Berlin to thank Vicky for the gifts which, with only the greatest stretch of the imagination one could envisage tucked under the Albertine tree. These included a large bust of his one-year-old grandson William and a boar's head from Fritz.

There is an odd final paragraph to this letter, which departs suddenly and inexplicably from the message of Christmas cheer. The comment brings to light Albert's humanist nature and his contempt for bigotry, something of which he found himself a victim, even after more than two decades in England, and which continued to cause him deep distress. It is worth quoting in its entirety.

> Prejudice walking to and fro in flesh and blood is my horror, and alas, a phenomenon so common. People plume themselves so much upon their prejudices, as signs of decision of character and greatness of mind, nay, of true patriotism. And all the while they are simply the product of narrowness of intellect and narrowness of heart.[32]

Albert could not neglect to send a letter to Baron Stockmar at this time of year. Along with his sincerest Christmas wishes and a nostalgic reminder of the birds they used to feed together on the professor's visits to England, the Prince broke the news that Bertie was off to Cambridge for a year to complete his formal studies. The Prince of Wales found his second stint at university a stifling business, after roaming the vast, exciting expanses of the New World. His thoughts therefore reverted, as in the past, to non-intellectual pursuits, such as the amateur dramatics club, hunting and his dream of joining the army, a career for which the Commander-in-Chief, the second Duke of Cambridge pronounced him totally unsuited. Bertie nevertheless went off for army training later that year, and managed to get himself involved in an incident that in Albert's horrified opinion came close to producing a royal catastrophe.

Albert and Victoria were preparing to start the new year with a visit to Osborne. But as the carriages were being made ready in the gravelled courtyard of Windsor Castle, news was brought of the death of the King of Prussia, Frederick William IV.[33] Saddened as they were by the King's death, Albert and Victoria carried on their way to Osborne, dispatching three high-ranking members of Court to battle their way through a snowbound and freezing Germany to represent the Queen at the funeral. Albert wrote to his cousin, now William I, who had been serving as regent since his brother's stroke in 1857, expressing his grief, but also with a sense of relief that Frederick William's years of suffering were at last ended.

In those early days of 1861, Osborne became the scene of a constant flow of visitors. Palmerston arrived to discuss, for once, an enjoyable and non-contentious item of business: the dowry to be allotted to Princess Alice on her marriage. Albert had not been eager to give away another daughter in early marriage − Alice was barely 18 − and conflicting views on the subject caused an exchange of sharp words with the Queen. But the secret engagement was no longer a secret, and it is testimony to Albert's enhanced stature in the country that, as had been the case with Vicky, not a dissenting voice was raised in Parliament on 2 May 1861 to the motion to grant Alice a £30,000 dowry, along with a £6000 annuity. This was three-quarters of what had been allotted to Vicky. Albert was somewhat disappointed with the amount granted to the younger daughter, but how he must have laughed to himself recalling the acrimonious debate in the House of Commons exactly 20 years earlier which had ended in a humiliating reduction in the Prince's proposed allowance.

Albert and Victoria were shortly to celebrate their twenty-first – and, as events were to prove, last – wedding anniversary. For all the bickering that had taken place over the years, and in spite of Victoria's periodic tantrums, the Prince's devotion to the Queen had remained unshaken. 'How many a storm has swept over it [his marriage],' he wrote to Stockmar in early February, 'and still it continues green and fresh, and throws out vigorous roots, from which I can, with gratitude to God, acknowledge that much good will yet be engendered for the world.'[34] He wrote to the Duchess of Kent in a similar vein: 'We have faithfully kept our pledge for better and for worse, and have only to thank God that he has vouchsafed so much happiness to us.'[35]

Victoria communicated her feelings to Uncle Leopold, her closest confidant after Albert, with equal fervour. She described the anniversary as the making of a day 'which has brought us, and I may say the *world at large*, much incalculable blessings! [Victoria's emphasis]'. For Victoria, Albert was, after 21 years of matrimony, full of 'the same tender love of the very first days of our marriage!'[36]

A mood of fatalism prevails in these letters. It was as if Albert and Victoria shared an unspoken sense of impending calamity, of an event far more tragic than the death of the Duchess of

Kent the following month, the loss of a mother that was to cast Victoria into 'terrible grief'.[37]

Albert's health was showing more and more the signs of overwork. To the recurrent stomach cramps was added an attack of toothache, on St Valentine's Day, which left his cheek puffed and inflamed. Ignoring this unpleasant development, he carried on with his punishing work schedule, with the result that by the next day the pain and swelling were worse. Common sense dictated that he cancel his public engagements. Instead, as president of the Fine Art Commissions, he went to chair a meeting in Chelsea, essentially to mediate in a wrangle with the Government over funding for the works of art that decorate the Houses of Parliament. The effort proved too much for him − by the following morning he was unable to step foot outside the Palace, so he took to his writing desk to share his afflictions with the ever-supportive Stockmar. 'I have been suffering greatly with toothache … Sleepless nights and pain have pulled me down very much.'[38]

In spite of peace talks, the European war over Italian unification was still on the boil. The conflict added to Albert's political responsibilities, requiring him to dispatch almost daily with Russell over matters of foreign policy. The Prince was certain there would soon be a new Mediterranean kingdom to deal with. He was still in the throes of his toothache torment when the telegraph brought news of the capitulation of Gaeta. It was in this fortified Italian seaport that Francis II of the Two Sicilies made his last stand against the forces of unification. The surrender brought about the merger of his realms with Sardinia to create the unified Kingdom of Italy.

Things could not have worked out more in Albert's favour. On the one hand, Prussia came out in support of the new Italy while Britain, in defiance of French obstinacy, granted King Victor Emmanuel immediate recognition. Albert was confident an independent Italy would act as a counterweight to Louis Napoleon's expansionist designs. The Prince hoped the new *realpolitik* in Europe would ease the movement towards the next great European political unification, that of Germany. This, he held, would require a liberal and generous policy on the part of Prussia as a precondition for an alliance with Britain and for Prussian hegemony in Germany. In 1871, the Treaty of Versailles on German unification, which gathered together princes of the German states to proclaim Fritz Emperor William II, sealed Germany's political union. Had he lived to see it, it would have marked the fulfilment of Albert's dream, that which he had always wished for and striven to achieve. The Prussian marriage in which he had put his faith and hopes would bring about Germany's union, and Vicky was destined to perpetuate his ideas in the following generation. The Prince was convinced that his daughter had learnt the political lessons her father had taught her, and that she had inherited his vision of Germany as a future force in Europe. 'Prince Albert was confident that she would prove a powerful emissary for the ideas of constitutional government in Germany.'[39] All this came about as the Prince had wished, but not until ten years after his death.

In comparison with the taxing events of the first half of 1861 − the death of the King of Prussia, planning for Alice's wedding, the end of the fight for Italian unification, the Prince's illnesses − the summer months brought a promise of more tranquil days ahead. Not that Albert's diary left much room for leisure, apart from stealing a few evening hours for light reading of some of his favourite authors, such as George Eliot or Wilkie

Collins. A typical day would see the Prince trotting out the gates of Buckingham Palace in his carriage before nine o'clock to attend meetings and officiate at events, rarely returning home before seven in the evening. However, these days were for the most part taken up with agreeable duties. Appropriately for a man who always longed to place cultural pursuits at the top of his agenda, the last public ceremony at which Albert presided was the opening, on 5 June, of the Royal Horticultural Gardens.[40]

Bertie once again loomed large in Albert's thoughts that summer, and in a most unwelcome way. The Prince of Wales had developed into a vigorous, gregarious man of 20, and he was in a state of euphoria at the prospect of ten weeks' training with the Grenadier Guards at Curragh Camp in Ireland. The boy who had spent his childhood yearning for his mother's love found in the fellowship of his brother officers a sense of self-esteem, even though, as has been noted, he had been pronounced unqualified for military life.

One night several of these brother officers, most probably the worse for wear through drink, decided to play a prank on Bertie by introducing an Irish actress, Nellie Clifden, into his tent. The sexually innocent Prince of Wales found his unexpected tryst a thoroughly enjoyable experience, so much so that he took a fancy to Nellie and allowed her to follow him to Windsor. Albert reacted with horror to his son's involvement with this commoner. When the story leaked out in November, he was certain it would blow up into a disaster of major proportions. The Prince spent sleepless nights fretting over the potential impact of this affair, which had caused him to lose faith in his son, and with it his interest in life. In the end, prudish Victorian society proved perfectly up to shrugging off the scandal, just as it treated with a bemused smirk his subsequent flings as King Edward VII.

Albert fired off a letter of admonishment to Bertie, following this up with a visit to Cambridge on 25 November. The Prince and his family had just been to the Duchess of Kent's mausoleum at Frogmore. The cold, blustery autumn was not an auspicious time for Albert, given his delicate state of health, to be out and about. His only diary entry for that morning walk to Frogmore reads, 'Am full of rheumatic pains, and feel thoroughly unwell. Have scarcely closed my eyes at night for the last fortnight.'[41] It was another wet and stormy morning when he boarded the train to Cambridge, feeling 'still greatly out of sorts'.[42] The Prince took Bertie for a long walk under a steady drizzle, on which he pleaded with his son to come to his senses and throw up this obviously manipulative woman − Bertie's personal honour and that of his family, not to mention the horror of a public smear campaign, hung in the balance.

Bertie was shocked to see his father in such an extreme state of anguish, and he agreed to draw a line under the affair. Albert walked away from this, his last meeting with his son, a contented man. He was equally proud that Bertie refused to reveal the identity of the officers who had got him into this scrape. 'Bertie's abject and heartfelt contrition made amends so far as Albert was concerned, but his mother was not to be so forgiving.'[43] Victoria was later convinced that the angst Albert suffered as a result of Bertie's exploit had hastened his death. 'Oh! That boy − much as I pity him I never can or shall look at him without a shudder,' she wrote rather heartlessly to Vicky.[44] She even went as far as to claim in unvarnished terms that Albert 'had been killed by that dreadful business'.[45]

The Queen tried to keep an iron grip on both her sons, though with Alfred the attitude was more autocratic than based on aversion. She wrote to Vicky in December 1860, ahead of a visit to Germany by the two princes, asking her to look after Alfred, 'a great darling – but he must be looked after and is never allowed to go out alone'. As for Bertie, who had just been granted Albert's permission to smoke, Victoria's only mention was to stipulate that her son must not be allowed to do so 'in public or in the house'.[46]

For her part, Vicky was unsympathetic to her mother's callous denigration of her brother. 'Only one thing pains me – when I think of it and that is the relation between you and Bertie!...I can only hope and pray that there may never be an estrangement between him and you – as it would be the source of endless misery to both.'[47]

Before her death in March, the Duchess of Kent had advised Albert that marriage was the time-honoured remedy for Bertie's erring ways. It was time to seek a woman fit to bear the title of Queen of Great Britain. Bertie was all for it. The Prince, however, was sceptical: future monarch or not, the fact remained that his son bore no resemblance to the handsome prince image of fairy tales. Albert brought the subject up with Victoria, who was prepared to resort to any expedient, short of a mother's compassion, which might reform her wayward son. The task of hunting down a suitable candidate was entrusted to Vicky, who, after drawing up a shortlist of Protestant women of noble birth, came up with Princess Alexandra of Schleswig-Holstein-Sonderburg-Glücksburg, daughter of the future King Christian IX. Anna of Hesse was 'not pretty' and had not 'a fine figure but a passable one'. However, the poor girl suffered from 'an incipient twitching in her eyes...and her teeth are nearly all spoilt'. The

Weimar girls she looked over 'are very nice but delicate and not pretty'. Alexandra, on the other hand, was 'a dear little girl, pretty and nice, but of course much too young [16] for Bertie'.[48]

This wife-hunt took place before the Duchess of Kent's death, and the still influential Victoria Marie Louise, Princess of Saxe-Coburg-Saalfeld, had serious reservations about this Anglo-Danish alliance: Victoria's mother had been brought up on 'terrible stories about the goings-on at … family gatherings'.[49] Albert himself was worried about the reaction in Prussia to a marital alliance between the Danish and British crowns, in light of Prussia's ongoing territorial dispute with Denmark.[50]

Bertie met his future bride in September 1861 when, not entirely by chance, both made trips to Germany. Rumours of a royal match had been grabbing headlines in the European press for weeks beforehand. Albert was not particularly put off by the newspaper gossip, for he had grown more enthusiastic about the idea of the union: 'We hear nothing but excellent accounts of the Princess Alexandra,' he noted in his diary. 'The young people seem to have taken a warm liking to each other.'[51] But he was furious with his brother Ernest, who opposed the marriage, for discussing the matter openly even before the couple had met, and he vented his anger in the most scathing terms. Ernest may have been entitled to a

> real interest in Bertie's affairs … But I do complain of your discussing matters of so private and delicate a nature with third parties, and sending me a Memorandum written by a secretary …
> I have always been worried by fear that the public might get wind of the plan, therefore I am sorry that you know about it.[52]

Bertie and Alexandra were married at Windsor Castle in March 1863, and the couple spent a brief honeymoon at Osborne.

Bertie may have settled down to the life of a family man − following in her mother-in-law's footsteps, Alexandra bore him six children in seven years − but this failed to soften Victoria's attitude towards her son. The Queen refused to allow him to take on public duties or represent her at public occasions. Once, when Bertie turned up late for a dinner party, a stiff glance from the Queen sent him hiding behind a pillar until the party broke up. He was over fifty at the time.

The final weeks of Albert's life were marked by further tragedy. Where Bertie had offered him little but distress, King Pedro V of Portugal, the Prince's protégé and cousin, was a man with the virtues lacking in his own son. Only four years Bertie's senior, Pedro had thrown himself body and soul into instilling modernisation and reform into his poverty-stricken, backward country. Pedro greatly admired Albert, and when the time came to find a bride for the young king, he unquestioningly accepted the Prince's preference for Stephanie of Hohenzollern, daughter of Karl Anton, head of the House of Hohenzollern-Sigmaringen. The marriage took place in May 1858, but it was shortlived: Albert was shattered a year later when Stephanie succumbed to diphtheria. This was, however, a minor blow compared with the death of Pedro from typhoid in 1861, at the age of 24. In his last letter to Fritz, Albert tells his son-in-law that Pedro's death had shaken him in an extraordinary way, 'for I loved and valued him greatly, and had great hopes that his influence might contribute towards setting on its legs a State and nation which had fallen low'.[53]

The terrible news of Pedro's death, the exhaustion and rheumatic pains the Prince was left with after the outing to the Duchess of Kent's mausoleum, an exhausting visit to Sandhurst on a rainswept day to inspect the new Staff College and Royal

Military Academy, the search for a successor to Prince Leopold's Governor, Sir Edward Bowater, who lay on his deathbed, and finally the strain of dealing with Bertie's sordid dalliance – the coming together of these events within the space of a few weeks would have taxed the strength of the most robust of men. For Albert, it proved all too much. Those weeks had taken him to the edge of death. He now began to complain of pains in his back and legs, and he was almost constantly weak and listless.

Albert knew in his heart that he had not long to live, yet he was unable to summon the will to resist. 'I do not cling to life,' he told Victoria. 'You do: but I set no store by it...I am sure if I had a severe illness I should give up at once, I should not struggle for life. I have no tenacity of life.'[54]

Even now, drifting towards death's door, the Prince was not spared the burden of official duties. Albert's last political act was, for that matter, no trifling matter: he was called on by the Government to intervene in an international diplomatic incident to avoid war between Britain and the United States.

The so-called *Trent* affair in November 1861, seven months after the outbreak of the American Civil War, took the two countries to the brink of armed conflict. Towards the end of November word spread throughout England that the American gunboat *San Jacinto* had intercepted the British mail packet *Trent* on the high seas. American officers boarded the *Trent* and arrested two Confederate envoys, James Mason and John Slidell, bound for Europe to press the Confederacy's case for diplomatic recognition by Britain and France. The Confederacy came close to achieving one of its aims, a rupture in British relations with Washington, when an outraged Palmerston dispatched eight thousand troops to Canada in preparation for hostilities with the US. At 77, Palmerston was still his old bellicose self, if anything more so, having advised Victoria to demand immediate reparation and redress from the American Government.

The British Government was not an ally of the American North, which Palmerston's Foreign Secretary Lord Russell dismissed as bent on conquest more than liberation. There were well-founded fears of the war disrupting the cotton trade. The economy of north-west England relied entirely on this commodity, which was landed in Liverpool and distributed to Lancashire mills. The South also provided Britain with much of its tobacco. There were also financial ties with the Southern states, as well as a good deal of popular support for the Southern cause.

> In March 1863, the Confederate government put a seven per cent loan worth £3 million on the market…allowing individuals to invest in the Confederacy and its war efforts. The loan was oversubscribed five times and accrued £16 million (the equivalent of £690.5 million today) worth of bonds, nearly all of them sold in London.[55]

Albert's task was to defuse anger in Britain and at the same time offer the US a way out of the diplomatic skirmish with honour. The Prince marshalled his diplomatic skills to tone down a belligerent Government memorandum before it was sent to Washington. On 30 November, ill as he was, Albert rose at seven to deliver the reworded document to Victoria for her signature. The Prince's version deleted comments that would have manifestly offended Washington, while making it clear that the US Navy captain had acted with an excess of zeal. This brought a satisfactory response: the Lincoln Administration released the two envoys and disavowed the captain's action, without having to take the humiliating step of issuing a formal apology. Mason and Slidell eventually reached England, but were rebuffed in their mission to achieve diplomatic recognition for their Government.

Even as Albert carried on with his work, the signs of deterioration were evident. In 1861, the Prince was still corresponding with Sir Charles Eastlake of the Commission on the Fine Arts regarding the decoration of the Houses of Parliament. Compared with his clearly written letters of the 1840s, the handwriting is shaky and in some instances barely legible.[56]

Albert's end came swiftly. Confined to his bedroom at Windsor, Albert attempted to write a letter to his son Leopold, but had to lay down his pen after the first few lines. The doctors attending him now had to acknowledge their patient's condition as serious, but they tried to reassure Victoria that there was yet hope of a recovery.

On 7 December, the characteristic pink rash of typhoid appeared. 'Dr William Jenner explained its implications to the Queen in the most optimistic manner, saying that "the fever must have its course, viz. a month…that he was not alarmed, and that there were no bad symptoms, but [Albert] could not be better until the fever left him."'[57]

By the second week in December, the press was preparing the public for the worst, putting out bulletins on the Prince's fevers and the likelihood that he was suffering from a grave illness. *The Times* reported an increase in the Prince's 'feverish symptoms' which were 'likely to continue for some time longer'. Three days later the paper gave a statement by Dr Thomas Watson, one of the two physicians Palmerston had persuaded Victoria to add to the medical team, who said that Albert was 'very ill…the malady is very grave…it is impossible not to be anxious'.[58]

The Prince hardly slept, and only with extreme difficulty managed to keep any food or drink down. His doctors plied him with brandy, of all things, which undoubtedly shortened his wretched agony by a few days. It is worthy of note that the medical team was led by Sir James Clark, the physician who in 1839 had falsely diagnosed Lady Hastings, from her appearance, as being pregnant. It is a testimony to the Queen's robust constitution that she herself managed to survive to 81. A wooden medicine chest in her bedroom at Osborne House contains an array of Clark-approved, potentially lethal concoctions, including laudanum, meconate of morphine, chloroforum belladonnae and pure chloroform.

By 12 December, Albert's breathing had become quicker and more laborious. There was no alternative but to inform the rest of the family and the Government of the imminent end. When Palmerston was told that Albert was sinking, his old antagonist was so horrified that one is left wondering how relations between the two men could ever have been so strained. 'Your telegram and letter have come upon me like a thunderbolt,' he wrote to Albert's private secretary Sir Charles Phipps. 'One can only hope that Providence may yet spare us so overwhelming a calamity.'[59]

Such hopes were in vain. Bertie arrived at Windsor in the pre-dawn hours of 14 December to join his sisters. Four of Albert's nine children were not able to be present in the final hours. Alfred was at sea, Leopold in France, Vicky in Germany and Beatrice, who was only four, was kept away from the deathbed scene.

Later that day, Albert began in an almost macabre fashion to arrange his hair and then folded his arms, which Victoria took as a sign that he was preparing himself for the journey. He muttered a few words in French, and uttered some endearing terms to Victoria in German as, one by one, his children came up to kiss his hand. So too did Phipps, General George Grey and Master of the Queen's Household Sir Thomas Biddulph. Victoria left the room for a few moments to compose herself for the final drama, but not before she bent low over Albert and whispered, 'Es ist kleines Frauchen!' ("Tis your little wife'). She asked if he would give her 'ein Kuss' ('a kiss'), and he did so.[60]

It was after ten o'clock that night when Princess Alice came out to summon Victoria back into the bedroom. The Queen took Albert's hand, which was already cold, and she drew close to listen to his quiet, gentle breathing as she sat by his side. The Castle clock chimed three bells of a quarter to eleven, Albert took two or three long breaths, and he was gone, eight months short of his forty-third birthday. Quiet sobbing, deep sighs were heard in the room. Victoria dropped to her knees by the bedside, speechless, gazing at her departed husband.

The official medical report listed the cause of death as typhoid,[61] though the symptoms the Prince suffered in the final months would suggest that his body was wasting away from another disease, possibly a cancer. The nation was stunned by his death, 'this man, the very centre of our social system, the pillar of our State', as the commanding voice of *The Times* put it, 'suddenly snatched from us, without even warning sufficient to prepare us for a blow so abrupt and so terrible'. The paper went on to remind its readers that the shock of his loss would not be confined to the British Isles. 'Wherever throughout the world the character and influence of the Prince Consort are understood, there will be regret and pity, astonishment to the full, as much as among ourselves.'[62] The list of foreign dignitaries at the funeral bore witness to this statement. Mourners came from all parts of Europe, and even India, to pay their last respects to the Prince. Albert's brother Ernest, of course, marched behind the Prince of Wales, in the company of leading members of the nobility of France, the Netherlands, Portugal, Prussia and Belgium.

'Oh, my poor child, why has the earth not swallowed us up?' Victoria wrote to her daughter Vicky. On the saddest Christmas Eve of her life, she described herself to Uncle Leopold as 'your poor forlorn, desolate child, who drags on a weary, pleasureless existence'.[63] From the moment of Albert's death, Victoria showed herself perfectly collected, resolved, as she told Leopold, 'to carry out the Prince's wishes and plans. And no human power will make me swerve from what he decided and wished.'[64]

Albert's funeral ceremony took place on 23 December in St George's Chapel. A guard of honour of the Grenadier Guards was mounted at the entrance to the state apartments of Windsor Castle. The hearse bearing Albert's remains was preceded by nine mourning coaches with representatives of three European monarchs and an assortment of the Prince's attendants, from valets and bailiffs to the Prince's apothecary and his physicians. Victoria brought up the rear in a carriage drawn by six horses. The elaborate funeral obsequies were precisely the sort of affair Albert would have detested. His casket was taken to the Frogmore Mausoleum, where he and Victoria now rest side by side. From the moment Albert breathed his last, a cloak of macabre sadness descended on the Court. The Queen lived on another forty years, yet she never discarded her mourning colours. Every day the servants at Windsor Castle would change the bed linen and put out fresh towels in the Blue Room in which the Prince had expired.

On a sunny August morning in 1862 in the Scottish Highlands, Victoria and her children set off on a trek, in pony cart and on foot, to the summit of Craig Lowrigan. 'The view was so fine, the day so bright, and the heather so beautifully pink – but no pleasure, no joy! all dead!' she wrote of the excursion.[65] On the summit, the family gathered at a cairn, 35 feet high, to carve their initials in stone all around the mound. The inscription reads, 'To the Beloved Memory of Albert, the Great and Good Prince Consort, Raised by his Broken-Hearted Widow, Victoria R.'

7

'We have buried our sovereign'

There is an inscription on a plain stone plaque in a corner of the crypt of St Paul's Cathedral in London which reads, 'Lector, Si Monumentum Requiris, Circumspice'. It translates from Latin as 'Reader, if you seek his memorial, look about you'. The tablet is above the tomb of Sir Christopher Wren, one of Britain's most celebrated architects. But it could equally have served as an epitaph to Prince Albert – with better cause, perhaps, because Wren's influence, though undeniably great, was less enduring than Albert's. St Paul's Cathedral and Kensington Palace stand as lasting monuments to the architect's genius. But Wren was superseded by newer generations, and his baroque style would today fire the imagination of few architects.

Albert's presence, on the other hand, is very much alive and visible in today's Britain. At the trivial end, his name has been widely commercialised, from the Albert Square of the BBC television programme *EastEnders* to towns across Britain that are awash with pubs bearing the name 'Prince Albert', 'Royal

Albert' or simply 'Albert'. The Prince was famously transported to literary fiction by George Macdonald Fraser in one of his 'Flashman' novels, German accent and all.[1] Greater indeed are the Prince's achievements, for Albert was an outsider, disliked by many in government and the aristocracy, a man who found himself having to struggle for years against the widespread mistrust of foreigners. Even before he arrived in Britain for his marriage to Victoria, the Queen had forewarned him of the cool reception he could expect. 'The English are very jealous of any foreigner interfering in the government of this country, and have already in some of the papers … expressed a hope that you would not interfere.'[2]

Albert's renown was recognised, however, at home and throughout the Empire, after his death. Towns and provinces bearing his name are to be found in Canada, Australia, South Africa and in almost every former British colony. There are lakes named after the Prince in Africa, Australia and the US, and four regiments of the British army that bore his name until the very recent reorganisation of the British forces: 11th (Prince Albert's Own) Hussars, Prince Albert's Light Infantry, Prince Albert's Own Leicestershire Regiment of Yeomanry Cavalry and The Prince Consort's Own Rifle Brigade. Given the Prince's preponderance in so many sectors of public life, from industry and politics to art and agriculture, it was with some justification that on Albert's death Disraeli was moved to exclaim, 'We have buried our sovereign.'[3]

Victoria's grief at her husband's death knew no bounds, to the extent that in celebrating Albert's legacy she made every effort – unhealthily, one might argue – to create a demigod in the place of a mortal. The Queen was overjoyed when the Poet

Laureate Lord Alfred Tennyson[4] dedicated his King Arthur saga, *Idylls of the King*, completed in 1885, to Albert's memory. As a work that recounts the unblemished King Arthur's attempt and failure to lift up mankind and create a perfect realm, the poem's association with Albert is an unfortunate one. The Prince was not perfection personified: he could easily sink into ill-temper and gloom, he took a severe hand to his children's upbringing, and he was highly sensitive to criticism. But these personality shortcomings hardly invalidate his kindness, wisdom and high moral principles. Those who came into contact with Albert invariably took away an impression of basic goodness. The diarist Charles Greville first met Albert in 1849, on a visit to Balmoral. Greville recounts that he was having breakfast with Lord Russell one morning when the Prince came in and sat down with them for nearly an hour. 'I was greatly struck with him,' Greville wrote. 'I saw at once (what I had always heard) that he is very intelligent and highly cultivated, and moreover that he has a thoughtful mind, and thinks of subjects worth thinking about. He seemed very much at ease, very gay, pleasant, and without the least stiffness or air of dignity.'[5]

Yet it would be mistaken to consign Albert to the Pantheon of the Gods atop Mount Olympus, though there is evidence that the Prince himself extolled the chivalric virtues of King Arthur. In a letter to Sir Charles Eastlake, secretary of the Commission on the Fine Arts for the decoration of the Houses of Parliament, Albert refers to the painter William Dyce's[6] proposed frescos for the robing room of the House of Lords, which depict Arthur and his knights of the round table. 'I am clearly of the opinion that it ought to be the widest circle of the legend of Arthur…

particularly from those scenes which exemplify the moral qualities venerated in chivalry.'[7]

This admiration, and indeed emulation, of chivalric conduct was to be found in Albert's nature from an early age. As a child, Albert and some of his friends were playing at the Rosenau one afternoon, pretending to be knights preparing to storm an old ruined tower on the side of the castle. As previously mentioned, one of the boys suggested they move to a place at the back where they could enter without being seen, and thus capture the castle without difficulty. Albert declared that 'this would be most unbecoming in a Saxon knight, who should always attack the enemy in front'.[8]

Albert took a lifelong interest in military affairs, and, as has been documented in an earlier chapter, his work behind the scenes to put the British army on an even footing with other European powers, specifically France, was another facet of his legacy: an organised, disciplined and well-equipped fighting force. But it was not enough to put soldiers into battalions and regiments. It was necessary to educate them as well. The Prince Consort Library at Aldershot, with its 65,000 volumes of military history and strategy, including most of the thousand books Albert himself donated, stands as a tribute to this task.

The Prince was a man of inherent humility. He was a devoted fan of Tennyson, and once wrote to him humbly begging his forgiveness for intruding 'upon your leisure', with a request to the Poet Laureate to write his name in a copy of *Idylls of the King*, which he enclosed with the letter.[9]

Albert was always resolute that no monuments or statues should ever be raised to his memory, and in the days of his final illness he reiterated this wish to Victoria. If the Queen was determined 'to carry out the Prince's wishes and plans', as she had stated in her letter to Leopold, this was one request she could not bring herself to observe. 'The rest of time would henceforth be to her only a memorial to the husband she had lost, a building up of duty on duty, in his honour and for his sake,' writes the poet Edith Sitwell. 'He must, he should, be known to her people for the man he was. Books must be written extolling his memory, statues and memorials must be raised with his image and bearing his name.'[10]

Victoria could not fail to immortalise her departed husband in granite and marble. He had been the driving force of her life, the person she depended on for love and guidance, whose advice was almost always accepted without question. 'He drafted her letters and dispatches, she never chose a bonnet or dress without his approval, after twenty years of marriage she grudged every hour they were apart. And now he was gone forever.'[11] Largely through Victoria's efforts and patronage, within a short period of time after the Prince's death there arose a cult of Albert that saw a proliferation of testimonials even greater in number than any erected to Wellington or Nelson. There was more to this than Victoria's stubborn wilfulness: Albert's death opened the floodgates to a wave of sympathy for the widowed Queen, along with, it need hardly be said, widespread grief at the loss of a man of acknowledged benevolence and generous heart. 'Within weeks of Prince Albert's death, schemes to commemorate him were being considered by towns, cities and institutions throughout Great Britain. No previous individual had been so widely honoured.'[12]

Given the intensity of grief that took hold of the country,[13] it will come as no surprise that most of Albert's monuments were funded by public subscription. The purpose expressed in most cases was to provide the British people with a reminder of the Prince's noble qualities. Victoria herself was present at the unveiling of several of these statues, including the one in Perth (Scotland), which took place nearly three years after Albert's death. The Queen was deeply touched by this display of public gratitude and affection for the Prince, which she took to be part of the rewarding progress of her endeavour to 'stimulate future generations to the practice of those virtues which have rendered the memory of [Albert] so dear to the people'.[14] Victoria's greatest reward was to witness what Sir Charles Wood, her Secretary of State for India, described as 'the demeanour of the people at these occasions, which showed how completely they felt the character of the day's proceedings'.[15]

Mayoral committees were set up across the country to raise funds for memorials, the majority of these in the form of statues, though many commemorative plaques and portraits were also executed in those years. Albert's image came to adorn the walls of churches, famously the carved portrait above a stone dedication tablet in St Mildred's, Victoria's parish church on the Isle of Wight. Portraits of the Prince were added to the collections of the National Portrait Gallery, which had opened its doors less than a decade earlier, as well as the Royal Collection. There also arose a burgeoning industry of Albert memorabilia, from medals and belt clasps bearing the Prince's portrait, to embroidered handkerchiefs and a silk bookmark with a likeness of Albert surrounded by his daughters – but curiously not his sons – now on display at the Victoria and Albert Museum.

Equestrian statues were erected in the main squares of Liverpool, Glasgow, Wolverhampton and Dublin, as well as

London's Holborn Circus, to name but a few places. Prince Albert statues and effigies multiplied not only in British cities but also in France, as far afield as Bombay and Sydney – with the inscription 'Albert the Good' – and of course in Coburg. Coincidentally, the two latter statues show the Prince holding a scroll depicting the Crystal Palace in London.

In spite of the great variety in form and shape of the testaments to the Prince's memory, we are persistently taken back to the Gothic-revival motif of Albert as the knight in shining armour: quite literally, in fact, as this is how he is depicted in portraits such as those by Robert Thornburn and Edward Henry Corbould that hang in the Royal Collection. Another striking example of Albert's idealised image is the marble resting effigy of the Prince with armour and broadsword, designed by Henri de Triqueti, in the Albert Memorial Chapel at Windsor Castle.

> Albert was regarded as an exemplar of modern chivalry, a peculiarly British response to popular medievalism. It was not Albert's deeds, but his character – his high moral ideals, his impeccable conduct and his unstinting devotion to the nation – that earned him his knightly public image.[16]

Victoria cherished the chivalric allusion, her King Arthur, and she as Gloriana, Edmund Spenser's Fairie Queen. Leaving mortal life, he could forever after live in legend, 'a knight who would never abandon her'.[17]

It must be taken into account that this knightly image had a great popular appeal in mid-nineteenth-century Britain. Albert's death came only 13 years after the foundation of the Pre-Raphaelite Brotherhood, while the country was still under the influence of the Romantic period and its veneration of medievalism, and moreover Britain was basking in the power and self-confidence of an Empire that held dominion over an immense portion of the world's landmass.

Albert's sense of duty, personal humbleness and respect for the institutions of parliamentary government served to buttress the country's political stability. He raised the British monarchy to the highest prestige it had ever enjoyed, so that Britain was spared the ravages of 1848, which had been brought on by public outrage in Europe at the corrupt regimes of monarchs who ruled by divine right rather than with the consent of their subjects. Things could have been different for the British monarchy had the louche and dissolute George IV, or his successor the ineffectual and elderly William IV, been on the throne in the year of European revolution. Albert and Victoria's propriety was never put in doubt, nor was there ever any hint of scandal or corruption in their lives, not even from their most vociferous detractors.

Albert's union with Victoria was to the everlasting good fortune of the British monarchy, for had she married another of the suitors who were sent knocking at the gates of Kensington Palace, the Crown would surely have sustained irreparable damage. It is distressing to think of the outcome had William IV had his way in marrying off his niece to William of Orange, for instance, a man much given to extramarital enthusiasm and once described as 'the greatest debauchee of the age'. Albert's brother had been given very long odds as a candidate, but it is more than likely that Victoria would have had to spend her days keeping him out of mischief of one sort or another. It was enough that Albert wasted precious time rebuking his brother for his constant demands for money. 'We must have a decided promise from you,' he once told Ernest, 'that you will pay off your debts and arrange your household in such a manner that you need no assistance out of the *Fideikommis* [family funds]…If you cannot see your way now, what would it be if you were to have children?'[18] That Ernest's marriage never yielded any offspring gave rise to speculation that he was suffering from venereal disease. William Duke of Brunswick, another of the hopefuls, who never married but fathered a number of illegitimate children, would hardly have made a creditable Prince Consort. Would he or Victoria have grasped the need to take the monarchy to the common people? Who would have been there to stand between a juvenile, impressionable queen and the towering political figures of the day? Who but Albert could have steered her through the turbulent events at home and abroad? Would the Duke of Wellington have taken one of these rogues under his wing and put him forward for the post of Commander-in-Chief? How would Victoria have stood up to Palmerston's bullying without Albert's strength of character to support her? Who else would have looked up to the monarchy as defender of the poor and downtrodden, as a campaigner for social justice, an advocate of education in the arts and science for all?

Yet Albert the Humble never lost sight of the fact that his duty was to the sovereign. There was no hint of self-aggrandisement in his labours, only the ceaseless effort to secure the moral dignity of the Court. For the Prince, this was only possible through 'the personal character of the Sovereign. When a person enjoys complete confidence, we desire for him more power and influence in the conduct of affairs.'[19]

The grandest of all monuments to the Prince's memory is the Gothic-revival Albert Memorial in London's Kensington

Gardens, facing the Royal Albert Hall. The Prince's devotion to schemes for social and educational advancement made his former associates turn initially to some institutional form of commemoration. One of the first to formulate a plan was Henry Cole of the South Kensington Museum. He wanted to develop an idea of the Prince's own by establishing an 'Albert University' at South Kensington for the award of diplomas to practising technologists and manufacturers.[20] The idea never came to fruition, but what did emerge on the site was Imperial College, founded in 1907 under a royal charter in the reign of the Prince's son Edward VII. This was the fulfilment of Albert's dream of a cultural centre for science and the arts.

From Edinburgh, one of the Prince's former advisers, Professor Lyon Playfair, recommended a further scheme of the Prince's: the establishment of a system of international exchange scholarships. It immediately became clear, however, that the general wish, and also the Queen's, was for a memorial 'in the common sense of the word', whether or not this 'personal memorial' were combined with an institution or 'work of utility'.[21] The memorial to the 1851 Exhibition had been sponsored by the Lord Mayor in 1853, and nine years later another Lord Mayor, William Cubitt, who had been the chief engineer of the Crystal Palace, took on the same duties. He called a meeting on 14 January 1862, and a committee was appointed to raise a subscription for building a memorial to a design to be approved by the Queen. It was around Victoria's secretary Charles Grey and his colleague Sir Charles Phipps, keeper of the privy purse, that ideas for the memorial were to be effectively discussed. They recalled that the Prince's qualities had been more readily appreciated by the middle classes than by the political aristocracy, hence the preference for a monument accessible to all, visitors and passers-by alike. A very strong motive with Grey and his associates at that time was a wish to avoid controversy and competition. This was largely out of respect for the Prince's opinion that competition among artists excluded the best work.[22]

The memorial, designed by Sir George Gilbert Scott, one of Britain's most prolific architects, took more than ten years to complete and was opened in 1872 by Victoria, though it was another three years before Albert was 'seated' under the canopy as we see him today.[23]

Since its inauguration, the Albert Memorial has been praised by many, including Victoria, as a magnificent tribute to Albert, who is depicted holding a catalogue of the 1851 Exhibition and robed as a Knight of the Garter. It has also been condemned as overly ornate, ostentatious, even tasteless – all valid criticism, depending on one's taste in shrines to the deceased. The fact is that there has been sufficient enthusiasm and pride in this classic piece of London iconography to have merited two major restorations, the last one as recent as 2006. A far greater manifestation of acclaim for the Albert Memorial is that the project was carried out entirely through public subscription, and at the fabulous cost of £120,000, a sum equivalent to roughly £10 million in today's money. More than £1200 was raised in a single day by contributions from peers, notables of the City, and town-hall authorities across the country.

A more faithful reflection of Albert's popularity with the people would be the donations that poured in from the working classes, in gratitude for the Prince having striven to lift them out of poverty and ignorance. Four months after Albert's death, the Working Men's Albert Memorial opened an account at the Bank of London to raise funds for the monuments they judged most appropriate to honour his memory: 'lodging houses with educational and institutional facilities, free libraries, etc., in memory of the late Prince Albert'.[24]

Albert's legacy is present in many spheres of contemporary British society. In the sciences, his paramount concern was for continuous and bold advancement, even if this provoked a confrontation with established prejudices. Hence his attempt to secure a knighthood for Charles Darwin, which failed in the face of ecclesiastical opposition. The quest for knowledge was a driving force in Albert's life. He cherished the belief that without advancement through knowledge, society is 'condemned to do things just as our fathers did, and for no better reason than because they did so'.[25] It is illustrative that these remarks were made when the Prince laid the first stone of the still-thriving Birmingham and Midland Institute in 1854. The Institute's founding maxim reads, 'The diffusion of and advancement of science, literature and art amongst all classes of persons'. It could have been composed by Albert himself.

Then, of course, there is the living legacy of the Great Exhibition of 1851. The Exhibition was the first in what was to become a spectacular sequence of events. During the second half of the nineteenth century some forty international exhibitions were staged worldwide from Dublin to Paris, New York to Vienna and Sydney to Guatemala City. These expositions expanded the scope of the original concept to embrace every aspect of human activity. The successful revival of the Olympic Games in 1896, for example, can be traced to this source. Indeed, the second, third, and fourth Olympiads were all held in conjunction with expositions – in Paris, St Louis, and London, respectively. The two nations to take up the exhibition idea most competitively were France and the United States, which between them staged some 14 major events before 1900.

More than anything else, the Great Exhibition ushered in a new age of art and design criticism. From 1851, design reform grew steadily in Britain as a professionalised activity, with exhibitions and publications on the subject proliferating. After the Great Exhibition, the *Art Journal* predicted that 'when His Royal Highness Prince Albert issues his summons to another competition, British supremacy will be manifested in every branch of Industrial art'.[26] Albert died the year before London's International Exhibition opened in 1862 in the grounds of what is now the Natural History Museum, but the prophecy was correct. The medal count revealed British design standards to have improved to the point where they rivalled those of the French. Albert's Exhibition is the only one whose legacy lives on, benefiting students and scholars today as it enlightened and enthralled millions more than a century and a half ago.

The 1851 Royal Commission now grants 24 scholarships a year for post-doctoral research, industrial fellowships and industrial design. The programme is aimed at benefiting Britain's manufacturing industry. 'Albert's influence is all around us and we like to think he'd be proud of the way we're carrying on his work, in the way we help scientists and engineers to make their way in society,' says the Commission's Secretary Nigel Williams.[27] The Commission has granted 2500 awards since the programme was launched in 1891, and its recipients include 12 Nobel laureates and 150 fellows of the Royal Society.

One writer draws an interesting comparison between Albert's Great Exhibition and the last Labour Government's plans, which took form in the mid-1990s, to stage another huge exhibition to celebrate the Millennium. For a start, it is pointed out, the planning process of the two events was entirely different: in 1851, the nature of the Exhibition was decided first, followed by discussion of the site and the building to house it. In the case of the Millennium project, the site was selected first, then the Dome was chosen to house the event. 'The Dome, with its emphasis on feelings, attitudes and ideas rather than on objects...was in most respects the exact opposite of the Crystal Palace. It recognised that in the twenty-first century Britain lives by its wits more than by the sweat of its brow.'[28] The Dome, like the Crystal Palace, suffered from bad publicity. But the Dome was also handicapped by a political outcry at the amount of public money being lavished on a project that clearly was not going to meet its financial targets, and the Government finally had to concede failure. The Great Exhibition was funded by private donation, while nearly a quarter of the Dome funding came from commercial sponsors who demanded a return on their investment. The spirit that motivated the disastrous Millennium Dome had nothing in common with the altruism that inspired the planners and supporters of the 1851 Exhibition. In short, the 1851 Exhibition was intended to enlighten, the Dome to make money.

Albert's enduring crusade to promote the application of science to manufacturing and industry was acknowledged in the number of institutions and schools that have since taken his name. At a town meeting in Sheffield held only weeks after the Prince's death, Mayor John Brown proposed that the name of the Sheffield School be changed to the Albert Memorial School of Science. His speech drew 'much cheering' from the crowd in attendance.[29] Framlingham College in Suffolk was founded in 1863 as the Albert Middle Class College, established as 'a school for the scientific and practical instruction of the middle classes at a moderate cost'.[30] The Albert Memorial Industrial School in Birkenhead was opened in 1866 with the poignant mission to further 'the education, industrial training and maintenance...of children who, through poverty or parental neglect...are left without instruction, or are in danger of contamination from vicious or criminal associates'.[31]

Schools, colleges, industrial and scientific institutes all scrambled to add 'Albert', with or without his royal title, to their names. It was, of course, the least costly way to endow their establishments with a lasting tribute to the Prince, as was the case with the many streets and bridges that became Albert Road, Albert Court, Albert Place and Albert Square.[32] But this in no way diminishes the gesture: there never appeared any charges in the press that this reflected an attempt to honour the Prince on the cheap.

Over the course of the years, Albert's name came to be attached to almshouses, hospitals, railway stations, obelisks and major city arteries, such as London's Albert Embankment, which runs parallel to the Victoria Embankment along the south side of the Thames. Cleopatra's Needle, gifted to Britain in 1819 by the ruler of Egypt, was rescued by the Prince and later erected on the Victoria Embankment. A short walk away is Nelson's Column in Trafalgar Square, facing the National Gallery, whose carved lions were also Albert's inspiration. Each year on the occasion of the Trooping the Colour ceremony on the Queen's official birthday,

Elizabeth II watches the RAF fly-past over Buckingham Palace, standing with her family on the Royal Balcony whose design and construction was inspired by Albert.

The progressive movements in British industry and science had good cause to mourn the loss of a friend, as well as one of their most ardent and influential supporters. Albert's interest in progress was not motivated by a material fascination with gadgetry and inventions – the telegraph, steam engine or power loom, for instance – emerging from the workshops of the Industrial Revolution. His concern was how these whirring, thudding and hissing contraptions could be employed to improve mankind's condition, specifically that of the downtrodden. Sir Arthur Helps, Clerk of the Privy Council and a close friend of Albert, as well as an associate in the struggle to abolish slavery, once said,

> If any man in England cared for the working classes, it was the Prince. He understood the great difficulty of the time as regards these classes, namely the providing for them of fitting habitations. He was a beneficent landlord and his first care was to build good cottages for all the labouring men on his estates.[33]

Albert went so far as to calculate in minute detail what he considered the amount of illness that could be prevented by ensuring the poor had proper dwellings constructed of weatherproof materials.

Albert had a perennial love affair with art, for personal pleasure but also as a means of education. His great cause was to take art to the common people, engage their interest in it and show how art can be employed to elevate and improve their lives. He believed that an appreciation and understanding of art would help soften the edges of the working classes' harsh existence. 'To restore the pride of the workman in the product of his hands and to strip toil of half its irksomeness by emancipating it from the monotony of mechanical work, was one of his cherished aims.'[34] Exposing the less fortunate members of society to museum collections would enable them to know what art as well as science had achieved. Once their interest and curiosity had been aroused, he reasoned, they would seek further knowledge elsewhere, and perhaps come to value the subtleness and beauty of the machines that dominated their working days.

Albert held that the arrangement of museums of art and science should be such as to afford the means of methodical study. He applied this principle to the national art collections, with results for which students of art must always be grateful. The Prince was instrumental in having his friend Sir Charles Eastlake appointed the National Gallery's first director in 1855. Around that time Albert drew up a plan for a national collection of paintings which he felt should be illustrative of the history of art, and which would be arranged so as to afford 'the best means of instruction and education in art to those who wish to study it scientifically in its history and progress'.[35] This has been adopted as the fundamental criterion in the National Gallery's acquisition and arrangement of pictures, and was enshrined in government policy even in Albert's day. The Parliamentary Commission of 1857 stated, 'The existence of the pictures is not the end purpose of this collection, but the means only to give the people an ennobling enjoyment.'[36] Albert was likewise responsible for having the Crown Surveyor of Pictures facilitate people's understanding of the works at Hampton Court, by the obvious but overlooked procedure of displaying a legible label next to every work of art.

Thus the study of art in public galleries was simplified thanks to Albert's direct, or in some cases indirect, intercession. This was acknowledged by George Scharf, the first director of the National Portrait Gallery, when Albert encouraged systematising the arrangement of great works on public display. For Scharf, these changes are the result of 'a thoroughly matured scheme laid down by the late Prince Consort and it may indeed be said that all the good now performed in respect to our national collections of art, is a realisation of his wise and beneficent intentions'.[37]

The idea that artistic works should be set forth in a systematic fashion for the education of the masses was characteristic of Albert's orderly, Germanic mind. It was a recurrent feature of his approach to all manifestations of art. In a speech he gave at the opening of the Manchester Exhibition of Art Treasures in 1857, an event which attracted more than 1.3 million visitors, the Prince praised the organisers for not having aimed at a mere accumulation of works of art and objects of general interest, 'but to give your collection, by a scientific and historical arrangement, an educational character – thus not losing the opportunity of teaching the mind, as well as gratifying the senses'.[38] Hardly any aspect of society was left untouched by this remarkable man, the Prince, whose sole ambition throughout his brief life was the betterment of the condition of his wife's subjects.

Circumspice – look about you. Look at what Albert achieved, always as a guiding spirit, taking care never to step outside his boundaries as consort to the sovereign, eschewing the role of protagonist, selflessly asking nothing in return. Albert was the British monarchy's great moderniser. While men like Peel, Russell and Palmerston bickered and squabbled to all hours in the House, the Prince calmly understood that as a unifying force, indeed for it to survive, the monarchy needed to accept political evolution and develop in tandem with the growing power of Parliament. Albert made these views known only in private, quite frequently in letters to Stockmar and to his brother Ernest, and sometimes with a tinge of irony. 'The English Government is a popular one and the constitution is becoming more and more democratic…Since 1830,[39] democracy has been getting the upper hand in England.'[40]

Albert came on the scene at a time when the monarchy was, in the opinion of British society at large, at a very low ebb. Victoria's predecessors, the wenching, sybaritic George IV and his younger brother, the extravagant William IV, known for his habit of spitting in public, had justifiably attracted the wrath of the press and the public at large. The Prince succeeded in 're-inventing' the monarchy by establishing in his wife's reign the image of guardian and benefactor of the people's welfare. Albert created the template for royal benevolence, as well as unimpeachable decency, that has been adhered to by Victoria's successors.

Lord Clarendon, who in 1857 served as Foreign Secretary in the Palmerston ministry, could scarcely contain his praise for the wisdom with which the Prince guided the monarchy. Clarendon's views were shared, openly or in confidence, by a sufficient number of people in government to confer upon Albert a stature comparable to that which had been held by Wellington, as the ultimate arbiter of matters of state.

> She [Victoria] acts in everything by his inspiration and never writes a letter that he does not dictate every word of. His knowledge and information are astonishing, and there is not a department of the Government regarding all the details and management of which he is not much better informed and more

capable than the Minister at the head of it. That in foreign affairs particularly he has prevented a great deal of mischief and kept the Government out of innumerable scrapes.[41]

Along with the modern concept of the art museum and his endeavours to bring art and science into the products of industry, the greatest gift to the nation of this 'most kind, eccentric, infallible and unfathomable German',[42] was to make of Victoria an admirable and successful monarch. We see in the young Victoria an egotistical, hot-tempered and somewhat bewildered woman, transformed by this remarkable partnership into the Queen-Empress who dispatched at ease with titans like Disraeli and Gladstone, endearing herself to the one and, when necessary, unflinchingly putting the other in his place. Victoria's popularity was secure after Albert's death, for in her deep mourning people came to appreciate his virtues, which became hers, and the value of having a permanent figure at the head of state to remind them that history did not begin yesterday. It was, moreover, these values that transcended Victoria's reign and enabled her successors to rule with the consent of their subjects. It is worth noting that no serious anti-monarchist movement has ever taken hold in Britain.

Bertie the irremediable socialite continued to slip on a frilly banana skin here and there, but despite these failings, after becoming Edward VII he achieved great popularity as a liberal, well-intentioned ruler. His son George V was lauded for the tenacious work he carried out for his country during the First World War. As King, George ushered in a redesign of the monarchy's social role, to be more inclusive of the working class and its representatives, adopting a more democratic stance that crossed class lines and brought the monarchy closer to the public. In his shortlived reign, Edward VIII could count on considerable sympathy from his subjects, which perhaps reflects a certain public soft spot for a man who would give up his crown for love. The Wallis Simpson episode aside, as King he showed a genuine concern for the social problems of post-war Britain. In spite of the constitutional crisis brought on in the British Empire and Government opposition to Edward's marriage to the twice-divorced American socialite, an outraged MP's proposed amendment that the monarchy should be done away with altogether was massively defeated in Parliament. If nothing else, the dapper Edward conformed admirably to Albert's standards of good taste in dress. Edward's younger brother George VI took an active interest in welfare projects and industrial conditions. As Duke of York, before acceding to the throne, he set up camps aimed at bringing together the different social classes for outdoor activities. During the Second World War, George's popularity was enhanced by staying in London despite the Blitz, and he worked tirelessly and bravely throughout those years. His wife, the late Queen Mother, greatly endeared herself to the public by saying she was glad Buckingham Palace had been bombed, for now she 'could look the East End in the face'.[43]

The reign of Elizabeth II, Victoria's great-great granddaughter, has seen its share of Bertie-esque episodes, well known to every adult in Great Britain and indeed to newspaper readers and television viewers across the world. Never before has the monarchy been so intensively under the spotlight. The prying skills of the media have reached prodigious levels, yet ferret as they may there has never been a hint of scandal or impropriety involving the person of the Queen. This is not due to any 'gentleman's agreement' between the press and Government to treat the monarch as sacrosanct, while enjoying a free hand with her offspring. The media do not accept those strictures.[44] It is an acknowledged fact that service and duty to the nation are built into every day of the Queen's life. In 2010, Elizabeth and her Prince Consort, the Duke of Edinburgh, both well into their eighties, undertook between them eight hundred official engagements, be these opening ceremonies, meetings, official visits or overseas tours. This in itself belies any notion of royal frivolity or indifference towards the country. Except for Christmas Day and Easter Day each year, the Queen has never had a day off from the official red boxes that pursue her everywhere.

Lytton Strachey maintains that had Albert been granted another thirty years of life 'the whole development of the English polity would have been changed'. He asserts that the Prince's influence would have enormously increased in this time, since he enjoyed the advantage of being perpetually installed at the centre of affairs, unlike politicians of his day, who treated the door of 10 Downing Street as a revolving one. 'If in his youth, he [Albert] had been able to pit the Crown against the mighty Palmerston and come off with equal honours from the contest, of what might he not have been capable in his old age?'[45] The 'what if' school of history is unsatisfactory because of its blindness to reality and its tendency to trivialise what has been. What is past is done, and the legacy that Albert left to the nation after two decades as Prince Consort is truly monumental in terms of its historical consequences. His patriotism, honesty and benevolence established the criteria that were to be followed by his wife and, to a suitable extent, the Queen's heirs. Albert can rest in peace, content at having created the modern British monarchy and endowed it with a lasting prestige.

Postscript

On 22 January 1901, a crowd of reporters stood outside the gates of Osborne House, huddled against the cold Channel wind, waiting for the final medical bulletin announcing the death of Queen Victoria. By the start of the year it had become clear that her health was deteriorating. She was 82, suffering the ravages of old age, including failing eyesight which required Princess Beatrice to be called in to read documents to her. Victoria was aware that her end was approaching, and often in those final days she would speak with a faint smile on her lips of her coming reunion with Albert. Her last diary entries showed that she had lost the will to live, a state of despondency made greater by the loss of three of her adult children.

Messages of concern flooded the telegraph room at Buckingham Palace, from South Africa, Hong Kong, Australia, New Zealand, Canada and every corner of the Empire. Even *The Times* correspondent in New York reported that 'God save the Queen is heard from American lips not less devoutly than from British.'[1] Victoria had been on the throne for nearly 64 years, Britain's longest-reigning monarch. The Queen came to love her subjects, and when at her last great public appearance, the Diamond Jubilee of 1897, she received the cheers of the multitude that turned out for the occasion, she could not hold back the tears that welled in her eyes. 'How kind they are to me! How kind they are!' she repeated.[2]

The week before her death, Victoria had been out for a carriage ride with another widow, the Duchess of Saxe-Coburg and Gotha. Both women had lived through the dawn of a new era in their respective countries. Germany was a unified nation, as Albert had dreamt it would one day become. Victoria could look with justifiable pride at a reinvigorated and popular British monarchy. Albert had been so right, she always reflected, in insisting that the Crown must remain always neutral. The people must wake up in the morning knowing that a nation's life did not begin with the last general election, that there exists a supreme arbiter above party politics, and that the sovereign genuinely cares for their welfare. As the Duke of Wellington was inclined to say, 'It is the better way.'

Victoria died at half past six that January evening, surrounded by her children and grandchildren. Her physicians reported that the Queen had slipped away peacefully, without a struggle, as well she might, in the knowledge that she had left her country and her subjects, the vast majority of whom had never known another monarch, in a state of prosperity and glory as had never been known before.

The power behind the power behind the throne, Baron Christian Friedrich Stockmar, had died in his native Coburg in July 1863, at age 76. His health had been in steady decline for some time, and in 1856, the year of his daughter's death, Stockmar made what he foresaw would be his last trip to London. The year before he passed away, Queen Victoria had paid a visit to Coburg, where together they looked over old photographs of Albert. Stockmar burst into tears and exclaimed, 'My dear, my good Prince, how I should dearly love to see you again. It will be soon.'[3] In the decades that he served the British Crown, Stockmar moulded Albert to his own image, and through the Prince, and in his personal dealings with the Queen, his high moral values had a profound influence on Victoria's character. Stockmar won over the great politicians of the day, Melbourne and Peel, to his views on social and political policy. It was largely through Stockmar's persuasion that Albert and Victoria saw to it that their children never forgot their Germanic heritage and were brought up speaking both languages, and it was the Prince himself who decided that German was to be his *lingua franca* with the Queen. One is at a loss to find a monument in Coburg to one of its most illustrious citizens, apart from a plaque over the door of his house in the centre of town, itself an unremarkable three-storey, stone-fronted affair, reflecting the life of a modest man who with much discretion wielded great power in Europe.

Stockmar was not alone, as we have seen, in exerting moral and political authority over Albert and, to an even greater extent, Victoria. The handsome and debonair Leopold I, King of the Belgians, was, with the doctor from Coburg, instrumental in arranging Albert's marriage to Victoria. Even before she succeeded to the throne, Leopold had been advising Princess Victoria by letter, and after her accession, he was one of the great figures of authority in the early days of her reign. It was natural for affairs concerning the British Crown to dominate Leopold's life, for through his marriage to Princess Charlotte of Wales, the only legitimate child of George IV and therefore heiress to the throne, he had been destined to assume the title of Prince Consort which devolved to Albert. Charlotte's untimely death a year after the marriage deprived Leopold of that role, and he spent nearly the next half century dispensing avuncular guidance to his niece and nephew. From the time of her girlhood, Victoria depended greatly on Leopold's counsel. At 18, she wrote seeking his views on the dynastic struggle taking place in Spain, and with adolescent charm enquired, 'Pray, dear Uncle, may I ask you a silly question – is not the Queen of Spain rather clever?'[4] Nearly twenty-five years later, within days of Albert's death, Victoria was still reliant on her uncle, for he must come to England 'to tell people what they ought to do' in this hour of unbearable affliction.[5]

In 1829, Leopold married Stockmar's cousin, the actress Caroline Bauer, in nuptials of doubtful validity. The union was dissolved two years later, and within months Leopold took as his recognised second wife Princess Louise-Marie of France. The King of the Belgians' personal life continued to be marred by tragedy: Louise-Marie died of tuberculosis at age 38, leaving him with two sons and a daughter, the future Empress of Mexico, Charlotte, named after his first wife. The death of Leopold in 1865, at 74, following the passing of Stockmar and the Prince, all within a four-year period, meant that the position of family mentor and counsellor fell to Victoria.

Poor Johan Christoph Florschütz, so overshadowed in Albert's upbringing and later life by the colossal figures of his fellow Coburgers Stockmar and Leopold. Albert's official biographer writes off the Prince's tutor in a few lines, with a mention of the two brothers having received from him instruction in the humanities. Even Victoria's commissioned work on Albert's early life contains barely a specific mention of the Prince's tutor. The Queen never forgot Florschütz, however, and she felt for his sadness after Albert's death. She wrote, 'You saw this great soul in its development and you may be proud of having educated him!'[6] Albert never lost touch with his old tutor, the retiring young man who had inspired in the Prince a thirst for humanist knowledge and a reverence for liberal thought. On his last visit to Coburg a year before his death, Albert stopped in to visit Florschütz, at the house which the Prince and his brother Ernest had built for him and his family. Florschütz lived out his days in obscure retirement in Coburg, where he died in 1882 at the grand old age of 88, surrounded by his books and loving wife Therese.

Vicky, the Princess Royal, became a prevailing figure in her own right, as semi-official family scout for suitable spouses for her siblings and ultimately, when her husband Frederick III ascended the throne, as Her Imperial and Royal Majesty the German Empress. It was fortunate for Queen Victoria that she did not live to have to endure the heartbreak of losing another child. Vicky, who herself had to cope with the death of two young sons, was diagnosed with breast cancer in 1899, and followed her mother to the grave seven months after Victoria's death. In common with the Queen, Vicky spent most of her middle age in mourning. Her happy marriage was cut short in 1888 when the Emperor died of throat cancer, after ruling only 99 days. She and the Queen would spend long hours together, solemnly gazing at photos of their departed husbands.

Before and after Albert's death, Vicky regarded her father with boundless admiration, the guiding light of her life. Albert passed on to her a devotion to art, literature and European history, and she, in turn, never failed to coax a cheerful smile from her father on those days when he found himself weighed down under official drudgery. The years of separation after

Vicky's marriage to the Prussian prince were almost too much for father and daughter to bear.

Much has already been said about Bertie, whose volatile, troublesome disposition once motivated Stockmar to sound the alarm, warning that the family might be in for a replay of the madness of George III, the Prince of Wales's great-grandfather. Other somewhat less insightful appraisals took the view that bumps in Bertie's skull betrayed tendencies towards aggression, egotism and other alarming character flaws. Albert Edward ascended the throne in 1901 as Edward VII, the first British monarch of the House of Saxe-Coburg and Gotha, renamed House of Windsor by his son, George V. Bertie confounded all the quackery, showing himself to be a benign and enlightened monarch, in many respects ahead of his time − his proposed reform of the House of Lords, as well as his endeavours to bring Britain closer to continental European affairs than any monarch had previously attempted, serve as examples. The King's habit of alternating between cigars and cigarettes throughout his waking hours brought on an attack of bronchitis, followed by several heart attacks in one day, which he did his utmost to ignore, insisting to his aides that he was determined to carry on working to the end. This came on the following day, 6 May 1910, at age 59, ending a reign of only nine years. Upwards of a quarter of a million people filed through London's Westminster Hall, where the King's body lay in state.

The remainder of the royal brood that came along between 1843 and 1857 never reached so exalted an echelon as Empress of Germany or King of Great Britain. But Albert and Victoria looked after their children's upbringing judiciously, instilling in each of them an awareness of a higher calling and a sense of duty to their country. It is to their parents' credit that none of the royal children was ever tainted by political scandal, and all made their contribution to public life, at home and abroad.

Alice was one of the more heartbreaking cases: at 19, her hopes were pinned to a happy marriage with Prince Louis of Hesse, a union that she anticipated would rescue her from the oppressive life at Court, as informal secretary to her despondent mother, permanently attired in black. Once she achieved her liberation, Alice devoted herself with passion to women's causes, becoming a follower of Florence Nightingale, whom Albert and the Queen had received in 1856 at Balmoral. Alice nursed the wounded in field hospitals during the Austro–Prussian War, and when an outbreak of diphtheria swept through Hesse in 1878, she was struck down with the disease and died at the age of 35.

To Alice's younger brother Alfred went the title Duke of Saxe-Coburg and Gotha in 1893, as Albert's brother Ernest had died without issue. Alfred's marriage to the Grand Duchess Maria Alexandrovna brought about a union with the Russian royal family (an occasion that inspired the London bakery Peek Freans to produce the popular Marie biscuit), and during his comparatively short lifetime Alfred Duke of Edinburgh served with distinction and great skill as a naval officer, rising to become Admiral of the Fleet. With Alfred, Victoria was to see another of her children into the grave in 1900, one year before her own death, when he succumbed to throat cancer at the Rosenau.

Princess Helena Augusta came along two years after Alfred, and, like her older siblings, she had to put up with a cheerless family atmosphere cloaked in perpetual mourning. Lenchen, as she was dubbed, kept her counsel, always patient and helpful in the household. Despite misgivings about her plainness, Lenchen managed to attract the attentions of a minor German prince, Christian of Schleswig-Holstein, whom she married and lived with in Britain. She remained close to her mother, while at the same time leading an active life as charity patron, and was one of the founding members of the Red Cross, though she came into conflict with Florence Nightingale as a supporter of nurse registration. Lenchen had the qualities of a loner, and kept little contact with the rest of her family. She was widowed a year after her fiftieth wedding anniversary, and died in London at the age of 77.

The next child was another daughter, Princess Louise, born in the turbulent year of 1848. She was destined to witness her country go through some of the most terrible bloodlettings of its modern history, from the Anglo-Boer War to both world wars. This is perhaps what deepened Louise's reclusive character − she preferred to devote herself to sculpture and art, though she made a foray into the early age of the feminist movement, maintaining a correspondence with some of the leading women activists of her day. Louise and her younger brother Arthur uncannily lived to exactly the same age, 91 years, eight months and 15 days.

Prince Arthur was two years Louise's junior, but, unlike his sister, his was a thoroughly outgoing temperament. His whole childhood was a preparation for the life of a soldier, and after attending the Royal Military College at Woolwich he served as Governor General of Canada and then spent the next forty years in the British army. He reinforced the family's German ties by marrying Princess Louise Margaret of Prussia, a grand-niece of the German Emperor, Arthur's godfather William I. Arthur saw active service throughout the Empire, though to his deep disappointment he was refused permission to fight in the

Anglo-Boer War. Arthur began to wind down his public life before the outbreak of the Second World War, and he died in 1942 at Bagshot Park, near Windsor.

Prince Leopold's life story was one of the most painful of any of Albert and Victoria's children. In a more primitive age of medicine, Leopold hardly stood a chance after being diagnosed with haemophilia as a baby. Victoria tried to shelter him under her wing, but young Leopold was having no part of it: he was determined to put a brave face on his illness, and try to lead as normal a life as possible in the years allotted to him. He sought a wife, and it is said that one of the candidates was Alice Liddell, for whom Lewis Carroll wrote *Alice's Adventures in Wonderland*. Victoria was not prepared to see her son married to an academic's daughter. The Queen stepped in to arrange a marriage with Princess Helene Friederike, which took place in 1882, two years before Leopold's death. Yet he lived long enough to see the birth of his daughter, tellingly named Alice, though he never got to know his son, Charles Edward, whom Helene was carrying when Leopold died at the age of 31.

Beatrice was the last of Albert and Victoria's issue. Born in 1857, four years before her father's death, she was also the last of the royal children to die. Beatrice was bright, healthy and attractive, but her early years became a struggle to secure her mother's permission to find a husband and embark on a life of her own. Finally in 1885, when she had reached the perilously advanced age of 28, the Queen relented and gave her blessing to a betrothal to the Hessian Prince Henry of Battenberg. There were strings attached to the marriage: Victoria insisted that the couple make their home at Court, where Beatrice was to serve as the Queen's unofficial secretary. Prince Henry died early of malaria, fighting in the Anglo-Ashanti War in what is now Ghana. Her loss drew Beatrice closer to her mother's side, where she remained until the Queen's death. Those wishing to study Queen Victoria's reign owe a great debt of gratitude to Beatrice, the great-grandmother of King Juan Carlos of Spain, who spent thirty years of her life editing her mother's journals.

Notes

Introduction

1   Kurt Jagow (ed.), *Letters of the Prince Consort*, John Murray, London, 1938, p. 141.

2   Theodore Martin, *The Life of HRH the Prince Consort* (People's Edition), Smith, Elder & Co., London, 1882, vol. II, p. 11.

Chapter 1

1   Quoted in Marshall-Cavendish Collection, *Royal Romances*, London, 1990, p. 5.

2   Quoted in Stanley Weintraub, *Albert, Uncrowned King*, John Murray, London, 1997, p. 28.

3   Quoted in Charles Grey, *The Early Years of the Prince Consort*, Smith, Elder & Co., London, 1867, p. 16.

4   Theodore Martin, *The Life of HRH the Prince Consort* (People's Edition), Smith, Elder & Co., London, 1882, vol. I, p. 1.

5   Grey, *The Early Years of the Prince Consort*, p. 19.

6   Robert Rhodes James, *Albert Prince Consort*, Hamish Hamilton, London, 1983, p. 24.

7   Ibid., pp. 32–33.

8   Grey, *The Early Years of the Prince Consort*, p. 56.

9   Ibid., p. 32.

10   Ibid., p. 29.

11   Florschütz letter to Victoria, 16 March 1863, quoted in Grey, *The Early Years of the Prince Consort*, p. 56.

12   Florschütz quoted in Grey, *The Early Years of the Prince Consort*, p. 96.

13   Martin, *The Life of HRH the Prince Consort*, vol. I, p. 2.

14   Grey, *The Early Years of the Prince Consort*, p. 124.

15   Martin, *The Life of HRH the Prince Consort*, vol. I, p. 3.

16   Grey, *The Early Years of the Prince Consort*, p. 213.

17   Max Müller (ed.), *Memoirs of Baron Stockmar*, Longman, London, 1871, vol. I, p. xli.

18   Lord Palmerston, never overly generous with his praise, said, 'I have come in my life across only one absolutely disinterested man – Stockmar.' Quoted in Martin, *The Life of HRH the Prince Consort*, vol. I, p. 3

19   Martin, *The Life of HRH the Prince Consort*, vol. I, p. 3.

20   Müller (ed.), *Memoirs of Baron Stockmar*, vol. II, p. 6.

21   Grey, *The Early Years of the Prince Consort*, p. 206.

22   Staatsarchiv Coburg, Letters to Ernest II, LAA 6969, 31 March 1839.

23   Kurt Jagow (ed.), *Letters of the Prince Consort*, John Murray, London, 1938, p. 14.

24   Martin, *The Life of HRH the Prince Consort*, vol. I, p. 4.

25   Ibid.

26   The Prince of Orange accused Leopold of having stolen his wife as well as his kingdom, for he had wished to marry Princess Charlotte, and the Kingdom of Belgium had been carved out of the Netherlands.

27   William was outraged to learn that the Duchess had taken a suite of 17 rooms at Kensington Palace. He used the occasion of a banquet held to celebrate his birthday to launch into a violent tirade against her in the presence of more than a hundred guests, shouting at the top of his voice that she was 'incompetent to act with propriety'. Edith Sitwell, *Victoria of England*, Faber & Faber, London, 1936, p. 64.

28   Victoria grew to hate Conroy over the oppressive system he and her mother tried to impose, and immediately expelled him from Court life when she became Queen. The Court was rife with rumours of Conroy being the Duchess's lover, but this was wholly unsubstantiated gossip.

29   Weintraub, *Albert, Uncrowned King*, p. 58.

30   Arthur Benson (ed.), *Letters of Queen Victoria*, John Murray, London, 1908, vol. I, p. 48.

31   The dog died four and a half years after Albert's marriage and was buried at Windsor, where a bronze model of her now marks the spot.

32   Jagow (ed.), *Letters of the Prince Consort*, p. 130.

33   Benson (ed.), *Letters of Queen Victoria*, vol. I, p. 46.

34   Ibid., p. 48.

35   Ibid., p. 49.

36   Quoted in Sitwell, *Victoria of England*, p. 59.

37   Benson (ed.), *Letters of Queen Victoria*, vol. I, p. 49.

38   Staatsarchiv Coburg, Letters of Prince Albert to Florschütz, Copy 104.

39   Jagow (ed.), *Letters of the Prince Consort*, p. 13.

40   Ibid.

41   The King's German Legion was a British Army unit of expatriate German soldiers. It was the only German force to fight without interruption against the French during the Napoleonic Wars. It was formed in 1803 under the Hanoverian George III and played a vital role in several campaigns, including the Peninsular War. The Legion was disbanded in 1816.

42   Sir Arthur Helps (ed.), *The Principal Speeches and Addresses of HRH the Prince Consort*, John Murray, London, 1862, p. 252.

43   Martin, *The Life of HRH the Prince Consort*, vol. I, p. 4.

44   Jagow (ed.), *Letters of the Prince Consort*, p. 14.

45   Marshall-Cavendish Collection, *Royal Romances*, p. 10.

46   Ibid., pp. 14–15.

47   Grey, *The Early Years of the Prince Consort*, p. 158.

48   Jagow (ed.), *Letters of the Prince Consort*, p. 18.

49   Martin, *The Life of HRH the Prince Consort*, vol. I, p. 7.

50   Grey, *The Early Years of the Prince Consort*, p. 200.

51   Staatsarchiv Coburg, Letters to Ernest II, LAA 6969, 19 February 1839.

52   Ibid.

53   Daphne Bennett, *King Without a Crown*, Book Club Associates, London, 1977, p. 28.

54   *The Times*, 16 May 1839, p. 4.

55   Benson (ed.), *Letters of Queen Victoria*, vol. I, pp. 177–78

56   James, *Albert Prince Consort*, p. 81.

57   Grey, *The Early Years of the Prince Consort*, p. 224.

58   Benson (ed.), *Letters of Queen Victoria*, vol. I, p. 188.

59   Charles Greville, *The Greville Memoirs*, Longman, London, 1875, vol. II, p. 114.

60   Jagow (ed.), *Letters of the Prince Consort*, p. 23.

61   Ibid., p. 24.

62   Ibid., p. 27.

63   Ibid., p. 40.

64   Grey, *The Early Years of the Prince Consort*, p. 324.

Chapter 2

1   *The Times*, 11 February 1840, p. 4.

2   Ibid.

3   Arthur Benson (ed.), *Letters of Queen Victoria*, John Murray, London, 1908, vol. I, p. 213.

4   Robert Rhodes James, *Albert Prince Consort*, Hamish Hamilton, London, 1983, p. 101.

5   Staatsarchiv Coburg, Letters to Ernest II, LAA 6970, 20 June 1840.

6   Kurt Jagow (ed.), *Letters of the Prince Consort*, John Murray, London, 1938, p. 69.

7   Theodore Martin, *The Life of HRH the Prince Consort* (People's Edition), Smith, Elder & Co., London, 1882, vol. I, p. 14.

8   Frank Eyck, *The Prince Consort: A political biography*, Cedric Chivers Ltd, Bath, 1975, p. 21.

9   Albert encouraged Victoria to become a keen reader, along with himself, of Henry Hallam's *Constitutional History of England*.

10 Martin, *The Life of HRH the Prince Consort*, vol. I, p. 11.

11 Hector Bolitho, *The Prince Consort and His Brother*, Cobden-Sanderson, London, 1933, p. 21.

12 Daphne Bennett, *King Without a Crown*, Book Club Associates, London, 1977, p. 56.

13 Martin, *The Life of HRH the Prince Consort*, vol. I, p. 15.

14 Ibid.

15 Ibid., p. 17.

16 In Britain the Slavery Abolition Act was passed in 1833, and slavery was officially abolished in most of the British Empire on 18 August 1834, with the exception of the territories of the East India Company and the Islands of Ceylon and Saint Helena. Slavery continued to be practised in other countries, such as the United States, Cuba and Brazil, until the late nineteenth century.

17 Sir Arthur Helps (ed.), *The Principal Speeches and Addresses of HRH the Prince Consort*, John Murray, London, 1862, p. 81.

18 Jagow (ed.), *Letters of the Prince Consort*, p. 69.

19 Ibid., p. 70.

20 Ibid.

21 Quoted in Edith Sitwell, *Victoria of England*, Faber & Faber, London, 1936, p. 252.

22   Quoted in Hector Bolitho, *Albert Prince Consort*, Max Parrish, London, 1964, p. 52.

23   Lady Augusta Stanley was an exuberant, sympathetic and profoundly religious person, an eminence in royal circles who brought the outside world into an enclosed Court. For years, she occupied the place of daughter in the Duchess's affections and was also in regular contact with Victoria. After the Duchess's death, Lady Augusta entered Victoria's service as resident bedchamber woman.

24   Dean of Windsor and Hector Bolitho (eds), *Letters of Lady Augusta Stanley*, Gerald Howe, London, 1927, p. 117.

25   Eyck, *The Prince Consort*, p. 19.

26   Edith Sitwell, *Victoria of England*, p. 33.

27   Lytton Strachey, *Queen Victoria*, Chatto & Windus, London, 1921, p. 51.

28   Arthur Benson (ed.), *Letters of Queen Victoria*, vol. I, p. 122.

29   Kate Williams, *Becoming Queen*, Arrow Books, London, 2009, pp. 284–85.

30   Administered as a purgative and diuretic in Britain until 1954, when it was found to be the cause of widespread mercury poisoning.

31   Martin, *The Life of HRH the Prince Consort*, vol. I, p. 12.

32   The Lord Steward is always a peer and until 1924 was also a member of the Government. He is the first dignitary of the Court. The Lord Chamberlain is likewise a peer as well as a privy councillor, and before 1782 he was of Cabinet rank. He is the chief functionary of the Court and is generally responsible for organising all Court functions. He is considered the senior official of the royal household. The Master of the Horse is the third dignitary of the court, a peer and a privy councillor. All matters connected with the horses and formerly also the hounds of the sovereign, as well as the stables and coach houses, the stud, mews and previously the kennels, are within his jurisdiction. The Master of the Household is the operational head of the 'below stairs' elements of the royal household. He has charge of the domestic staff, from the royal kitchens, the pages and footmen, to the housekeeper and her staff.

33   Martin, *The Life of HRH the Prince Consort*, vol. I, p. 27.

34   Bolitho, *Albert Prince Consort*, p. 67.

35   Jagow (ed.), *Letters of the Prince Consort*, p. 355.

36   Malcolm Hay, Curator of Works of Art at the Houses of Parliament, in conversation with the author.

37 John Steegman, *Consort of Taste*, Sidgwick & Jackson, London, 1950, p.134.

38 William Dyce was a Scottish artist who played a significant part in the formation of public art education in Britain, as perhaps the true parent of the South Kensington Schools system.

39 The water-glass technique involves applying plaster to the entire wall and keeping the wall wet with lime water while applying the paint. Liquid silica is sprayed on top to bond with the plaster and hold the pigment in place. The technique was largely, but not entirely, successful in preserving the paintings.

40 Letter quoted in Justin O'Driscoll, *A Memoir of Daniel Maclise*, Longman, London, 1871, p.149.

41 Jagow (ed.), *Letters of the Prince Consort*, p.88.

42 Ibid., p.89.

43 Martin, *The Life of HRH the Prince Consort*, vol. V, p.82.

44 Public Record Office, JER/OSBORNE/17 1845.

45 Winslow Ames, *Prince Albert and Victorian Taste*, Viking, New York, 1968, p.61.

46 Mary Miers, 'Osborne House, Isle of Wight', *Country Life* 195/13 (2001), p.87.

47 Quoted in Martin, *The Life of HRH the Prince Consort*, vol.I, p.42.

48 Martin, *The Life of HRH the Prince Consort*, vol.I, p.25.

49 Jagow (ed.), *Letters of the Prince Consort*, p.81.

50 Ibid.

51 Ibid., p.95.

52 Arthur Helps (ed.), *Leaves From the Journal of Our Life in the Highlands*, Smith, Elder & Co., London, 1868, pp.101–2.

53 Charles Greville, *The Greville Memoirs*, Longman, London, 1875, vol.VI, p.303.

54 Ames, *Prince Albert and Victorian Taste*, p.106.

55 Ibid., p.105.

56 Helps (ed.), *Leaves From the Journal of Our Life in the Highlands*, p.149.

57 Ibid., p.158.

58 Jagow (ed.), *Letters of the Prince Consort*, p.144.

59 Michael Lynch, *Scotland: A new history*, Pimlico, London, 1992, p.146

Chapter 3

1   Theodore Martin, *The Life of HRH the Prince Consort* (People's Edition), Smith, Elder & Co., London, 1882, vol. I, p. 65.

2   Quoted in Stanley Weintraub, *Albert, Uncrowned King*, John Murray, London, 1997, p. 185.

3   Ibid., p. 66.

4   Robert Rhodes James, *Albert Prince Consort*, Hamish Hamilton, London, 1983, p. xii.

5   Teaching has existed at Oxford since 1096, and in 1204 Cambridge was founded by scholars who left Oxford after a dispute arising from the execution of two of their colleagues. Bologna ranks as the world's oldest degree-granting institution, having received its charter eight years before Oxford.

6   Peel was horrified to learn that William Whewell, Master of Trinity College, was in favour of waiting a century before a new scientific discovery should be admitted into the curriculum. He told Albert that in his view such an attitude 'exceeds in absurdity anything which the bitterest enemy of university education would have imputed to its advocates'. Martin, *The Life of HRH the Prince Consort*, vol. II, p. 20.

7   *The Times*, 9 April 1848, p. 8.

8   Lytton Strachey, *Queen Victoria*, Chatto & Windus, London, 1921, p. 153.

9   Vicky's governess was chosen by Stockmar himself. This was Sarah Anne Hildyard, nicknamed 'Tilla', the daughter of a clergyman who was 'intelligent, well-read and a stimulating teacher'. Vicky and her brother Bertie were placed under the 'supervision and authority of one person for the development of character'. Quoted in Hannah Pakula, *An Uncommon Woman*, Orion, London, 1997, p. 42.

10   Martin, *The Life of HRH the Prince Consort*, vol. I, p. 17.

11   Ibid., p. 33.

12   Sir Arthur Helps (ed.), *The Principal Speeches and Addresses of HRH the Prince Consort*, John Murray, London, 1862, p. 126.

13   Kurt Jagow (ed.), *Letters of the Prince Consort*, John Murray, London, 1938, p. 124.

14   Ibid., p. 125.

15   Ibid., p. 126.

16   The six principles were universal suffrage for men (excluding women), the ballot, equal electoral districts, abolition of property qualifications for MPs, payment for MPs and annual parliaments.

17   In the early years of Chartist disturbances the Prime Minister, Arthur Wellesley, an opponent of parliamentary reform, had iron shutters fixed to the windows of his house in Hyde Park Corner to stop the pro-reform mob breaking in, and was given the epithet the Iron Duke.

18   Jagow (ed.), *Letters of the Prince Consort*, p. 135.

19   *The Times*, 22 March 1848, p. 5.

20   Ibid.

21   Other societies engaged in providing affordable working-class housing, included the Metropolitan Association for Improving the Dwellings of the Industrious Classes, the East End Dwelling Company and the celebrated Peabody Trust, founded in 1862 with an unprecedented £150,000 donation from the American banker and Puritan bachelor George Peabody. The latter resembled a quasi-monastic institution, with a night-time curfew, a set of rigid moral standards and strict restrictions on trades that could be carried out at the dwellings.

22   Jagow (ed.), *Letters of the Prince Consort*, p. 88.

23   Ibid., p. 89.

24   Britain's state pension was introduced in 1908 by David Lloyd George, who was Chancellor of the Exchequer at the time. Before that, the task of relieving the plight of the poor and the defenceless was entirely in the hands of private philanthropy. Numerous organisations were working towards this end, from the British Beneficent Institution, which advertised itself in urgent need of funds to support 38 aged ladies receiving annuities from the society, and the Model Soup Kitchen, which in one month distributed 1722 gallons of soup and 8724 loaves of bread to 14,824 destitute individuals, to the Royal Agricultural Benevolent College for the Relief of Decayed Farmers, Their Widows and Orphans.

25   Quoted in Edith Kenyon, *Albert the Good*, W. Nicholson and Sons, London, 1887, pp. 212–13.

26   Martin, *The Life of HRH the Prince Consort*, vol. II, p. 38.

27   Hector Bolitho, *The Prince Consort and His Brother*, Cobden-Sanderson, London, 1933, p. 109.

28   Ian Bradley, *God Save the Queen*, Darton, Longman & Todd, London, 2002, p. 121.

29   Martin, *The Life of HRH the Prince Consort*, vol. II, p. 31.

30 The permanent presidency of the German Confederation was in the hands of Austria, which, along with its ally Russia, feared the creation of a German state and did all in its power to thwart its establishment.

31 Jagow (ed.), *Letters of the Prince Consort*, p. 101.

Chapter 4

1 The Lord President of the Council is the fourth of the great officers of state, ranking beneath the Lord High Treasurer and above the Lord Privy Seal. The Lord President usually attends each meeting of the Privy Council, presenting business for the monarch's approval. Today, the holder is by convention always a member of one of the Houses of Parliament and the office is a Cabinet post.

2 Charles Greville, *The Greville Memoirs*, Longman, London, 1875, vol. V, p. 330.

3 Lytton Strachey, *Queen Victoria*, Chatto & Windus, London, 1921, p. 114.

4 Ibid., p. 117.

5 Archives of the Royal Commission 1851, H/1, vol. II, p. 81.

6 Ibid., vol. I, p. 15.

7 Robert Rhodes James, *Albert Prince Consort*, Hamish Hamilton, London, 1983, p. 201.

8 Sir Arthur Helps (ed.), *The Principal Speeches and Addresses of HRH the Prince Consort*, John Murray, London, 1862, p. 108.

9 Ibid., pp. 110–12.

10 *The Times*, 26 January 1850.

11 While there is no statutory barrier to a peer being prime minister, it has been an accepted constitutional convention ever since the Parliament Act in 1911 established the supremacy of the House of Commons. The last member of the House of Lords to serve as Prime Minister was Lord Salisbury in 1902.

12 James, *Albert Prince Consort*, p. 196.

13 *The Times*, 6 February 1850.

14 Ibid., 15 March 1850.

15 Archives of the Royal Commission 1851, H/1, vol. III, p. 70.

16 Ibid., H/1, vol. II, p. 43.

17 For an authoritative and detailed account of Paxton's life, see Kate Colquhoun, *A Thing in Disguise: the Visionary Life of Joseph Paxton*, Fourth Estate, London, 2004.

18 *The Times*, 20 March 1850.

19 Sibthorp was not the only member of the House to vote for a cut in the Prince's allowance, and in fact the £30,000 he favoured was more generous than the £17,000 that had been proposed by the Radical MP Charles Hume. The sum of £50,000 had by tradition been granted to the consorts of George II and William IV, and in the more closely analogous case of Prince Leopold, on his marriage to Princess Charlotte. The British economy was in crisis in 1850, making it far from likely that the proposal for a £50,000 allowance should pass unchallenged.

20 *The Times*, 2 December 1850.

21 Ibid., 17 April 1851.

22 Kurt Jagow (ed.), *Letters of the Prince Consort*, John Murray, London, 1938, p. 176.

23 Ibid., pp. 162–63.

24 Ibid., p. 162.

25 Arthur Benson (ed.), *Letters of Queen Victoria*, John Murray, London, 1908, vol. II, p. 255.

26 Ibid., p. 256.

27 Theodore Martin, *The Life of HRH the Prince Consort* (People's Edition), Smith, Elder & Co., London, 1882, vol. II, p. 50.

28 *The Times*, 5 July 1850.

29 Stanley Weintraub, *Albert, Uncrowned King*, John Murray, London, 1997, p. 240.

30 Martin, *The Life of HRH the Prince Consort*, vol. II, p. 41.

31 Ibid.

32 Ibid., vol. II, p. 48.

33 Benson (ed.), *Letters of Queen Victoria*, vol. II, p. 253.

35 Martin, *The Life of HRH the Prince Consort*, vol. II, p. 44.

36 Kenneth Morgan, *The Oxford History of Britain*, OUP, London, 1988, p. 251.

37 James, *Albert Prince Consort*, p. 212.

38 Royal Archives C 17/55.

39 James, *Albert Prince Consort*, p. 210.

40 Schleswig-Holstein had been claimed by Germany as an integral part of its territory, and a war between Denmark and Germany was in progress. Palmerston was said to be one of only three people in Europe who understood the complexities of this dispute.

41 James, *Albert Prince Consort*, p. 211.

42   Benson (ed.), *Letters of Queen Victoria*, vol. II, p. 235.

43   Public Record Office, PRO 30/22/9J, 17 December 1851, p. 127.

44   *Dictionary of National Biography*, Smith, Elder & Co., London, 1898, vol. LVI, pp. 26.

45   In 1850, in response to the Catholic-emancipation legislation that had been in force since 1829, Pope Pius IX set up a Roman Catholic hierarchy of bishops in Britain. This was met with widespread hostility, and many characterised it as an act of 'papal aggression'. The Ecclesiastical Titles Act 1851 was passed in response, making it a criminal offence for anyone outside the Church of England to use a territorial episcopal title, and providing that any property passed to a person under such a title would be forfeit to the Crown.

46   William Makepeace Thackeray, *May Day Ode*, published in *The Times*, 1 May 1851.

47   *The Times*, 1 April 1851.

48   *Bombay Times*, 14 February 1851.

49   *The Times*, 27 September 1851.

50   *Apalachicola Advertiser*, 6 September 1851.

51   Jagow (ed.), *Letters of the Prince Consort*, pp. 175–76.

52   *The Times*, 2 May 1851.

53   Benson (ed.), *Letters of Queen Victoria*, vol. II, p. 318.

54   It was decided to conduct the salute from the north side of the Serpentine, for fear that the peal of the cannons might cause the Crystal Palace to shatter.

55   John Steegman, *Consort of Taste*, Sidgwick & Jackson, London, 1950, p. 230.

56   Martin, *The Life of HRH the Prince Consort*, vol. II, p. 67.

Chapter 5

1   Charles Greville was appointed to a clerkship-in-ordinary to the Privy Council, an appointment that gave him an unrivalled opportunity to enter the most influential political circles of the day and, in the course of a long career, to enjoy the confidence of leading figures like Wellington, Melbourne, Palmerston and Peel. The eight volumes of his diaries comprise an extremely important source for the history of British politics from the Regency to the Crimean War, as well as a social document of wide range and the most acute observation. In his first meeting with Albert in 1839,

Greville pronounced the Prince 'handsome without much expression, rather a slouching air and though tall, clumsily made'. Charles Greville, *The Greville Memoirs*, Longman, London, 1875, vol. II, p. 114.

2   Greville, *The Greville Memoirs*, vol. V, p. 330.

3   Ibid., vol. VI, p. 413.

4   International exhibitions of this sort were much in vogue in nineteenth-century Europe, but they were not always a success story. A notable example of failure was the Barcelona Universal Exhibition of 1888, which was open three months longer than London and attracted one-third the number of visitors. It took the Barcelona City Council years to pay off the debts the Exhibition incurred.

5   Theodore Martin, *The Life of HRH the Prince Consort* (People's Edition), Smith, Elder & Co., London, 1882, vol. II, p. 96.

6   John Steegman, *Consort of Taste*, Sidgwick & Jackson, London, 1950, p. 320.

7   Sir Arthur Helps (ed.), *The Principal Speeches and Addresses of HRH the Prince Consort*, John Murray, London, pp. 110–11.

8   Ibid., p. 112.

9   Francis Sheppard, *Survey of London: South Kensington Museums Area*, 1975, vol. 38, p. 1.

10   Ibid., p. 2.

11   Martin, *The Life of HRH the Prince Consort*, vol. II, p. 90.

12   Hermione Hobhouse, *Prince Albert: His Life and Work*, Hamish Hamilton, London, 1983, p. 110.

13   John Physick, *The Victoria and Albert Museum: The history of its building*, Phaidon, London, 1982, p. 35.

14   Roger Williams, *The Royal Albert Hall*, Fitzhardinge Press, London, 2003, p. 10.

15   *40th Report of the Department of Science and Art*, London, 1893, p. xxxiii.

16   Martin, *The Life of HRH the Prince Consort*, vol. II, p. 39.

17   Ibid, p. 78.

18   Ibid.

19   The Battle of Sinope, which brought Britain and France into the conflict, is generally taken to be the last major naval engagement during the age of sail.

20   Greville, *The Greville Memoirs*, vol. VII, p. 128.

21   Lytton Strachey, *Queen Victoria*, Chatto & Windus, London, 1921, p. 144.

22   To Fitzroy Somerset, later Lord Raglan, goes the distinction of having ordered the disastrous charge of the Light Brigade at Balaclava.

23   Hector Bolitho, *The Prince Consort and His Brother*, Cobden-Sanderson, London, 1933, p.141.

24   Kurt Jagow (ed.), *Letters of the Prince Consort*, John Murray, London, 1938, p.203.

25   Martin, *The Life of HRH the Prince Consort*, vol.II, p.91.

26   Quoted in Daphne Bennett, *King Without a Crown*, Book Club Associates, London, 1977, p.252.

27   Ibid., vol.II, p.95.

28   Jagow (ed.), *Letters of the Prince Consort*, pp.205–6.

29   Robert Rhodes James, *Albert Prince Consort*, Hamish Hamilton, London, 1983, p.219.

30   Bolitho, *The Prince Consort and His Brother*, p.146.

31   Ibid., p.147

32   The report's primary objective was to highlight Britain's vulnerability to an invasion by France, which the Government considered the 'one power in the world against which we need any especial preparations for the possible contingency of war'. Fortunately, this perceived threat vanished when the two nations formed an alliance to fight Russia.

33   Public Record Office, PRO 30/22/9J, Part I, 11 December 1851, pp.100–18.

34   The purchase of commissions dated back to the reign of Charles II in the seventeenth century. Two hundred years later, in Albert's time, the cost of a commission ranged from £450 for an infantry ensign to £9000 for a lieutenant colonel of the Foot Guards. One of the most outrageous purchases was Lord Cadogan's colonelcy of the fashionable regiment of cavalry the 11th Dragoon Guards, which later became Albert's 11th Hussars. Cadogan paid nearly £40,000 for his commission, at a time when £50 a year was considered a reasonable income.

35   Martin, *The Life of HRH the Prince Consort*, vol.III, p.32.

36   Bennett, *King Without a Crown*, p.256.

37   The Prince was an enthusiastic library supporter. When the London Library opened its doors in 1841, Albert, its first patron, donated a collection of books along with a cheque for £50. The catalogue of the library's German Collections makes mention of 'a valuable selection of the best German authors from His Royal Highness Prince Albert, the Patron of the Institution, and they [the Committee] look forward with some confidence to this source, as likely to bring many important editions to the stores of the library'. Albert made a further donation to the library in 1861, shortly before his death.

38 James, *Albert Prince Consort*, p. 225.

39 The first Crimean War veterans to receive a backdated Victoria Cross were Charles Lumley of the 97th Regiment of Foot, William Johnstone of HMS *Arrogant*, Charles Wooden of the 17th Lancers and Robert Shields of the 23rd Regiment.

40 Quoted in Stanley Weintraub, *Albert, Uncrowned King*, John Murray, London, 1997, p. 295.

41 *The Times*, 26 June 1857, p. 9.

42 Martin, *The Life of HRH the Prince Consort*, vol. IV, p. 15.

43 British India at that time was comprised of three colonial regions. The Bengal Presidency consisted of present-day West Bengal and Bangladesh, as well as the states of Assam, Bihar, Meghalaya, Orissa and Tripura. Several princely states were later added to its jurisdiction, including the North-West Frontier Province, Punjab and Burma. The Madras Presidency was also directly under East India Company control. It encompassed much of southern India, which included Tamil Nadu, the Malabar region of North Kerala, parts of Andhra Pradesh and other regional districts. The Bombay Presidency at its greatest extent comprised the present-day state of Gujarat, the western two-thirds of Maharashtra state, including the regions of Konkan, Desh and Kandesh, and north-western part of Karnataka state; It also included Pakistan's Sindh province and the British territory of Aden in Yemen.

44 Jagow (ed.), *Letters of the Prince Consort*, p. 313.

45 The title of Empress was bestowed on Victoria in part to ensure that the Queen remained in station above her daughter Vicky, who would have the title Queen when her husband ascended the German throne. Victoria would thereby also continue to outrank the various rulers of India's princely states.

46 Arthur Benson (ed.), *Letters of Queen Victoria*, John Murray, London, 1908, vol. III, p. 298.

47 Letter by Clabon quoted in Martin, *The Life of HRH the Prince Consort*, vol. IV, p. 2.

48 Ibid.

49 The ballast heavers were dock workers who, as their name implied, loaded ballast onto ships. London's Docklands abounded with workers of colourful job descriptions − lumper, coal whipper, bobber, to name a few − though their daily labour was far less amusing than their titles would imply.

50   Martin, *The Life of HRH the Prince Consort*, vol. IV, pp. 1–2.

51   Benson (ed.), *Letters of Queen Victoria*, vol. III, p. 264.

52   Jagow (ed.), *Letters of the Prince Consort*, p. 317.

53   Bennett, *King Without a Crown*, p. 324.

Chapter 6

1   Theodore Martin, *The Life of HRH the Prince Consort* (People's Edition), Smith, Elder & Co., London, 1882, vol. IV, p. 78.

2   Kurt Jagow (ed.), *Letters of the Prince Consort*, John Murray, London, 1938, p. 335.

3   Martin, *The Life of HRH the Prince Consort*, vol. IV, p. 21.

4   Ibid., p. 20.

5   Jagow (ed.), *Letters of the Prince Consort*, p. 289.

6   *The Times*, 16 February 1858, p. 12.

7   Granville memorandum in Arthur Benson (ed.), *Letters of Queen Victoria*, John Murray, London, 1908, vol. 3, p. 343.

8   As early as 1856, at the conclusion of the Crimean War, Victoria expressed her satisfaction at the way the Government had upheld the honour and interests of Britain 'under the zealous and able guidance of Lord Palmerston'. Arthur Benson (ed.), *Letters of Queen Victoria*, vol. 3, p. 186. In that year she invested Palmerston with the Order of the Garter.

9   The position was not created until after Albert's death. Sir Charles Grey was appointed Victoria's first private secretary.

10   Martin, *The Life of HRH the Prince Consort*, vol. IV, p. 78.

11   Jagow (ed.), *Letters of the Prince Consort*, p. 319.

12   Ibid., p. 336.

13   Ibid., p. 319

14   Martin, *The Life of HRH the Prince Consort*, vol. IV, p. 74.

15   Jagow (ed.), *Letters of the Prince Consort*, p. 332.

16   The title of Lord Lieutenant is given to the monarch's personal representatives, usually in a county or similar circumscription. In Albert's day the Lord Lieutenant was head of the county militia. The office is now usually invested in a retired local notable, senior military officer, peer or business leader.

17   Martin, *The Life of HRH the Prince Consort*, vol. IV, p. 80.

18 The colour red, the dominant colour of Prince Albert's royal crest, has remained the traditional covering of the boxes.

19 Martin, *The Life of HRH the Prince Consort*, vol. IV, p. 62.

20 A fall during the princess's pregnancy was believed to have been the cause of the damage to the child's left arm, which, despite desperate efforts at a cure, remained shorter than the right.

21 Martin, *The Life of HRH the Prince Consort*, vol. V, p. 25.

22 The twice-married Princess Victoria of Saxe-Coburg-Saalfeld was one of the more controversial members of the royal family, and the subject of much speculation about an affair with John Conroy, an Irish officer who served as her private secretary. Conroy was said to be the instigator of a long-running feud between his patroness and Victoria's uncle, King William II. This generated a good deal of bad blood between the Queen and her mother, though the Duchess was taken back into Victoria's confidence after the birth of the Princess Royal.

23 Jagow (ed.), *Letters of the Prince Consort*, p. 351.

24 Karina Urbach, *Bismark's Favourite Englishman*, I.B.Tauris, 1999, p. 108.

25 Martin, *The Life of HRH the Prince Consort*, vol. V, p. 37.

26 Ibid., p. 44.

27 Ibid.

28 Temperatures dipped to minus 15 degrees Fahrenheit (minus 26 degrees Centigrade) near Edinburgh, the lowest on record for fifty years.

29 Victoria mentions in her memoirs that she took a little water with whisky to refresh herself, 'as the people declared pure water would be too chilling'. Quoted in Arthur Helps (ed.), *Leaves From the Journal of Our Life in the Highlands*, Smith, Elder & Co., London, 1868, p. 186.

30 Helps (ed.), *Leaves From the Journal of Our Life in the Highlands*, p. 187.

31 Roger Fulford (ed.), *Dearest Child: Letters between Queen Victoria and the Princess Royal*, Evans Bros, London, 1964, pp. 173–74.

32 Jagow (ed.), *Letters of the Prince Consort*, p. 357.

33 The title King of Prussia had only been in existence since the early eighteenth century, when it was sold by the Emperor of Austria to the Duke of Prussia, Frederick William's son, who became Frederick I. The purchase price was 8000 soldiers and an undertaking of perpetual loyalty to the Hapsburgs.

34 Ibid., p. 358.

35 Ibid., p. 359.

36 Benson (ed.), *Letters of Queen Victoria*, vol. III, p. 433.

37 Jagow (ed.), *Letters of the Prince Consort*, p. 359.

38 Martin, *The Life of HRH the Prince Consort*, vol. V, p. 50.

39 Frank Eyck, *The Prince Consort*, Cedric Chivers Ltd, Bath, 1975, p. 238.

40 The garden over whose opening Prince Albert, the Society's fourth president, presided, no longer exists. It lay between what is now the Natural History Museum and the Royal Albert Hall. It lasted until 1888, when the Royal Horticultural Society abandoned the site to their landlords, the Royal Commissioners, and Imperial College was built on it.

41 Martin, *The Life of HRH the Prince Consort*, vol. V, p. 71.

42 Ibid.

43 Robert Rhodes James, *Albert Prince Consort*, Hamish Hamilton, London, 1983, p. 268.

44 Fulford (ed.), *Dearest Child*, p. 30.

45 Christopher Hibbert, *Queen Victoria: A personal history*, HarperCollins, London, 2000, p. 346.

46 Ibid., p. 295.

47 Ibid., p. 318.

48 Ibid., pp. 293–94.

49 Daphne Bennett, *King Without a Crown*, Book Club Associates, London, 1977, p. 357.

50 The Schleswig-Holstein question flared up for a second time in 1864, though Albert could have rested easy on this issue, for Denmark was defeated and forced to cede the contested territories to Prussia and Austria.

51 Martin, *The Life of HRH the Prince Consort*, vol. V, p. 67.

52 Jagow (ed.), *Letters of the Prince Consort*, pp. 364–65.

53 Ibid., p. 370.

54 Cecil Woodham-Smith, *Queen Victoria*, Alfred A. Knoph, New York, 1972, vol. I, p. 417.

55 Thomas Sebrell, 'Lincoln's British Enemies', *BBC History Magazine* 12/4, 2011, pp. 23–26.

56 See correspondence in the Victoria and Albert Museum Archive, Letters to Sir Charles Eastlake, Mss. 86/GG/18.

57 William Schupbach, 'The Last Moments of HRH the Prince Consort', *Medical History* XXVI (1982), p. 322.

58 *The Times*, 8 and 9 December 1861.

59 Jagow (ed.), *Letters of the Prince Consort*, p. 258.

60 Martin, *The Life of HRH the Prince Consort*, vol. V, p. 77.

61   On 21 December 1861, the Registrar-General listed the official cause of death as 'typhoid fever, duration twenty-one days'. *The Times*, 24 December 1861, p. 6.

62   *The Times*, 16 December 1861, p. 8.

63   Benson (ed.), *Letters of Queen Victoria*, vol. III, p. 476.

64   Ibid.

65   Queen Victoria, *More Leaves From the Journal of a Life in the Highlands*, Smith, Elder & Co., London, 1884, p. 1.

Chapter 7

1   Rugby School was, for Macdonald Fraser's Albert, 'of the kind which turns younk boys like yourself into men like Colonel Flash-mann here.' *Flashman at the Charge*, HarperCollins, 2006, p. 36.

2   Kurt Jagow (ed.), *Letters of the Prince Consort*, John Murray, London, 1938, p. 66.

3   George Earl Buckle, *The Life of Benjamin Disraeli*, John Murray, 1916, vol. 4, p. 383.

4   Tennyson held the tenure of Poet Laureate for 35 years, until his death in 1892. He was greatly admired by the royal couple, who commissioned him to compose a verse to greet Alexandra of Denmark when she arrived in Britain to marry Bertie. Tennyson also wrote the ode sung at the opening of the Great Exhibition.

5   Charles Greville, *The Greville Memoirs*, Longman, London, 1875, vol. VI, p. 303.

6   Dyce's paintings of the 1840s were influenced by the Nazarene School, a pseudo-monastic group of German artists based in Rome. Albert greatly admired Dyce's work, and in 1848 he managed to secure him a fee of £800 a year, a small fortune in nineteenth-century Britain, for the duration of his work on the Houses of Parliament.

7   V&A Museum Archive, Letters to Charles Eastlake, Mss. 86/GG/18, p. 33.

8   Theodore Martin, *The Life of HRH the Prince Consort* (People's Edition), Smith, Elder & Co., London, 1882, vol. I, p. 2.

9   Jagow (ed.), *Letters of the Prince Consort*, p. 347.

10   Edith Sitwell, *Victoria of England*, Faber & Faber, London, 1936, p. 247.

11   Cecil Woodham-Smith, *Queen Victoria*, Alfred A. Knopf, New York, 1972, p. 437.

12 Elisabeth Darby and Nicola Smith, *The Cult of the Prince Consort*, Yale University Press, London and New Haven, CT, 1983, p.58.

13 One historian maintains that the cult of Albert's death reached 'an intensity not known again until Princess Diana's time'. John R. Davis, *The Great Exhibition*, Sutton, Stroud, 1999, p. 212. The comparison might seem somewhat contrived when considering the extent to which people's lives were touched by these two figures and the material benefits of their respective legacies. Those who experienced the disturbing days of 1997 might likewise reflect on what will remain of Princess Diana's work in 150 years' time. Moreover, the pitch of grief heard at the time of her death was, in a digital age, deafening but shortlived.

14 *The Times*, 6 September 1864, p.7.

15 Ibid.

16 Debra A. Mancoff, 'Albert the Good', *Biography* 15/2 (Spring 1992), University of Hawaii, pp.141–42.

17 Ibid., p.153.

18 Hector Bolitho, *The Prince Consort and His Brother*, Cobden-Sanderson, London, 1933, p.143.

19 Jagow (ed.), *Letters of the Prince Consort*, p.99.

20 V&A Museum Archive, Miscellanies of Henry Cole 1861–6, f. 24: RA Add. H2/2.

21 *The Times*, 3 January 1862, p.7.

22 Francis Sheppard, *Survey of London: South Kensington Museums Area*, 1975, vol.38, p.148.

23 The Memorial suffered serious damage from various causes, including bunged up rainwater sumps and anti-aircraft fire during the Second World War, which blew off the top of the spire. Beginning in 1994, English Heritage undertook an £11 million restoration programme. Hedley Pavett, consultant architect, said the decay was so severe that 'the spire was actually held together by rust'. The monument was returned to its original splendour and was unveiled by Queen Elizabeth II in October 1998. *Perspectives on Architecture*, I/6 (1994), p.9.

24 Ibid., 1 April 1862, p.8.

25 Sir Arthur Helps (ed.), *The Principal Speeches and Addresses of HRH the Prince Consort*, John Murray, London, 1862, p.20.

26 *Art Journal*, facsimile edition of the 1851 Great Exhibition catalogue, 1995, p.viii.

27 Nigel Williams, Secretary of the 1851 Royal Commission, in conversation with the author.

28   Michael Leapman, *The World for a Shilling*, Headline, London, 2001, p.291.

29   *The Times*, 25 January 1862, p.10.

30   Darby and Smith, *The Cult of the Prince Consort*, p.87.

31   Joseph Hooker Dalton, *A Sketch of the Life and Labours of Sir William Jackson*, London: Cambridge Library Collection, 1876, p.21.

32   There are 36 Albert Roads in London alone. This poses the difficulty of ascertaining which were named for the Prince Consort and which for his son Bertie, who was also referred to as Albert when Prince of Wales.

33   Helps (ed.), *The Principal Speeches and Addresses of HRH the Prince Consort*, p.48.

34   Martin, *The Life of HRH the Prince Consort*, vol.IV, p.3.

35   Ibid.

36   Quoted in Erika Langmuir, *The National Gallery Companion Guide*, Yale University Press, London and New Haven, CT, 2005, p.11.

37   George Scharf, 'Essay on the Royal Picture Galleries', *Old London* (journal), 1867, p.376.

38   Helps (ed.), *The Principal Speeches and Addresses of HRH the Prince Consort*, p.181.

39   This was the age of the railway and its democratising influence, as well as the introduction of the Great Reform Bill, which brought an enlarged franchise and a restructuring of parliamentary representation.

40   Bolitho, *The Prince Consort and His Brother*, pp.195–96.

41   Lytton Strachey and Roger Fulford (eds), *The Greville Memoirs 1814–1860*, Macmillan, London, 1938, vol.VII, pp.304–5.

42   Winslow Ames, *Prince Albert and Victorian Taste*, Viking, London, 1968, p.170.

43   Josephine Ross, *The Monarchy of Britain*, William Morrow, New York, 1982, p.175.

44   There was a time when the Government was less sensitive to the people's right to know. When the Queen Mother married the Duke of York, the future George VI, in 1923, it was reported that Stanley Baldwin's Cabinet debated whether the ceremony should be broadcast live on the radio. The decision was that it should not, on the grounds that men listening in pubs might not doff their caps.

45   Lytton Strachey, *Queen Victoria*, Chatto & Windus, London, 1921, pp.176–77.

Postscript

1   *The Times*, 22 January 1901, p. 5.
2   Quoted in Lytton Strachey, *Queen Victoria*, Chatto & Windus, London, 1921, p. 243.
3   Quoted in Pierre Crabitès, *Victoria's Guardian Angel*, George Routledge & Sons, London, 1937, p. 259.
4   Arthur Benson (ed.), *Letters of Queen Victoria*, John Murray, London, 1908, vol. I, p. 59.
5   Ibid., vol. III, p. 474.
6   Quoted in Robert Rhodes James, *Albert Prince Consort*, Hamish Hamilton, London, 1983, p. 277.

Bibliography

Aldous, Richard, *The Lion and the Unicorn*, Pimlico, London, 2007

Ames, Winslow, *Prince Albert and Victorian Taste*, Viking, New York, 1968

Art Journal, facsimile edition of the 1851 Great Exhibition catalogue, 1995

Bennett, Daphne, *King Without a Crown*, Book Club Associates, London, 1977

— *Queen Victoria's Children*, St Martin's Press, New York, 1980

Benson, Arthur (ed.), *Letters of Queen Victoria*, John Murray, London, 1908

Bolitho, Hector, *Albert Prince Consort*, Max Parrish, London, 1964

— *The Prince Consort and His Brother*, Cobden-Sanderson, London, 1933

— *Victoria And Albert*, Cobden-Sanderson, London, 1938

Bradley, Ian, *God Save the Queen*, Darton, Longman & Todd, London, 2002

Buckle, George Earl, *The Life of Benjamin Disraeli*, John Murray, London, 1916

Crabitès, Pierre, *Victoria's Guardian Angel*, George Routledge & Sons, London, 1937

Darby, Elisabeth and Nicola Smith, *The Cult of the Prince Consort*, Yale University Press, London and New Haven, CT, 1983

Davis, John R., *The Great Exhibition*, Sutton, Stroud, 1999

Dean of Windsor and Hector Bolitho (eds), *Letters of Lady Augusta Stanley*, Gerald Howe, London, 1927

Eyck, Frank, *The Prince Consort: A political biography*, Cedric Chivers, Bath, 1975

Feuchtwanger, Edgar, *Albert and Victoria*, Continuum, London, 2006

Fulford, Roger (ed.), *Dearest Child: Letters between Queen Victoria and the Princess Royal*, Evans Brothers, London, 1964

Greville, Charles, *The Greville Memoirs*, 8 vols, Longman, London, 1875

Grey, Charles, *The Early Years of the Prince Consort*, Smith, Elder & Co., London, 1867

Hay, Malcolm and Jacqueline Riding, *Art in Parliament*, Jarrold Publishing, Norfolk, 1996

Helps, Sir Arthur (ed.), *The Principal Speeches and Addresses of HRH the Prince Consort*, John Murray, London, 1862

— (ed.), *Leaves From the Journal of Our Life in the Highlands*, Smith, Elder & Co., London, 1868

Hibbert, Christopher, *Queen Victoria: A personal history*, HarperCollins, London, 2000

Hooker Dalton, Joseph, *A Sketch of the Life and Labours of Sir William Jackson*, London: Cambridge Library Collection , 1876

Ingle, Harold, *Nesselrode and the Russian Rapprochement with Britain*, University of California Press, Los Angeles, 1976

Kenyon, Edith, *Albert the Good*, W. Nicholson and Sons, London, 1887

Kiste, John Van Der, *Queen Victoria's Children*, Alan Sutton, Gloucester, 1986

Langmuir, Erika, *The National Gallery Companion Guide*, Yale University Press, London and New Haven, CT, 2005

Leapman, Michael, *The World for a Shilling*, Headline, London, 2001

Lorne, Marquis of, *Viscount Palmerston*, Nonsuch Publishing (reprint), Stroud, 2007

Lynch, Michael, *Scotland: A new history*, Pimlico, London, 1992

Magnus, Philip, *King Edward the Seventh*, John Murray, London, 1964

Marshall-Cavendish Collection, *Royal Romances*, London, 1990

Martin, Theodore, *The Life of HRH the Prince Consort* (People's Edition), Smith, Elder & Co., London, 1882

Medical History, vol. XXVI, 1982

Miers, Mary, 'Osborne House, Isle of Wight', *Country Life*, 195/13 (2001)

Müller, Max (ed.), *Memoirs of Baron Stockmar*, Longman, London, 1871

Nicklas, Thomas, *Das Haus Sachsen-Coburg*, Verlag W. Kohlhammer, Stuttgart, 2003

O'Driscoll, Justin, *A Memoir of Daniel Maclise*, Longman, London, 1871

Perspectives on Architecture, I/6, 1994

'Prince Albert and the Development of Education in England and Germany', *Prince Albert Studies* 18, K.G. Saur, Munich, 2000

Queen Victoria, *More Leaves From the Journal of a Life in the Highlands*, Smith, Elder & Co., London, 1884

Raymond, John (ed.), *Queen Victoria's Early Letters*, B.T. Batsford, London, 1963

Ross, Josephine, *The Monarchy of Britain*, William Morrow, New York, 1982

Scheele, Godfrey and Margaret, *The Prince Consort: Man of many facets*, Oresko Books, London, 1977

Sebrell, Thomas, 'Lincoln's British Enemies', *BBC History Magazine* 12/4, 2011

Sheppard, Francis, *Survey of London: South Kensington Museums Area*, 1975, vol. 38

Shorberl, Frederic, *Prince Albert and the House of Saxony*, Henry Colburn, London, 1840

Sitwell, Edith, *Victoria of England*, Faber & Faber, London, 1936

Staatsarchiv Coburg (Coburg State Archive), various documents, letters and memos

Strachey, Lytton, *Queen Victoria*, Chatto & Windus, London, 1921

Strachey, Lytton and Roger Fulford, *The Greville Memoirs 1814–1860*, Macmillan, London, 1938

Steegman, John, *Consort of Taste*, Sidgwick & Jackson, London, 1950

The Times, various quotations throughout

Thompson, Brian, *Imperial Vanities*, HarperCollins, London, 2003

Urbach, Karina, *Bismark's Favourite Englishman*, I.B. Tauris, 1999

— *Queen Victoria*, Verlag C.H. Beck, Munich, 2011

Victoria and Albert Museum Archive, Miscellanies of Henry Cole 1861–6, f. 24: RA Add. H2/2

Warner, Marina, *Queen Victoria's Sketchbook*, Macmillan, London, 1979

Weintraub, Stanley, *Albert, Uncrowned King*, John Murray, London, 1997

Williams, Kate, *Becoming Queen*, Arrow Books, London, 2009

Williams, Roger, *The Royal Albert Hall*, Fitzhardinge Press, London, 2003

Woodham-Smith, Cecil, *Queen Victoria*, Alfred A. Knopf, New York, 1972

Index

'A' indicates Prince Albert and 'V' indicates Queen Victoria.